"I have long be ⟶ ⟶ fan of Ralph's work as a writer, teacher, and healer. In *Outshining Trauma*, he beautifully combines his training in two systems that belong together: Internal Family Systems and Buddhism. What results is a meaningful, intimate, and highly transformative book for working with your own wounds and stuck places. I'll be recommending this book to friends and students for years to come!"
—ETHAN NICHTERN, author of *Confidence:
Holding Your Seat through Life's Eight Worldly Winds*

"Packed with perspective on the pervasiveness of trauma and stress, this gem of a resource combines the ancient wisdom of Buddhism with modern psychotherapeutic methods and philosophy, gently guiding readers to know what it means to outshine their traumas and find freedom from the past."
—AMANDA GILBERT, author of *Kindness Now*

"Whether you're dealing with trauma yourself or supporting someone who is, *Outshining Trauma* offers invaluable insights and practical steps to guide you on your journey. Ralph De La Rosa's message is clear: healing is possible, and you have the power to outshine your trauma."
—ERIC ZIMMER, host of *The One You Feed* podcast

"Ralph De La Rosa masterfully blends trauma-informed Internal Family Systems (IFS), post-traumatic growth, and Buddhist meditation into a cohesive, practical, and beautiful book. His approach brilliantly teaches how to walk the long and crucial journey from head to heart in a manageable and enriching way. With insightful exercises and tools, De La Rosa takes us through the process of healing from trauma using IFS language, inviting us to see post-traumatic growth as a real possibility. Drawing from his personal experiences and professional expertise as a therapist and Buddhist meditator, he offers a fresh perspective on the challenging yet exhilarating path to recovery. This book is an invaluable companion for anyone seeking to heal and grow."
—DR. EDITH SHIRO, author of *The Unexpected Gift of Trauma:
The Path to Posttraumatic Growth*

"I have always appreciated Ralph's levelheaded honesty and down-to-earth perspective from which he so comfortably teaches as we navigate the traumas of our lives. In *Outshining Trauma*, Ralph's sharing of his own difficulties illuminates the recipes for transformation in a very relatable style that highlights each of our journeys to self-compassion. I am always happy to see a new addition to his excellent body of work."

—RAGHU MARKUS, Executive Director of Love Serve Remember Foundation and host of *Mindrolling* podcast on Ram Dass's Be Here Now Network

"*Outshining Trauma* is an essential read for anyone struggling to overcome trauma. Drawing on years of clinical experience, a deep commitment to spiritual practice, and his own healing journey, Ralph helps us understand that post-traumatic growth is indeed possible when we commit to radical self-compassion. He offers many practices that bring us into loving relationship with ourselves, and his writing style is so friendly and accessible—it's like he's walking the path with us and cheering us on."

—LINDA SPARROWE, author of *Yoga at Home* and *Yoga Mama*

"Offering profound insights and posing thought-provoking questions, De La Rosa creates a nurturing atmosphere where readers feel supported every step of the way. There are even jokes to lighten things up from time to time. His writing fosters a beautiful exchange, encouraging readers to engage actively in their personal growth. In the hands of Ralph De La Rosa, readers are assured a transformative opportunity to explore and understand themselves on deeper levels. As a person with almost zero spiritual practice, I felt myself engaged the full way through. Now, excuse me while I go on a Curiosity Walk."

—BONNIE PIPKIN, author of *Aftercare Instructions*

OUTSHINING TRAUMA

A New Vision *of* Radical
Self-Compassion

RALPH DE LA ROSA
Foreword by RICHARD SCHWARTZ

Integrating Internal Family Systems
and Buddhist Meditation

SHAMBHALA

Shambhala Publications, Inc.
2129 13th Street
Boulder, Colorado 80302
www.shambhala.com

Cover art: Dedraw Studio/iStock
Cover design: Amanda Weiss
Interior design: Kate Huber-Parker

9 8 7 6 5 4 3 2 1

First Edition
Printed in the United States of America

Shambhala Publications makes every effort
to print on acid-free, recycled paper.
Shambhala Publications is distributed worldwide by
Penguin Random House, Inc., and its subsidiaries.

Library of Congress Cataloging-in-Publication Data
Names: De La Rosa, Ralph, author.
Title: Outshining trauma: a new vision of radical self-compassion
integrating internal family systems and Buddhist meditation / Ralph De
La Rosa.
Description: First edition. | Boulder, Colorado: Shambhala, 2024 |
Includes bibliographical references. |
Identifiers: LCCN 2023038042 | ISBN 9781645472322 (trade paperback)
Subjects: LCSH: Posttraumatic growth—Popular works. | Psychic
trauma—Alternative treatment. | Psychotherapy—Methodology. | Buddhist
meditations—Popular works.
Classification: LCC RC552.P67 D398 2024 | DDC
616.85/2106—dc23/eng/20231114
LC record available at https://lccn.loc.gov/2023038042

For Bill

"Irony is the language of the Universe."
1976–2021

A mirror becomes a razor when it's broken,
a stick becomes a flute when it's loved.

—Yoko Ono

CONTENTS

FOREWORD

I feel honored by and thrilled with the contents of this book! To have such a respected author, meditation leader, and Buddhist scholar describe so beautifully and compellingly how he used my Internal Family Systems (IFS) model to heal his polarized inner system is gratifying in itself. Then to have him eloquently describe how others can integrate it with meditation practices and with Buddhist thought to heal trauma is a huge contribution. As Ralph writes in the introduction,

> We're not meant to get broken in life and then simply carry on in a compromised state, as generations before us have done. Radical self-compassion is attainable. It is our deeper nature. Post-traumatic growth is attainable. We are wired to manifest it. Creating space for joy is within reach. We are built for these things, built to overcome. The heartbreaks and betrayals we've suffered can, if we so choose, mark a new beginning, a new story of discovering freedom.

And, given all the trauma in Ralph's life, he knows of what he speaks. When you carry the level of emotional wounding he did, you do what it takes to contain or distract from it. Maybe, like him, you have spent years in the throes of addiction to hard drugs and alcohol with repeated rehabs and relapses. Maybe, like Ralph, you have reached the point where you wanted more from life and moved toward healthier ways to try to heal your pain and anxiety—meditation, yoga, spirituality, therapy—and found that while those practices helped you manage your trauma-based emotions enough to function without the need for the addictions, they didn't fully heal them. From his spiritual studies and practices, Ralph knew he was to give himself compassion but only had a vague idea of how to do that. "Like so many others, I believed compassion and self-love were the way but struggled with what this actually meant—and especially with how to actually *apply* self-love toward afflictions with any level of precision."

Consequently, he concluded that full healing isn't possible—the best you can hope for is to contain and get some respite from painful beliefs and emotions, but they're always lurking in the background and still spring forward at times when you are triggered. If any of that is familiar, then this book will inspire you to reconsider that assumption.

It is possible to heal and, as he puts it, to shine, despite having a terrible history and tortured present. I have forty years of experience helping heavily diagnosed and pathologized souls use IFS to bring compassion and love to the parts of themselves that they had been terrified of or hated and watching those parts transform from their destructive states into wonderful allies and advisers. In his metaphor of shining, Ralph emphasizes the dual nature of this healing. Not only does a part release the extreme beliefs and emotions it got from the trauma (unburdening), which allows it to transform into its naturally valuable and enjoyable state, but now you have access to the wonderful qualities it affords that weren't available to you while it was in exile or covered by burdens. As more and more of your traumatized parts are unburdened and come back home to you, you can't help but shine. As he writes poetically, you reclaim "the best of the childlike qualities you were born with—qualities such as effortless creativity, uninhibitedness, easy laughter, trust, endless imagination, in-the-moment-ness, eagerness to learn and explore, a big capacity to love, and unstoppable vitality."

And, again, he can be believed because he has lived it and generously lets us in on all he has gone through. I know Ralph to be a skilled IFS therapist and his inclusion of his clients' stories is useful, but each time he tells an aspect of his own, you will be as enthralled as I was. That's part of why I'm excited about this book—it contains a rare, first-person account of the IFS healing process from someone with a severe trauma and symptom history who tried many of the common approaches, including many versions of spiritual and intellectual bypassing (see chapter 13 for a great discussion of those), but didn't find real post-traumatic growth until he engaged with IFS.

Subsequently, he was able to see how to apply much of what he had learned in his years of Buddhist study to the healing endeavor without bypassing. The second part of the book is full of this wisdom and often elegantly integrates aspects of IFS with Buddhist teachings. Similarly, Ralph, who for years has taught meditation, has creatively included aspects of his meditative practices in his IFS work and has been impressed with the results. In this book he shares all of that and adds many exercises for you to try that combine both.

All of this can help you become more Self-led. Throughout Ralph's decades of spiritual seeking, a version of what IFS calls Self was implied in each tradition he explored but seen as elusive and distant. "For years, I thought the awakened state in me was something exotic, something romantic, something mysterious to only be glimpsed by true mystics and masters." In this book you learn that not only is it attainable, it's close by and can be immediately accessed when your parts open space for it. Once accessed, it becomes an inner leader, good parent, healer (retriever, unburdener—liberator of your parts), who can show your parts that they can stand down and let Self lead your life while they assist and enjoy. While the steps for doing all that can be found throughout the IFS literature, Ralph's descriptions are compelling and convincing because, as I said earlier, he's lived it and is so open about his past and his process.

I'm very honored to have Ralph as an influential and authentic partner in our effort to bring about collective awareness and healing through IFS. His journey from suffering to shining is inspiring and instructive, and his integrating of IFS with Buddhism and meditation makes his a uniquely valuable voice.

—*Richard Schwartz*

ACKNOWLEDGMENTS

Where would I be without you?

Richard Schwartz, Vinny Ferraro, Matt Zepelin, Peter Schumacher, Linda Sparrowe, Joelle Hann, Bess Lovejoy, Amanda Ludwig, Tess Felder, Kim Milone, Nicole Iverson, Hope Jansen, Eleanor Bell, Ethan Nichtern, Michael Hewett, Bonnie Pipkin, Jessica Stickler, Aimee Barr, Ambyr D'Amato, Eric Zimmer, Lorin Roche, Lisa Levine and Maha Rose, Shanna Honkomp, Rima Rabbath and Souk, Ariel Deva De Léon and Tigerlily Holistic, Adreanna Limbach, Lodro Rinzler, Adam Merkel, Brilliant Miller, Nick See, Shannon Myers, Edith Shiro, Will Johnson, Reggie Ray, Rick Hanson, Sharon Salzberg, Jack Kornfield, Renee LaRose and the Big Heart City sangha, Rasmani Orth and Kripalu, Jon Gingerich, Carol Haworth, Dennis Haworth, Joy Caesar, and all of our beautiful friends who celebrate Bill always and all ways.

The entire Amplify Teacher Training and Coming Home Lojong sangha whose practice and insights inspire me to no end. This book wouldn't exist without you:

Louise Egger, Michelle David, Michelle Smith, Joanne O'Brien, Joan Malloy, Ronnie Boehm, Robin Ressler, Nita Cabrera, Shivani Bhargava, Kristy Weidner, Jenna Hanlon, Dori Cohen, Alex Trivilino, Sheila Shulleeta, Laura Antonik, Zak Middleman, Holly Sass, Jody Hassel, Anna Dillingham, Alberta Dering, Amber Caldwell, Mousumi Mukerji, Kelly Lauder, Matthew Dugan, Gwen Frenzel, Katie Oldfield, Susie Bertie, Rebecca Friedman.

HOW TO USE THIS BOOK

This book is less about certain modalities and theoretical lenses and more about our shared experience of life itself. As such, I hope that you will engage with it in the way that feels right to you at this time. You are welcome to simply accrue more knowledge and conceptual insight here. You are also welcome to use this book as an experiential dive into your inner world, almost like a workbook or a course. If you choose the latter, I recommend keeping a journal to track the experiences you begin to have, what comes up in the meditations, and so forth. This will help you to integrate the material into your daily life much more deeply. When it comes to inner experiences, such as the meditations offered here, they are similar to dreams in that if after a meditation you get up and immediately move on, the experience evaporates. It will also take little effect. If you write down the experience, however, you open to a new world—the world of your embodied, inner workings. As with dreams, it is also best to do this right away.

For those who intend to take an experiential deep dive here, I'd urge you to not make this a big project. Hold this work lightly and keep the effort manageable so you're more likely to follow through to the end. Give yourself permission to be an imperfectionist about absolutely all of it.

You may find it most valuable to work through this book alongside a friend, whether near or far. Decide on a weekly meeting time and a reasonable number of chapters to accomplish in that time. This will help you to maintain your attention in addition to having a sense of mutual support.

ON UTILIZING MEDITATIONS IN PRINT

While you can find audio versions of many of the meditations offered in this book on my website and Insight Timer pages, you may want to simply use the print versions without getting more devices involved. There are a few ways to do this. My favorite approach is to read one instruction then close my eyes for some time to practice it, then read the next instruction and close my eyes to practice some more, and so on. That said, many of us might find we have the natural capacity to keep one eye on the instructions on the page with another "eye" on the world inside and thus won't need to pause so much. Finally, a third, powerful option, for those who are inspired to engage deeply and have the resources to do so: use the printed instructions to make recordings for yourself. You could do this right on the voice memo app on your phone. If you were to choose this option, the process of making the recording would deepen your familiarity with the instructions in a different way, and you'd have your own voice to guide you in all your future sessions. This falls right in line with the spirit of this book, which is getting to know ourselves in ever-deepening ways.

Please always remember that the point of the path is enhanced self-awareness and the rousing of love and compassion. If anything offered here does not point you in these directions, feel free to ignore it or set it aside to investigate later.

OUTSHINING TRAUMA

Introduction

THE THINGS WE CARRY

As a culture and as individuals, we are just now opening our eyes to the pervasiveness of traumatic stress. We are realizing that every one of us is affected by traumatic experience, whether directly or indirectly. We are finally admitting that experiences of crisis, loss, betrayal, and violence aren't just something to "get over"; they need to be met by well-informed responses and resources. They call for healing. Even if you don't consider yourself impacted by trauma presently, it is simply a matter of time. As we accrue years, we accrue experiences both beautiful and deeply adverse. Without knowing how to process and heal, we are often left holding the impact of such experiences in our bodies. Within a culture that values repression and self-medication, traumatic experiences often have a nasty way of piling up, ultimately obscuring our ability to perceive and appreciate life's beauty.

Given this pervasiveness, I know that trauma is also present in many of the people you love, people who touch and impact your life directly—friends, family members, coworkers, intimate partners. It can take the shape of the common, diagnosable symptoms such as intrusive thoughts and emotions, overwrought reactions, recurring nightmares, addictions, difficulty in relationships, depression, anxiety, and aversion to reminders of troubling events. It can also result in harder-to-recognize, cyclical patterns such as the wounded ways families pass down for generations, unquestioning adherence to harmful cultural norms, biases against groups and identities, loss of purpose, inability to sustain healthy habits, people-pleasing, attraction to emotionally unhealthy partners, and the inability to set and maintain boundaries. Trauma's effects aren't

1

always obvious. Too often, it sits quietly in the background, informing our experience like undetectable toxic fumes seeping out of a vent, slowly making life feel less tolerable, less livable. Our sense of possibility and the preciousness of life can shrink, even to the vanishing point, when unmet wounding remains in the body.

Like not being able to enjoy a favorite song because it reminds us of someone who broke our heart, trauma's overarching effect is one of narrowing—of options, of awareness, of hope. To hold unprocessed traumas in our bodies is an enormous liability. We end up with relationships that don't work; jobs that are unsatisfying; a decreasing ability to play, laugh, and feel free; increased physical illness—even shorter life spans.

The researchers Naomi Breslau and Ronald Kessler conducted a study that found that as many as 75 percent of American adults have experienced a traumatic event.[1] We don't need a study, however, to know that, in 2020, 100 percent of the global population experienced the COVID-19 pandemic and all the profound uncertainty, loss, social divisiveness, political violence—and sense of powerlessness—that came with it. In the wake of the global pandemic, the narrowing effect of trauma has been laid bare. Our social worlds have shrunk. Cutting off friendships has become a reflex for many. Entire communities and creative subcultures have disappeared. People are starved for touch and true interpersonal closeness while spending far more time staring at screens.

We must also acknowledge that the way trauma unfolds for any given person has everything to do with social context. Our lives don't happen in a vacuum and our experiences are anything but one-dimensional. Rather, experiences unfold against a backdrop of an encroaching climate crisis, an epidemic of loneliness, institutionalized bigotry, widening economic inequality, dehumanizing social media culture, political animus, and religious extremists legislating a holy war against entire populations. These conditions matter to everyone, but for the marginalized among us, they bear a deeper significance and harsher impacts. When adverse experiences fall against a tapestry of heightened stress, exposure, and unsafety, they subjectively carry much more weight and depth.

It's impossible for them not to. Thus, what is traumatic for one person might not be for the next person—and the difference is often due to unseen and unexamined factors.

The Buddha's famous Noble Truths point out the obvious: uncertainty and pain are simply core aspects of existence—we will never find some kind of impregnable safety from unexpected crises and losses in our lives. Given this fact of life, why do so few of us know what to do when trauma befalls us or our loved ones? Here, now, in what I've been calling "the golden age of mental health," this is changing, and I see this book as a contribution to this crucial dialogue. As the Four Noble Truths go on to indicate, suffering is born of causes and conditions, and those conditions can be vanquished.

ON OUTSHINING

The most important thing about our broadening recognition of trauma is that it has allowed for the development of methods of healing and transformation that are reliable, *that actually work*. This stands in sharp contrast to how things used to be, even rather recently. For instance, Martin Seligman, the head of the American Psychiatric Association for decades and the "father of positive psychology," admitted on a TED Talk that the field of Western psychology, from its inception until recent years, has largely been "smoke and mirrors," involving a great deal of guesswork.[2] Perhaps this is why Bessel van der Kolk's landmark book on trauma, *The Body Keeps the Score*, has remained at the top of the *New York Times* bestseller list, at the time of this writing, for over 250 weeks. Its outlining of efficacious therapeutic modalities such as Somatic Experiencing and Internal Family Systems (IFS) is a springboard for innumerable people to finally find resolution and peace.[3] In this book, we will be exploring IFS alongside somatically focused mindfulness meditation—and the Buddhist worldviews that underpin it. It's an integration I've taught to tens of thousands of students worldwide, and with startling results.

While trauma is in us and around us at all times, so is the outshining of it.

OUTSHINING: THE ANTIDOTE
TO NARROWING

To outshine trauma is to allow our hearts, minds, and lives to grow bigger and brighter than any of the troubles we've ever faced. That's the promise of healing work when done well: we naturally emerge from it wiser, better equipped to handle future calamity, and moving in the direction of self-actualization. We become less susceptible to ills of all kinds. Healing self-work is an invitation to heighten our emotional intelligence, and it's a more skillful approach to life and relationships. The real benefit, however, is the full reclamation of our embodied experience—the basis of all human spirituality, the basis of all joy.

We can recover so much of what we lose to the narrowing of trauma. We can reclaim our childlike vitality, sense of wonder, dreams for the future, ability to trust and feel uninhibited, creative spark, and love of learning and growth. All of this not only can be recovered but is meant to be so. We are built for it. We have the natural capacity to do the inner work that leads to such an integration. While I won't tell you such work is necessarily easy—little in life that's worthwhile is—I will tell you that it can become quite compelling when we access genuine, heart-expanding compassion and infuse the process with it.

"Outshining" means a release of the full, unfettered energies of the heart such that they outsize what we struggle with. For most of us, those heart energies lay hidden, covered over. Yet they are not lost, even if we've lost the experience of them. In this way, compassion-centered healing work organically nurtures the best in us as we unburden the weights we carry. We can not only expand where once we had narrowed but also continue that expansion all the way toward ever-deepening purpose and spiritual radiance. Traumatic experience, when met resourcefully, can become our biggest asset, the very fodder for previously unimagined goodness.

We're not meant to get broken in life and then simply carry on in a compromised state, as generations before us have done. Radical self-compassion is attainable. It is our deeper nature. Post-traumatic growth is attainable. We are wired to manifest it. Clearing space for joy is within reach. We are built for these things, built to overcome. The heartbreaks and betrayals we've suffered can, if we so choose, mark a new beginning, a new story of discovering freedom.

Trauma needn't be more than your prologue.

STARTED FROM THE BOTTOM: MY STORY

As those who've read my previous books *The Monkey Is the Messenger* and *Don't Tell Me to Relax* know, trauma was once the center of my story as well. I am no stranger to being abused and abandoned by an alcoholic caregiver. I know the texture of social alienation and humiliation at the hands of peers. I know the terror of weapons being held against my body as men bigger than me issued credible threats. I know what it is to freeze against my own will, hoping the person punching me would tire out. I remember vividly what it's like to be told in the aftermath of such things that it was my fault for dressing differently or "acting like you're gay"— and that I must like the attention since it happened so often. I also remember the night I walked in on my first love in bed with another man, an emotional betrayal leaving an impression more indelible than fists ever could. I know consuming rage, radical numbness, terrible panic, and the abyss of depression.

I know what it is to look everywhere for answers—to really and truly seek. I've knocked on the doors of Christianity, Hinduism, Buddhism, and endless healers and therapists. I've pored over stacks of self-help books hoping they'd have The Answer—some missing link that would make it all make sense and take the pain away. And each of them did have pieces of *an* answer for me, but never the final one. It turns out that no one thing can have The Answer for any of us. Healing can only come through a process of truly getting to know yourself. No one else's method can do that for you. No one else knows exactly what it's going to take for you. What modalities and wisdom traditions *can* offer you are methods and insights that help you to discover who and what you truly are. But it will always be up to you to discover for yourself how it needs to work. Ultimately, this is an empowering truth. "It's up to you" can also be a tough pill to swallow when you're at your wit's end—or smashing through the glass floor of every rock bottom.

That's another thing I did a lot of: bottoming out. For a long time, cocaine and heroin were my Answer. They made the pain go away enough that I could go out and dance, play in bands, feel charming, and find friends and lovers. Drugs felt like the only way for me to have a life at all, really. They kept the rickety vehicle of my life patched up enough to get from one place to another. That is, until my father died suddenly and I went on a mission to destroy myself completely. Soon after, I began shooting drugs intravenously. I knew on day one of this development that this would be my undoing. My lifestyle was a slow suicide; I knew it, and I couldn't have cared less.

It took a village to pull me out of the 100-foot hole I had dug for myself. Nearly homeless, penniless, and with a heart full of insatiable craving, a merciful partner did the footwork to get me into rehab. Once there, I did die—I died unto myself, unto my old life. I also found a rebirth; one imbued by a new, grounded form of spirituality rooted in getting to know myself as an ordinary human. Its foundations were the most immediate aspects of my life: body, breath, thoughts, emotions, memories, and relationships. The practice: learning how to love myself, right in the middle of the mess, just as I was. This practice was cultivated in the arenas of daily meditation, yoga, community, and trauma-focused therapy. It left me with more questions than answers and yet it became my road map out of hell, the way out of the 100-foot hole.

Less than a year later I enrolled in school with the intention of helping other trauma survivors someday. I had no money, no outside support, no real belief in myself, and it was going to take a long time. Yet, if drugs had taught me anything, it was how to say "Fuck it" in the face of consequences. So why not one last, very healthy "Fuck it" in the face of student loans and hard work? Deep down, I knew that helping others was the real way to save myself from ever going back to my old life. I was right.

To this day, it's the trauma survivors I serve that keep me honest and earnest. There is no accountability (and no joy) quite like altruistic service. After all, I know the road map of hell, having been there and back too many times to count. Today that knowledge is my superpower, for I can walk with anyone into the darkest neighborhoods of their minds, know what to do once we're there, and how to find our way home. That's an outshining I wouldn't trade for anything.

Imagine feeling utterly hopeless and permanently damaged and then discovering that all of it—*all of it*—is treatable. That's what happened to me. Daily meditation quickly became most indispensable. Therapy was still essential—but what about the six days and twenty-three hours a week one *isn't* in therapy? Meditation is immediately available and costs nothing (aside from some morning snoozes). Daily practice is what truly allowed me the space to become familiar with my inner life. Though it was a world of both wonders and horrors, I began to see that love was always the appropriate response no matter what I bumped into inside. I slowly began confirming my suspicion—the exhaustion and damage of this world didn't have to be the end of the story. A sense of trust in the unfolding path began to arise. With time and consistency, what was tangled in me began to unfurl, what was confused began to clarify. Woundedness and rage still abounded, yet instead of feeling hopeless in the face of how extensive it was, I started to perceive it as fuel to keep going—keep meditating, keep showing up at therapy, and keep finding friends who were walking a path similar to my own. I just *had* to find out what a life without all this pain might be like.

I was in a position I see so many in today: Having done good work on myself, having healed so very much, but still prone to reactive emotions, self-defeating beliefs, and compulsive behaviors. I'd sifted through all the memories in therapy and attended a number of silent retreats and yet I was somehow only half-healed. I'd experienced the most miraculous of turnarounds and yet big emotions still eclipsed me rather routinely and my relationships were rife with confusing dynamics and fallouts. A decade after I'd traded heroin for a healing lifestyle, trauma was still lodged in my body, surreptitiously shaping and limiting my world.

I guess some things aren't meant to be healed, I'd tell myself. *I suppose life is just so mysterious, there are just some questions that will never be answered. I'll have to carry on this way, managing as best as I can and in therapy for the rest of my life.* That's when IFS entered the picture, offering me the processes that would help me discover the rest of the road home.

INTERNAL FAMILY SYSTEMS:
AN ANATOMY OF OUR INNER WORLD

Just prior to encountering IFS, I had been immersed in the Vietnamese Zen monk Thich Nhat Hanh's method of working with your inner child through accessing and holding deep emotions with a caring attitude. In meditation, I had learned the simple, revolutionary skill of splitting my awareness by experiencing things like pain and anger and then offering love and compassion to those afflictions. Our brains organically have this capacity! Meditating in this way was like walking into a room that was filled with a rich array of decorations. Then IFS came along and whispered in my ear: *You know, there's a whole house.* So I walked out into that house and discovered it was a mansion.

Like so many others, I believed compassion and self-love were the way but struggled with what this actually meant—and especially with how to actually *apply* self-love to afflictions with any level of precision. What IFS offers is a step-by-step process for experiencing these things directly—room by room, hallway by hallway, you can study the mansion of your mind, heart, and body for yourself. You do this by getting to know the living psychological energies that occupy such corridors. In IFS, we call these *parts*.

IFS begins with honoring that we are made of many parts and subpersonalities. To take a simple example, most people manifest a certain personality while at work that's quite different from the personalities that might manifest with their partner, friends, or when they're feeling lonely or anxious. You might also notice while ordering at a restaurant that one part of you wants to order the cheeseburger and feel celebratory while another wants to order a salad and feel healthy. It isn't that either part is better or worse—each part is real and has its own wisdom and voice. While there are parts of ourselves we hold in good favor and those we'd rather excise with a pair of tweezers, they all serve a purpose.

IFS is one of a number of psychotherapeutic methods that use a *parts work* approach to understand our human experience. Parts work is a process of self-inquiry that allows us to get to know the multitudes we hold inside. It facilitates a shift into appreciation and caring for all that we are.

It turns out that healing isn't a matter of fixing ourselves or getting rid of the parts of us that make messes. Healing is, rather, a natural by-product of getting to know the parts of our psyche in a compassionate way. This often comes about through inner "conversations" (I use quotes here because they don't always happen in words), which IFS offers many transformative scripts for.

As we begin to acknowledge that we each have a veritable cosmos of parts and personalities inside, some of us begin to feel daunted. The notion of healing each member of our inner household can make us think, *This is going to take forever.* What I want you to know is, this process, specifically as it's presented in IFS, can quickly turn into a real source of joy. If we can look through the lens of fascination with how complex and intricate we are as beings, if we approach healing as a heartfelt process of discovery and not some therapeutic drudgery, then what might formerly have looked like a marathon starts to look like an adventure.

> **Insight:** When we feel resistance to doing healing work, that's actually a part of us that fears what might happen if we start to change. Can you imagine what it would be like to kindly acknowledge that part of you inside, take a breath, and trust your deeper instinct? The true thing to fear isn't change; it's things staying the same.

I initially engaged parts work in meditation and not with a therapist. I began with my angriest parts. I figured I had one or two—and quickly discovered an unruly mob. Whereas I'd previously attempted (and failed) to meditate these intense energies into obedience, the suggestion of IFS was to allow them to take up some space. So, I welcomed this host of "spiritually incorrect" parts and the intense thoughts and feelings that came with them. I used IFS's steps (described in chapter 3) for developing curiosity about these long-held resentments and overwrought defense mechanisms. Curious exploration of my anger brought realizations about why I acted the way I did sometimes (I'm sensitive and anger shields hurt), why my intimate relationships weren't working (the wounds I hadn't processed from the past were being projected onto the present), and why my years in therapy had only helped so much (we were addressing the underlying hurt but without my own self-compassion involved). I also discovered many positive things. My angry parts had wisdom; for example, they were often seekers of justice, wanting to right wrongs. I also discovered that when my anger turned inward, such as with depression and inner critics, I could find creative ways of conversing within to help these energies see that beating myself up really wasn't the way forward.

Fascinated and relieved, I lay on the floor of my tiny shrine room for weeks intensively processing my traumas in new ways. Things I had felt stuck with for years began moving toward unburdening very quickly. Parts of me I had long considered neurotic and unwanted began dancing in my awareness, revitalized in feeling seen.

IFS propelled me into feeling truly at home with myself. It showed me how to access an openheartedness I thought was the stuff of fairy tales and ancient yoga masters. More importantly, it showed me how to *apply* openhearted self-compassion in a manner that released the emotional and energetic residue of trauma from my body. With each burden that released came open space—space to reclaim and integrate some of my more connected and courageous qualities that had fallen away as pain had accumulated.

I couldn't keep it to myself. I started offering some basic IFS steps in the embodied mindfulness meditation classes I offered. The results were astonishing. I repeatedly received feedback that went something like, "I have no idea what that was, but it did more for me than the last year of therapy sessions combined." My Saturday-morning parts work meditation class became the most popular class at a premier NYC meditation studio with three locations. More recently, I led a dedicated group of parts work meditators into a yearlong, experiential intensive exploring IFS in the context of the Mahayana Buddhist *lojong* (mind training) teachings—something we'll explore in part three of this book. We found ourselves flabbergasted with the overlapping insights. New approaches to meditation organically emerged. Most importantly, students began unburdening their traumas within their daily practice of meditation and feeling liberated in new ways.

The vast majority of these students weren't Buddhist, either. In fact, we had a few lifelong Christians in the mix. Something curious about both Buddhism and IFS is that they're inherently flexible and adaptable. IFS is a model built for life, not just the therapy room. While there's definitely some complexity and sophistication to the model as a whole, the rudiments of it are fairly easy to grasp and can be applied in infinite ways. This quality had also fueled my initial fascination with Buddhism. The heart-centered practices and worldviews that Buddhism offers have grown roots in a broad spectrum of countries and cultures and have managed to speak directly to the people of each within their context. This was just as true for ancient China as it turned out to be for the modern West. In North America, Buddhist mindfulness-based practices have mixed with Christianity, Judaism, and Indigenous American ceremonies, just as they've proliferated in corporate boardrooms and preschool classrooms. And now this kind of organic mixing is happening with IFS; it's being applied in career coaching, weight-lifting classes, nutrition counseling, educational tutoring—hell, I even have an IFS voice coach. These porous and permeable qualities mindfulness meditation and parts work have in common allow for a rather seamless integration. Buddhist meditation and IFS, it turns out, go together like baby carrots and hummus.

WHAT'S COMING YOUR WAY

You do not need to have a background in either IFS or meditation to use this book, as the concepts and exercises we'll be exploring are open to beginners. For those who do have a background in IFS, Buddhist meditation, or both, you might want to skim some sections that will be review for you, while other sections will still offer you new ground.

This book works with a two-way thesis:

1. The *inner technology* of IFS has the capacity to bring deeper healing into the sphere of Buddhist approaches to meditation practice.
2. The *worldview, philosophy, and meditative techniques* of Buddhism complement and amplify the processes and road maps IFS gives us.

We'll also place good emphasis on somatic embodiment and breathwork throughout this adventure. Embodiment and simple breathwork set the stage for parts work to go deeper and be especially effective. We want to disrupt our habitual modus operandi of living in our thoughts, and embodied presence can help us get there. We also must acknowledge that, as trauma takes up residence within the body, many of us sense an alienation from our bodies. Hence, practices that bring compassionate attention to the living and breathing body help us reclaim a sense of home inside (albeit a little at a time).

They say the most difficult journey is often the eighteen inches from the head to the heart. That is, it can be one thing to develop insight at the cognitive level, and yet another thing entirely for insight to become a realization, an experience. The latter is where change and healing develop. Therefore, this book contains numerous exercises, journal prompts, and meditations designed to help us move from insight to realization, from the conceptual to the experiential. (As stated in the "How to Use This Book" section, I recommend dedicating a separate journal specifically for the good work about to unfold here.)

This book has three main elements:

1. Trauma theory and post-traumatic growth
2. IFS and its transformative processes
3. Buddhist worldview, philosophy, and meditation

Part one begins with an exploration of trauma, what it is, how it comes to be internalized, and how it can be rooted out of the nervous system. We also explore the essential tenets of IFS, including its model of the psyche, how to experience healing and compassionate "Self Energy" internally, and some of the rudimentary processes of the model. We'll look at some case studies as well as a story from my own history to help bring this material to life.

Part two is a primer in parts work meditation and a manual for integrating this practice into your daily life. This begins with establishing a somatically focused foundation of presence and self-regulation through breath and attentional techniques that take into account our parts and our trauma-focused aspirations. With this foundation established, we then go deeply into a variety of approaches to parts work meditation. This includes discovering a sense of secure refuge in life as well as some of the deepest processes IFS has to offer. We'll also explore a practice known as *parts mapping* that can engender continuous development with this approach.

Part three is a call to the post-traumatic growth of *reparenting* ourselves. We utilize aspects of the Buddhist lojong practice to address limiting beliefs we might hold, maintain motivation, reclaim play and joy, and walk through grief and loss. This section contains straightforward discussion of the most shadowy topics we'll approach in this book.

———

This book is about looking at yourself through the lens of love. What trauma comes down to, really, is the ways in which love was withheld and betrayed in your life. The antidote, then, is the restoration of love, here and now, in the body and nervous system and life you get to have for this short time.

While it's true that the body keeps the score and that trauma is an everyday reality, it's also true that our bodies are built for immense enjoyment, deep connection, and unsurpassable enlightenment. We can emerge wise, strong, brave, eloquent, and lighthearted from the experiences that could have broken us forever. When we outshine trauma, we extinguish the pain of intergenerational legacies we have inherited. When we outshine trauma, we rewire our nervous systems and fundamentally change what we can pass on to others, including future generations.

The engine of such possibility is closer than our own skin.

EXERCISE: IDENTIFY A REPETITIVE PATTERN
5–10 minutes

Take a moment to reflect on why you picked up this book. Chances are there is an issue in your life that you were hoping to move past. Chances are that issue has been repetitive: you keep meeting with some version of it over and over again. Chances are you've tried at least a few things in an attempt to root it out and achieve change.

- What is that issue, and how is it affecting your life?
- What's the earliest you can remember experiencing it?
- What's one thing that would be different if you were no longer holding the burdens surrounding this issue?

Answering these three questions will give you a taste of the work to come and give you a solid reason to work with this material earnestly.

PART ONE: ROOTS

The Lived Experience of Trauma and the Process of Healing

THE SOMA KEEPS THE SCORE

Understanding Trauma and
the Window of Consolidation

Shame dies when stories are told in safe spaces.

—*Ann Voskamp*

Caveat: In this book, I use diagnostic language to describe some of the more classical understandings of trauma. In my experience, such labels can help us to comprehend complex matters fairly easily—but they can also be a trap. Diagnostic language is sloppy shorthand, at best, for a rich array of lived experiences that could never be summed up by these terms. Diagnostic language is the stuff of insurance companies looking for whom to bill and audit. It intrinsically defies the tender aim and ethos of this book. Personally, I relate to Irvin Yalom, who wrote that diagnosis "does violence to the being of another. If we relate to people believing we can categorize them, we will neither identify nor nurture the parts, the vital parts, of the other that transcend category."[1] Therefore, while I'll use diagnostic language because it is helpful in giving us some shared language, it's only for lack of better, more all-encompassing terms. Please take only what is helpful to you and remember that human life is exquisitely beyond categorization.

The body itself wants to heal. The psyche itself wants to heal. No part of us wants to be trapped in the exhausting roles of reactivity, suppressing pain, or holding pain. What's more, at every level we are built to be strengthened through recovery. *Under the right conditions,* most traumatic experiences can be healed. (Note that the first part of that sentence is crucial.) Allow me to clarify, though, that when I use the words *healing* and *recovery*, I do not mean a return to a previously known status quo but rather an ascent to a new state of self-awareness and reclaimed vitality. Like the Japanese *wabi sabi* concept of repairing a broken ceramic pot with fine metals, we can be made more beautiful by filling in our cracks with gold. This is what's earned through the work healing asks of us.

Yet all too often, trauma becomes like a record skipping in the same spot, unable to complete the natural continuum of the song. It's when the compassionate conditions needed for resolution aren't present that we get stuck. The traumatic experience, then, is left to repeat itself through compulsive patterns in our lives. Over and over again we experience the same difficult emotions, the same confounding issues in relationships, the attraction to the same self-medicating and avoidance strategies, the same resistance to healthy habits, and the same thought loops. When trauma unfolds this way, it often becomes like an unending nightmare. In clinical settings, such nightmares go by the names *traumatic stress* and *post-traumatic stress (PTSD)* or *complex-PTSD (C-PTSD)*.

THE SPECTRUM MODEL OF TRAUMA

The appropriate use of the word *trauma* is a matter hotly debated in the field of mental health. Many clinicians are concerned not only that it is being overused but also that its prevalence is an insult to people who have survived things like wars, famine, migration, and real torture. I, however, agree with the clinical pioneer Gabor Maté: "In a society that constantly tells you you're not good enough, the very values of that society are traumatizing. . . . We exist on a spectrum of woundedness."[2]

Thinking of trauma as a spectrum is more closely aligned with the spirit of the word than seeing it as an either-or situation. It also allows us to honor the crucial role subjectivity plays in the forming of traumas. After all, our brains don't respond to *actualities* but to *perceptions*. We'll soon be exploring how trauma is less about *what happened* and more about someone's subjective experience of what happened within a complex array of situational variables. The matter is hardly black-

and-white in nature—so, who's to judge if an event in someone's life qualifies as validly traumatic or not? Viewing trauma as a broad range of experiences—that, of course, do result in a wide range of outcomes—also conforms more to the definition of the word as well as to where the current research points us.

Trauma is the Greek word for "wound," which seems to inform the *Oxford English Dictionary*'s definition: "A physical injury or wound, or a powerful psychological shock that has damaging effects."[3] This definition leaves room for variability. On one end of a continuum, we have extreme experiences such as war, torture, and assault; at the other, we have far less extreme but still subjectively significant experiences such as being ghosted by someone meaningful to you, growing up with "black sheep" status, or experiencing the effects of climate change while feeling powerless to stop it. The range encompasses the intensity of the experience along with the experience of powerlessness within it. The sense of powerlessness is indeed a defining line that helps us differentiate between "traumatic experience" and "adverse experience." That said, powerlessness comes in many forms and, again, a person's subjective perception is what governs whether or not the body generates traumatic stress.

Here is my own basic definition of trauma:

Trauma is any adverse experience in which our defense mechanisms are mobilized but rendered useless for any reason.

It's common for those of us who relate to the spectrum model of trauma to refer to "lowercase-*t* trauma" versus "capital-*T* trauma." Both ends of the trauma spectrum entail troubling experiences for which our bodies naturally generate neurochemicals associated with our defense mechanisms—adrenaline, cortisol, and the like. These neurochemicals produce intense states of mind and body that have nowhere to go, no effective outlet, no immediate resolution. Our nervous systems are left to stew in those chemicals; absent caring intervention, the resultant psychological and emotional states can become deeply internalized—we get stuck.

METABOLIZATION

Experiences are like food. Everything we consume through our senses is meant to be digested, metabolized into new vitality and life wisdom, and then let go of. It's all nutrition. It all affects us and changes us. In the same way that food can fuel a workout or block an artery, experiences can bolster resilience or shut us down at our core. When you eat or drink something toxic, whether by accident or on purpose, your body gets to work moving it out of your system. Your kidneys and liver collaborate to filter it all out and prepare it for removal, and your body temperature may rise as if cooking the toxins out of you. For most human bodies, detoxification is a well-oiled system that saves us from a lot of trouble. There are those of us, however, who aren't so lucky. Some of us live in environments or in lifestyles that are so toxic—or with illnesses and disabilities—such that our organs are overloaded and can't do their job. When met with conditions that counteract our natural propensity to move toward well-being, toxicity just sort of . . . sits there.

Traumatic stress, to follow the digestion analogy, is like food sitting in the system, waiting to be processed. Whether or not it will be metabolized and eliminated or left to calcify into post-traumatic stress disorder depends on a few factors.

What's needed for metabolization are environments wherein it's safe to do at least a few of the following:

- Feel what one needs to feel in an atmosphere of compassion.
- Tell the story and have it received with receptive caring.
- Reflect and distill insight and life lessons from what happened.
- Seek and attain justice.
- Make meaning by turning the experience into creative expression.
- Turn the experience into compassion by being of service to others in a similar position.

Notice that all of these factors rely heavily on relationships. The power of community and societal support is never to be underestimated. It's for this reason that caring and basic respect for each other ought to be both the baseline in our relationships as well as the guiding principle for governing bodies and institutions. If that sounds like this is asking a lot, well, that's just how dehumanizing our cultural norms have become. These mitigating factors aren't extensive. They're utterly humane, reasonable, and intuitive. They fall squarely in the category of basic decency. If you go through something horrific, you deserve the care and the resources to get through it—end of story. All too often, however, someone isn't believed; parties that could intervene don't; basic safety and support aren't available; someone hasn't been shown how to make meaning of experiences and process things; or someone is alone with no support. Then there's traumatic experience that gets stacked on top of other factors that aren't directly related—for example, when a disability or chronic illness comes into play, the trauma has to be shoved aside to get back to work; or when someone is struggling with systemic forms of violence. These too-common conditions are where post-traumatic stress tends to develop. The record begins to skip, and it will continue to skip until a gentle hand comes along to set the needle back on the right track. Thankfully, that hand can be our own.

The skipping of the record—that is, the repetitive patterns that form around the trauma such as intrusive thoughts, emotional upheavals, and compulsive avoidance strategies—first arrives as bad news. Conventional psychology tells us they are pathological symptoms to merely be managed and medicated. Make no mistake, however: the repetitive quality of the record skipping is the body itself saying, *Here's another chance to get the compassion we missed on the first round. Perhaps this time we'll feel heard and held.* The problem is when the people around someone whose trauma manifests as, say, rage attacks or dissociative episodes, have no awareness of how trauma works, they aren't likely to respond with the compassion needed. They might do quite the opposite. And the record continues to skip.

Capital-*T* traumas are likely to set off one version of this. Traumas on the lowercase end of the spectrum are likely to set off another. We must also take into account the great difference between single-event traumas and repeat traumas that form a continuum of experiences. For example, it's one thing for someone to be attacked, and it's quite another for someone to grow up in the hands of a caregiver who repeatedly attacks them. The clinical world accounts for this by adding the qualifier *complex* to the trauma, hence *C-PTSD*. While single-event traumas are enough to throw one's entire life off course, complex traumas commonly give rise to personality disorders and psychosis.

Even in severe cases, trauma doesn't always become traumatic stress, and traumatic stress doesn't necessarily turn into PTSD or C-PTSD. This is where the mitigating factors mentioned earlier come into play. Context both before and after traumatic experience impacts how it's all absorbed into the body. That process of absorption is called *consolidation*. In the rest of this chapter, we'll be looking at consolidation, because understanding how it works will help us in at least four ways:

1. Comprehending the trauma we hold
2. Discerning what we need in the face of a traumatic experience
3. Knowing how to heal and transform our unresolved wounds from the past
4. Knowing how to respond when someone else experiences something terrible

The best place to start in understanding how trauma consolidates is with the recognition that it never hits an inert person—trauma always meets a body, mind, and heart thrumming with innate aliveness.

Let's back up and start from the beginning.

THE FORCE OF LIFE

We are not born into the world as blank slates. The human psyche is not merely a product of its conditioning. Rather, we are born with a vast, complex vitality already coursing through us. In Buddhism this is often called *buddha nature*. IFS calls it *Self Energy*. And this vitality has an agenda: it wants to develop and flourish as best as the resources present will allow. (Of course, not everyone is born with the same biological or environmental resources.)

The vitality in us has an enormous job to do right out of the gate. In the first months of life, without anyone's intention or volition, the neural circuitry involved in vision, speech, basic movement and coordination, memory, and discipline is quickly forming. From there, the developmental process changes but never stops. We continue to develop and enjoy the most sophisticated thing known to science—the human brain—until the moment of death. Like so many plants forever growing in the direction of the sun, twisting and contorting as needed to bask in the light, so the force of life within us moves ever toward that which it perceives will support our becoming.

Our neural circuitry develops in tandem with the experiences we have—this is something called *neuroplasticity*. How wild is it that in every possible moment, what is happening outside of us is changing our bodies inside? What we experience leaves behind particles of neural structure; the subjective becomes something objective, the nontangible becomes utterly tangible. The Buddha famously taught about the ceaselessly changing and interdependent nature of things, and it turns out that isn't just philosophy—it is literal, biological reality.

There's a catch, though: once again, perception comes into play. A plant can be tricked with UV lighting to grow toward a light bulb rather than the sun. Baby sea turtles, just hatched in the sand, are instinctually guided by the stars and the moon toward the ocean. They often mistake city lights for these celestial bodies, though, and head in the wrong direction toward those lights, dying in the process. Similarly, we humans are instinctually motivated by three core needs: safety, feel-good rewards, and belonging. We too can be tripped up by facsimiles of these things. We often mistake comfort (and power) for safety. We erroneously seek the instant gratification of pleasures instead of the deeper satisfaction of learning and growth. We conflate validation with true belonging. In these ways, we get tricked like fledgling sea turtles, wending our way toward grimy asphalt when the vast expanse of the ocean is our true home.

Our seeking of safety, rewards, and belonging can also become endless. Like a billionaire who still craves more wealth, we too can enter into a crazy-making spiral of searching. This is in part because every solution we find will come with a new problem. It's just the way life works. The search for optimization is a seven-headed hydra.

When are we safe enough? When do we feel good enough? When do we belong enough? Though these questions are more rhetorical in nature than they are literal, we must ask them of ourselves. We must relate to the concepts of enoughness and contentment in order to protect ourselves from the bottomless pit of yearning for a life free of complications and drama.

DANGER SIGNALS INSIDE

When we begin to hold trauma in our bodies, the nervous system quite often gets tricked in another way. The consolidation of trauma in the body weaves danger signals into our cellular makeup. That means parts of the nervous system don't truly leave defense mode. Because our unprocessed trauma has internalized our perception of danger, we carry it everywhere and are likely to project that sense of threat into the external environment and the people we find there, *even if nothing threatening is actually happening.* If we find ourselves in the presence of a trauma reminder—the true meaning of the word *trigger*, which we'll discuss shortly—parts of us can respond as if the terrible past event is happening right now. The reactions we have to trauma-triggering situations occur in a flash, unconsciously and involuntarily. If you've ever overreacted to a situation, treated a loved one like a mortal enemy, or found yourself rationally knowing better but unable to stop yourself, it's likely a trauma reminder that set off without your volition or awareness.

REACTIONS TO TRAUMA REMINDERS AREN'T VOLUNTARY

A student shared an experience in class recently about a fight with their spouse. Their partner put on a song while driving that reminded my student of a traumatic experience. Their nervous system revved up and sought to eliminate the source of distress—by quickly shutting off the music. Their spouse thought it rude and went to turn the stereo back on. My student slapped their partner's hand away from the radio, not even understanding why. Of course, an argument ensued.

My student was distressed. "I've been meditating! *How could I possibly be acting like this?*" I won't soon forget the relief that washed over their face when I asked, "Did you choose to turn off the radio or slap your partner's hand away, or did it just sort of *happen* before you could think?" Of course, it was the latter. The incident wasn't actually the student's fault. Their automatic reaction came from a part inside of them that was terrified of anything resembling the trauma that had happened before. Yes, the student still needed to be mature enough to take accountability and repair the rift with their partner, but with the proper perspective, they could certainly understand and forgive themselves.

The involuntary nature of our trauma reactions highlights an important truth: we are not responsible for the cards we've been dealt, yet we are still accountable for how we play them. Trauma came to live in our bodies as the result of things that were deeply unfair, and yet it is up to us how we meet our ongoing situation and respond to it.

> **Insight:** Most of your thoughts are ones you've had before. They're on repeat—uncontrollably so. Yes, you can steer some of your thoughts—but not all of them and not all of the time. We are less in control of ourselves in the present moment than we like to think. For example, I definitely do not want you to imagine a tiger holding purple balloons right now. Try your very best not to think of that. And definitely do not imagine that tiger's a happy little bugger scampering about showing off those balloons to all her friends, either. That would be a terrible idea!
> . . . See what I mean?

THE WINDOW OF CONSOLIDATION

When a truly distressing event occurs, we tend to go into something of an altered state, what I call *the trauma tunnel of surreality*. All sense of normality is upended. Our needs for safety, feel-good rewards, and belonging have been shattered. Our bodies instinctually begin to shut down systems involved in digestion, detoxification, conscious awareness, and explicit memory to help us generate a reaction that might quickly get us back to safe harbor. When no perceived safe harbor is within reach, our bodies tend to clamp down even harder, sometimes causing a person to black out altogether. In this moment, the intense firing of neural circuitry along with the hormones and neurotransmitters associated with immense stress go into wild flux as the body seeks to address the emergency and find any inkling of homeostasis. A memory of the experience is actively being formed but has not yet coalesced. That much will take anywhere from twenty minutes to several hours. That period of time is what's called the *window of consolidation.*

> **The window of consolidation is the period of time after a traumatic event in which a memory of the experience is forming but can still be greatly influenced.**

What happens during this window of time impacts everything about the way the trauma begins to take shape in the nervous system. The context of the experience can exacerbate the trauma greatly or it can mitigate the internalization of traumatic stress altogether. It boils down to this: *Was compassion present?* If a child is being abused, it matters whether or not a loved one intervenes and addresses the abuser. If someone is victimized in public and has to go to the hospital and make a police report, how the hospital staff and police treat the victim matters. Whether someone is believed or not matters. Whether one has a comfortable home environment to return to or not matters. Whether one has a loving intimate partner or a solid sense of community matters. Whether the traumatized person loves themselves or hates themselves matters. If compassion is there in any of its myriad forms during the window of consolidation, the associated neurochemicals and subtle energies of that compassion get mixed into the actively coalescing memory. In IFS terms, we would say that Self Energy remained present to some degree in the aftermath of the trauma.

Remember, though, that conscious memory systems have been compromised during this time so that the nervous system can channel all energy toward survival needs. Where traumatic memories go to live, then, is in another memory system, known as *implicit memory.* Implicit memory doesn't hold the *story* of what happened but rather the *sensory information* present in the experience: the sights, smells, sounds, tactile sensations, and so on. This sensory data, once consolidated, then forms a trigger. Trigger formation happens for highly adaptive and healthy purposes. The traumatic event was related to one's survival, after all. For safety, the body needs to remember key sensory data in case the same circumstance arises again. A trigger is like an icon on your computer's desktop that, when clicked, reveals files and folders filled with all the data that's been stored there. For example, if someone was called a moron during a traumatic experience, the body might link the entire experience to just that one word. Should that person be called a moron again—even if jokingly and by someone who truly loves them—that word could well unlock an entire implicit memory and a host of reactions related to the original trauma as if it were all happening again. Such memories, being more sensory than verbal, are often so subtle or indirect that the person may not even be conscious that they have been triggered. They are reacting to the original trauma in the present moment without having a clue as to what started it.

If that sounds scary—or if you already know it's scary because it's happened to you—here's some potentially good news: whenever a traumatic memory gets triggered within a person, the window of consolidation opens again. The body is firing the same cylinders it was during the original experience. Again, parts of us may very well believe that we are back in the past in some way, under the same oppressive and hurtful conditions we've already survived. When this happens, it is either an opportunity or a liability. The difference, once again, is some form of compassion. That compassion could look like someone using their power to help you. It could look like an apology. It could look like being held. It could look like someone letting you know they really hear you and are trying to understand. Importantly, from a therapeutic standpoint, it can also look like *imagining* a compassionate intervention, even a fantastical one. In other words, that compassion doesn't have to come from someone else. It can come from you. This book is about training in methods that will help you know how to do this. Compassion has a thousand faces, a thousand forms.

If we don't find compassion in the new moment—if we're judged for being "too sensitive," if we're yelled at or told to relax, or if we're internally beating ourselves up—this new aggression will mix into the soup of memory reconsolidation. This amounts to retraumatization. However, if we *do* find compassion in the new moment as a traumatic memory is triggered, it will change the way that traumatic memory lives in the body. In chapter 14, we'll explore a deep process for rewiring the nervous system called *retrieval*, wherein we can go into traumatic memories armed with compassion to take the emotional charge out of such memories for good.

The guiding reality for healing trauma—and hence the North Star of this entire book—is that *we cannot go wrong with compassion*. Compassion is alchemical. When compassion finds a way into an adverse situation, it changes that situation for the better. It moves us in the direction of well-being and adaptive choices. When compassion mixes with traumatic stress, it has the power to reshape that suffering in surprising ways.

Despite the complexity of everything we've discussed here, I sometimes marvel at how simple it all really could be. *Our lives take shape around how we've been loved and the ways in which love has been withheld and betrayed.* If we could consistently care for one another and love ourselves, so much would be easier. Healing would come naturally over time. Our ethics would align themselves to situations organically. Our behavioral lives and habits wouldn't get so tangled up. Our relationships would naturally prosper. Our communities would enjoy harmony. Governing bodies could even institutionalize systems of compassion. Such conditions would give us all the space to really lighten up.

EXERCISE: CALLING IN COMPASSION

Think of a time when you've experienced compassion, whether that was feeling compassionate toward someone else or someone expressing it to you. It might have taken the form of a simple kindness. It might have been a courageous act of intervention. It might have been a moment of true listening and understanding. It might have been felt but never quite expressed. Whether large or small, take a moment to find a memory of when compassion was present in your life.

Now, ask yourself, *If I were able to feel this compassion fully, what would it be like? What would the sensations inside me be? What would it feel like in my body-mind?* And then imagine that for a few moments—really feel into it. Then ask yourself, *If I could turn the volume all the way up on this compassion—if it were big and bright and vivid—what would that be like? What would it feel like internally?* Take a few moments to linger with what comes up.

Notice what changed, if anything. Experiences can range from full-blown emotions to suddenly feeling blocked. There is no right or wrong here. At the very least you just planted a very useful seed within yourself, a seed that will bear fruit if you continue to water it.

Optional: Take five to ten minutes and journal about your experience to help it integrate into your system.

MORE THAN THE SUM OF YOUR PARTS

The Internal Family Systems Model of the Psyche

I learned that no thing in the world is one thing; that each thing in the world is two things at least, and probably many more than two things. I learned to find a queer pleasure in staring at a thing and dreaming of how many things it might be.

—*Gerald Murnane*

Now that we understand a little bit about how trauma works—including the window of consolidation and the critical role that the presence or absence of compassion plays in how that window sets into neural pathways—we're ready to explore Internal Family Systems. We'll spend the next two chapters getting to know the IFS map of the embodied psyche, broken down into the various parts of us, as well as its approach to healing and transformation.

Picture me at four years old as I dismantle a brand-new, state-of-the-art record player. Its pieces are scattered around me. It's like I'm on an archaeological dig, excavating bones and forgotten structures. Adults rush in and hover above, aghast at what I've done.

I'd recently fallen in love with music for the very first time. I'd heard the Carpenters the week before and, aside from being delighted by the sounds, I found my eyes glued to the record as it spun, the needle tracing its grooves. I became consumed with the question, *How did they get the music in there? How is it* in *the record player?* Clearly I was in the presence of confounding magic, a mystery of cosmic proportions.

I needed answers.

My family had been invited to lunch at another family's home after church. It was here that I committed the small crime of surgically dismembering the living room console while no one was looking. To my surprise, I didn't find music inside the device. I found neither sound nor Karen Carpenter nor guitars or drums. Instead, I was confronted by rubber belts, small motors, and wires. I found *parts* that, when they worked together, made something ineffable, dare I say, mystical: music. The plot thickened! My fascination doubled as I overheard my parents promising to cover the expense of my wonder-turned-vandalism.

While replacing record players is fairly easy, getting to the bottom of my original, nagging question became a lifelong quest. Today, I'm a musician who continues to be fascinated by the endless processes involved in a song being birthed, recorded, and eventually burned into the grooves of a record. Healing from trauma isn't so different, really. Such self-work, if done well, is an invitation to peer deeply into the nature of one's experience, to peel back the surface layers and uncover what's really going on inside us. Typically speaking, it's a process we endeavor for when the records played on the heart begin to skip. That is, when repetitive patterns abound and we feel cornered in some way. When we sense something is off but don't quite understand why. When we need answers.

Similar to my process with the actual record player, we might assume figuring this out ought to be a straightforward affair. We might expect to find music inside the record player. Or quick-fix answers in a therapist's online course. What we find instead is that there are many moving parts underneath what we experience on the surface. Once again, the plot thickens in a most curious fashion.

———

IFS is rooted in the view that the human *psyche* (Greek for "soul"), not unlike record players or bodies, is composed of parts. This simple-enough assertion has profound implications. If we begin with the view that we are not singular, solid entities but rather a dynamic system of interwoven parts, we start to gain clarity around how we could ever experience things like inner conflict, "standing in our own way," holding multiple perspectives in mind, and the like. All of our parts were meant to work together like the belt and motors inside a turntable to make the music of life happen. The suffering in our lives is commonly a product of our parts not working together harmoniously—often for reasons that aren't our fault—a product of trauma just about every time. We can begin to get curious about the reasons why it came to be this way. Perhaps most importantly, we can jettison the notion that anything about us needs to be "fixed" per se. Rather, the mission of transformative healing becomes a mission of wholeness, of reharmonization.

Your body-mind is the record player, made of parts. Your experiences are the music, both wonderful and strange. Your parts capture your experiences, recording them. The experiences that matter get burned into records. Your body stores the record collection, which piles up over time. Trauma forms scratches on some of the records. When traumatized records are played, they skip. They repeat the same note over and over again until someone compassionately removes the obscuration—or, better yet, helps to record a new memory that is healthy, free of scratches, loving and real.

THE BODY IS AN ANALOG

If you're having trouble grasping this view of yourself as made of living parts, let's look at a parallel. Even though your liver is just a part of your body, it doesn't sound wild for me to remark that your liver is alive. It is a living entity, doing things that you know nothing about. It has an agenda, a job, and communicates with the other organs without your awareness or volition. Your liver is affected by many of the choices you make, and it responds to those choices. Your liver has a certain sentience and volition, and you are in communication with this organ; there is something of a transactional dialogue happening there.

Similarly, if your psyche has aliveness, then so do each of your psychological parts. And if those parts possess aliveness, then the process of regaining wholeness begins with honoring your parts as having a certain sentience and volition as well, just like your liver. Isn't it true that we constantly find ourselves in a dialogue with ourselves? We say things like, *One part of me feels sad my plans are being canceled, but another part of me is relieved to have a night in.* That is us talking from two different parts of ourselves simultaneously. If we were to slow down and invite more from each part one at a time, we would likely unfold new connections and pieces of information—perhaps the sad part would generate thoughts about rescheduling with your friend, while the relieved part might respond with a sense of relaxation in the body.

Sidenote: Some people refer to *parts* as *objects*, using pronouns such as *it*. In order to keep firmly in mind their aliveness, I much prefer to talk about parts like I would other people and indicate this by using pronouns. For the sake of this book, you'll find in most cases I refer to parts as "they/them." Many practitioners actually find their parts have distinct genders. More times than not, the gender of the parts will match a person's gender identity, but not always. Men, for example, might find they have a female part inside. Women might find they have male parts inside. Curiously, many of my nonbinary clients and students often (but not always) find a real blend of gender presentations among their parts. I believe this could account for the way gender is experienced along a spectrum and not always in neat, boxed-in categories.

Parts communicate to us in four ways:

- Thoughts that come in words
- Thoughts that come in images
- Bodily sensations
- Emotions (sometimes experienced as a vague sense)

You might get a combination of any of these, or you might just get one. It can also change from part to part and from day to day.

Our inherent multiplicity allows for us to feel and think many things at once. It is this faculty that makes it possible for us to feel compassion while facing our own pain. It is this ability that makes us capable of self-love, which necessarily must entail being both the sender and receiver of that love. Most of us have never received any instructions or advice on how to have such an experience, but IFS gives us steps through a process called *parts work.*

Parts work is the central process of insight and healing in IFS. It's how we go behind the scenes and get to know all the moving pieces in the record players and vinyl discs of our lives. Here are some examples of how parts work can unfold in situations ranging from innocuous to profound.

Expressing Needs

I was staying at a friend's house recently when I found myself suddenly very anxious. I was enjoying my time with them and confused at first about the anxiety. Habitually, I went about stuffing down the anxiety while looking for little ways to feel better. *Was I dehydrated? Did I need a moment alone?* I finally took a breath and paused. I got curious about what was happening internally. In a flash, I realized that there were at least a few parts of me rumbling beneath the surface. I was a bit sleepy, and one part of me wanted to head downstairs to grab a coffee. Another part felt a bit insecure and didn't want to interrupt things. Yet another part of me was judging myself for being insecure—about wanting coffee of all things—and yet *another* part was very busy trying to stuff this internal conflict down. The result: anxiety.

> **Insight:** Anxiety is often the by-product of parts having a lot to repress in the name of functioning. Anxiety is rarely a primary emotion but rather the outcome of having lots of other emotions and thoughts that certain parts of us feel we can't allow to the surface. Anxiety is often not held by parts so much as it is a feeling generated by parts when they feel stressed about holding it together.

Seeing this offered me a small liberation. I had been focused on the wrong thing: the anxiety. The only real issue was the part of me feeling insecure about having needs (common for trauma survivors). So the insecure part and I agreed to take a chance: I asked my friend if we could go downstairs to the café, knowing the answer would be "Of course we can!" And that was that.

This might seem like a small thing, but we've all been in situations where we haven't been aware of or expressed our needs, making a situation more difficult to live through than necessary—which then often leads to resentment. Small things can become big things awfully fast—and small healings can have big implications.

George's Career Choice

This is a real example offered with permission. Names and details have been changed.

George initially came to therapy because he felt stuck in his career. He was burned out at his day job and had the ideas and resources to step out on his own as an entrepreneur. He just couldn't bring himself to start taking the steps he needed to. He believed his issues were depression, lack of motivation, and lack of confidence. I could've easily taken George's situation at face value and worked with him on alleviating the depression and cultivating motivation and confidence. In IFS, though, these issues are what's called a *trailhead*, like the opening of a hiking trail that leads into a forest worth exploring.

Similar to my own process at my friend's house, I asked George to pause and look inside at the emotions and thoughts he found there. He noticed that there were physical sensations involved as well, including a tightening in his solar plexus. It took a few steps, but George was able to find curiosity about the parts of him involved in this tightening. With this, George was ready to answer some key questions, such as "What do these parts fear might happen?" and "What's the earliest I can remember feeling this way?" What spontaneously emerged were memories of George's father, who was a very traditional head of household and worked for the same company his entire career. I had George ask inside, *What's the earliest message I heard about how careers work?* He remembered his dad saying things like, "This is how it is: you work hard, stay loyal, and you'll eventually make your way to the top"; "The most important thing in life is work and providing for your family"; and "Don't take chances; play by the rules."

These experiences aren't what we typically think of as traumas, and George's dad certainly wasn't being abusive. Nonetheless, these experiences were consolidated into George's nervous system as limiting beliefs about the nature of livelihood and career that were much more relevant to the work culture of previous, less entrepreneurial generations. Those beliefs were holding George back in a big way. Slowly, over the course of some sessions, I guided George into dialogues with the parts of him that held these beliefs. These parts needed to be reparented. They needed a new caring adult voice inside to help them update their awareness.

It was challenging for George to upend what his loving father had taught him, but we were able to walk through many examples that proved his dad wrong (e.g., most adults in the US have several careers over the course of their life). We helped his parts see the value in thinking bigger and taking well-informed risks. His parts needed something that so many of us need—to trust that even if we fail, even if we get hurt, we have what it takes to weather the storm, become stronger in the process, and get back on track if need be. George has since become an entrepreneur, started multiple companies, and is providing well for his family.

Rachelle's Difficulty Driving

*This is a real example offered with permission. Names and details have been changed. **Heads-up:** what follows is a much more intense example that includes child sexual abuse.*

Rachelle had tremendous difficulty driving. She could hardly stand to wear a seat belt and didn't understand why. She was able to manage her anxiety well enough if traffic flowed smoothly, but when she drove at rush hour, it was a different story. She'd have panic attacks when she found herself surrounded on all sides by other cars in stop-and-go traffic. She sometimes had to pull over to calm herself down. She usually had to talk herself through coping skills like remembering to breathe deeply all the way home. She also judged herself harshly for this, often asking, *What's wrong with me?*

Rachelle and I explored these trailheads together using the same steps and kinds of questions I facilitated for George: "What's the earliest you can remember feeling sensations similar to the seat belt? When you feel surrounded by other cars, does it remind you of anything?" We learned that Rachelle had been sexually assaulted repeatedly in early adolescence, leading to an unwanted pregnancy at the age of twelve, which she brought to term. The issues stemming from her assault and pregnancy were manifold, of course, but a key feature of this horrific experience was being in the stirrups while being cruelly yelled at by a nurse during the delivery of the baby. The sense of confinement along with verbal abuse in the context of bodily violation was all consolidated into her nervous system. The energy of this horror was being triggered by the constraint of seat belts. When she'd find herself surrounded by cars on all sides at rush hour, the feeling of being trapped would escalate. Her panic attacks weren't indication that something was wrong with her. They were evidence that her nervous system and protective parts were, in fact, doing their job very well.

What Rachelle struggled with on the surface was not the problem at all; the problem was that these underlying traumas had been left unaddressed for decades (and, of course, that Rachelle had been abused in the first place). Rachelle was initially unaware that these experiences were connected. It was only through compassionate inner inquiry that these associations were revealed. Rachelle was slowly able to bring compassion and caring to the young parts of her holding these experiences. We were eventually able to rescue that child trapped in the images flashing in Rachelle's mind utilizing the process of retrieval and unburdening (which we will cover in chapter 14 of this book). Over the course of these powerful sessions, Rachelle slowly experienced the anxiety of driving diminishing.

It's noteworthy that the first time I identified Rachelle's experience as "trauma," she didn't believe the term could possibly apply to her. Unfortunately, it is quite common for trauma survivors to downplay their past, even to themselves. Embracing the word *trauma* validated for Rachelle the gravity of what she had survived. I believe that this speaks to why the spectrum model of trauma is so humanizing. We need a model that avoids any sort of "yours is valid trauma versus yours isn't" dynamic. This is also an example of when the sloppy shorthand of diagnostic terms actually helped empower someone by giving them a way to name their experience.

PARTS, SELF, AND THEIR FUNCTIONS

Given the complexities of the human condition, we have many more parts within us than we might think. Yet IFS has found that, by and large, almost all parts can fit in one of four categories: Managers, Exiles, Firefighters, and Self Energy. Let's look at these in turn now.

Managers

Manager parts are the glue that hold our lives together. They are the parts of us that organize, plan, strategize, make lists, mentally rehearse conversations, prompt us to dress decently, and help us to comport ourselves appropriately for the situation we're in (e.g., work vs. a date vs. family gathering). When we're depressed, they're the parts of us that might tell us to stay indoors to limit disappointment—but they're also the parts that might nag us to do things to counteract the depression (exercise, call a friend, hydrate, etc.). When we're anxious, these are the parts that remind us repeatedly of our to-do list—but they're also the parts that fantasize about moving to a tropical island to start a new career selling piña coladas on the beach.

We have multitudes of managerial parts and many of them are *polarized*, meaning they generate opposing ideas about what we ought to do. These are the parts mentioned in the introduction of this book that get conflicted about whether we should have the salad for lunch (*it's healthy!*) or the burger (*it's delicious!*). However these parts of us manifest, they all have the same agenda: safety, rewards, and belonging.

Manager parts employ *preemptive defense mechanisms* to accomplish their end of this agenda. If you go back through the brief examples above, you'll notice a common theme of maintaining the status quo, limiting our risk of pain and embarrassment, avoiding triggers, and acting in accordance with our self-concept. Without these parts, we would absolutely fall apart. Yet Managers often get demonized as the "monkey mind" or the "ego"—the very subject of my first book *The Monkey Is the Messenger*. It's true that we could help these parts evolve, but that effort is only going to come through appreciation and building trust within ourselves, not enmity and pathologizing.

Seeing that these parts are motivated by safety, rewards, and belonging helps us to view these parts as nonpathological and nonneurotic. After all, *defense mechanism* is shorthand for "stuff I'm doing to keep myself safe and in the feel-good zone." There's wisdom in that, even if the wisdom gets tangled up and expressed in unwise ways. For example, the Manager activity repressing our emotions is one of the most unwise things we can do for our mental health. When we repress things, they don't go away; they go underground, accumulate, fester, and eventually manifest in ways that are much more intense. That said, there's also a wisdom in repressing our emotions as we have lives to lead, jobs to perform, and families (chosen or biological) to maintain. In such situations, we must find ways to set things aside in order to function. Thus, our Managers also have the task of holding down our Exile parts (which we'll come to), who hold our more vulnerable and painful emotions.

Problem is, our managerial defensive strategies generally form in childhood (when we are far less resourced and far more vulnerable to the world around us) and rarely get updated. This causes our managerial team inside to work far harder than it needs to, which results in our lives being more limited than they ought to.

The promising truth is that Manager parts don't actually *want* to be doing the jobs they do. We find with great consistency that they simply feel like they *must*—for example, repeat our to-do list over and over again or else bad things would happen; we'd fall apart in some way. If not for this fear, these parts would choose a role inside that feels better. Again, parts are just like people, and no one you know would really want the job repeating laundry lists or being vigilant about safety. They too would rather be at the beach. They too would rather be happy.

Hang on to this last part. You'll see it come into play when we explore the Six Fs in chapter 3.

Exiles

Exiles are the "inner children" of the inner family. Their function is to hold our pain, shame, and fear—the vulnerable emotions and memories we've experienced but haven't fully metabolized. They carry the burdensome material that we would rather ignore and wall off and, well, exile. These are the parts our Managers keep at bay in the name of maintaining our lives and protecting ourselves. Again, while there is wisdom is this strategy, these parts are often the youngest parts of us (even though, paradoxically, they often hold hurts accrued in adulthood). Richard Schwartz, in his book *You Are the One You've Been Waiting For*, remarks that the exiling of these parts is "insult added to injury. [Exiles] carry the memories, sensations, beliefs, and emotions of the hurtful experiences; then they are rejected by others as well as by us."[1]

My friend and teacher Vinny Ferraro made an astute point about this kind of inner activity in a talk titled "The Freedom of Forgiveness":

> I put an armor around my heart. I thought my heart was something I was supposed to hide from the world to protect it from the world. [I didn't know it was] my greatest gift . . . I didn't always know that. So, I put this armor around it. And biologically this makes sense. We want to protect ourselves. We want to get away from pain. But closing our hearts imprisons us. It's so tragic because it imprisons us with the very thing we're trying to escape from. Because the trauma's still in there with us . . . I can't think of a worse way to deal with things: *"A trauma has visited me, so I'm going to lock myself in with it."* . . . The good news is: if we locked the door, who else could possibly have the key?[2]

The most important thing to know about Exiles isn't that they hold our pain. These parts also hold our most lively and childlike qualities such as spontaneity, imaginativeness, vitality, sweetness, playfulness, and joy. When people talk about "growing up too fast" or "the loss of innocence," what they are really saying is that their Exiles hold burdens that have covered over these invaluable attributes. As I've been saying, outshining trauma is about getting these qualities back. Doing so is a natural by-product of outshining our trauma. We don't have to regress or surrender the wisdom and discernment of adult maturity either. That would be a disaster. Chapter 6 dives into what such an awakened life could look like.

Firefighters

When too much perceived hurt or vulnerability lands at our doorstep, our Exile parts activate and can overwhelm our preemptive managerial system. But we have a second line of protection, a *reactive defense system* made up of Firefighter parts. When trouble is in our face, when we're already exhausted, or when trauma is triggered, our Firefighters force their way to the front to fight, flee, freeze, or fawn (do whatever it takes to please an aggressor in hopes that they'll stop). Our Firefighters utilize either chaos or rigidity to eradicate the perceived threat and get the Exiles back underground so that the Managers can return to their post. Their strategies for accomplishing this are quite broad and can include dissociation, compulsive avoidance, self-medicating behaviors and substance use, lashing out with anger and rage, and making rules so "this never happens again!"

Strangely enough, Firefighter parts will resort to attacking *us* in this quest, such as with inner critics, self-sabotage, and even self-harm. When it comes to inner critics and saboteurs, theirs is generally a quest to keep a person small and to minimize taking chances. After all, if we achieve things, they can be taken away. If we are seen, we can be slandered. If we are successful, we will be exposed to a greater scrutiny. Self-harm, however, is a much more complex topic, but I find that most people engage in self-harm for the same reasons I once did—to express just how rotten everything inside feels; to make the invisible emotional wounds real and tangible. Of course, there are also the parts of us that shame us for our compulsive behaviors—or, depending on the person, for just about anything, really. Yet if we look through the lens of curiosity at this inner activity for long enough, we will find motivations in the direction of safety, growth, and belonging every time. These confounding psychological situations generally come down to choosing what one perceives as the lesser evil. Once again, perception and subjectivity play a big role here, therefore helping these parts to protect us in ways that feel better often comes down to helping them perceive things more clearly.

Firefighters are the most pathologized of all due to their involvement in things like addictive tendencies, rage attacks, and personality disorders. Yet the missions these parts go on are not intrinsically patho-logical. Like literal emergency personnel, Firefighter parts want to save the day, vie for justice, and shelter the Exiles. They deserve our apprecia-tion *and* they deserve to be introduced to better options for how to enact their missions. As with Manager parts, we find with great consistency that Firefighters are exhausted and would rather be doing something else. Their jobs aren't fun. However, they too hold the belief that if they dropped their guard, we'd be worse off in some way. For these reasons, they are not quick to give up their post. In the next chapter we'll ex-plore the Six Fs, a method of self-inquiry that helps our defensive parts, be they Managers or Firefighters, to see that another way is possible.

Self Energy

For years, I thought the awakened state in me was something exotic, something romantic, something mysterious to only be glimpsed by true mystics and masters. Plot twist: it is actually quite basic. We experience the divine spark of the spacious, awakened state all the time without rec-ognizing it. We wouldn't be sane without it. We touch this deeper nature at times through movement, dance, and art—whether making it or expe-riencing it. We feel it when we are receptively connected to nature. We are immersed in it when sex is full of genuine affection. We are directly connected to it anytime we see someone in pain and feel warmth toward them, perhaps desiring to become a resource for them. In IFS, this awak-ened, openhearted state is called Self Energy. In Buddhism, it has a di-rect correlation to buddha nature, unborn awareness, and teachings on the limitless qualities of the heart (which we will explore in chapter 13). (Speaking of Buddhism, if parts of you are hollering inside, *But the Bud-dha taught there is no self!*, this is addressed in the next chapter.)

Self Energy is not a part. It's the expression of our true nature. It's ex-perienced within the psyche and yet it transcends the psyche altogether. It's sensed inside as something spacious, fluid, sometimes tingly. It can manifest in any number of ways. Self Energy doesn't tend to have a clear voice or a unique personality like our parts do. It is a force, a presence, a certain radiance that can mix in with any of our parts (when our parts al-low space for it). For those of us who find the metaphysical connotations of the word *Energy* to be off-putting, we can veer toward its meaning in physics—a potential, a capacity, a vitality. Just as with many things in the world of physics, it is also not yet well understood, which doesn't make it any less real.

While Buddhism and many other spiritual systems do a great job of emphasizing this awakened state, they tend to not give us too much to go on when it comes to recognizing it subjectively. Thus, it is an absolute game-changer that IFS gives us specific, discernable qualities that become available inside when Self emerges. Being able to discern when Self is present opens the doorway to utilizing this inner resource. It also helps us to familiarize ourselves with what the mindstate of Self is like, which in turn allows us to deepen our experience of it over time.

HOW TO RECOGNIZE SELF ENERGY WITHIN

IFS delineates eight *C* qualities and five *P* qualities Self exudes. This is by no means exhaustive but gives us a lot to go on. When we recognize any of these qualities in an unforced, uncontrived way, Self Energy is on the scene.

The first four Cs are what we generally check for first:

1. Calm
2. Clarity
3. Curiosity
4. Compassion

I think of the first three *C*s here (calm, clarity, and curiosity) as the seedlings of the pivotal fourth *C* of compassion. To be in a calm state is synonymous with feeling spacious inside, like there's room for possibility. When we have clarity of mind, we are seeing beyond the surface of things, and liberating insight begins to dawn quite naturally. When we are curious and want to know more about a part of us or someone else, we are well on our way to understanding them better. It is when we understand where people are coming from that we begin to see that, to paraphrase Maya Angelou, we are much more alike than we are different. In such conditions, compassion naturally begins to dawn.

These four qualities lead us to four "outcome" qualities:

1. Courage
2. Confidence
3. Creativity
4. Connection

Self also has five P qualities:

1. Presence
2. Patience
3. Perspective
4. Persistence
5. Playfulness

Compassion contains the full expression of Self Energy. To express compassion is to also express courage, confidence, creativity, connection. Similarly, presence, patience, perspective, persistence, and even playfulness are either ingredients in compassion or where compassion will naturally lead us. Compassion is so spacious that it has room for all of these qualities (more examples of this are given in chapter 6). In essence, it is a state of genuine, expansive warmth. It is a trembling of the heart and the soft spot inside where we sense that all life is tender and of supreme importance. In this way, compassion can also be bittersweet at times. Because we see that life and our experience of it is invaluable, our hearts are a bit broken by the confusion and ignorance that robs people of their lives, opportunities, and dignity every day. Compassion is the source of every wish we've ever had to save the world. It is like the sun: no matter how covered over by the weather, it is there, radiant and effulgent, offering life-giving nutrients to everything and everyone without exception. Compassion outshines trauma like nothing else can. It is the path, the practice, and the goal.

> **Insight:** We tend to think of compassion as being something heavy and intense. Much like other human qualities, though, there are

many forms that we simply have not developed sufficient language for. Much like love, there are intense forms of compassion but also forms that are light and even humorous. Compassion can look like saying yes, and it can look like an unequivocal no. Compassion can take the shape of forgiveness, and it can be expressed as holy anger on behalf of the oppressed. Compassion correlates with the element of space itself; it can accommodate everything. What unifies all forms of compassion is that they originate from a soft spot in the heart (even when compassion is ultimately expressed in spicy ways).

EXERCISE: GET TO KNOW SOME OF YOUR PARTS

While you've been reading this chapter, various parts of you have been active. Some have been trying to focus on taking in the words. Some have been distracting you, perhaps reminding you to do the dishes. Some have been agreeing or disagreeing with what's being written here. It's likely that many agendas—all of them valid—have been at work in you while you simply tried to read.

Take a moment to reflect on your experience of reading this chapter. Can you identify parts that have been present, even if you were only faintly aware of them? Did they show up as a voice in your head? A feeling? An image? Sensations in the body?

If you'd like to take this a step further, see if you can get a little bit curious about what these parts of you are up to. If you find you can become curious or open to these inner parts, you could ask a question internally: *Is there anything you'd like me to know?* Try to not think of the answer or figure it out. Just ask the question from a place of sincere curiosity and see if anything comes back.

You might get more information. You might find that everything goes quiet inside. You might uncover resistance to doing this at all. It's all valid. Simply notice. You could even thank them for their input.

3

ROAD MAP TO WITHIN

Finding and Working
with Your Parts

Safety is not the absence of threat.
It is the presence of connection.

—*Gabor Maté*

Parts work is essentially a method of self-inquiry centered on establishing lines of communication within oneself. The results of this "inner relating" are often surprising. It turns out that our parts have been trying to communicate with us our whole lives, and few of us realize on our own that how we talk back really matters. The dialogues we have within (which don't just happen in words) can open doors of possibility and they can close them. They can lead us toward healing and they can deepen our wounding and confusion. It's said that the most important relationship we'll ever have is with ourselves; after all, who else is with you every second of every day? Thus, the quality of relationship we have with our parts impacts the quality of everything we experience and everything we do. The psyche is the filter through which all of our perceptions and decisions pass through and thus how we tend the psyche vis-à-vis our parts is of pivotal importance.

Later in this chapter we'll explore a tried-and-true method for engaging in such self-inquiry and conscious inner dialogues. First, I'd like to demystify the nature of parts a bit more so we can enter this work with more clarity.

I've found these two simple insights to be most helpful in understanding how to engage with parts:

1. Parts are like people. Parts simply want what everyone wants: to feel safe, loved, respected, listened to, valued, and supported. We all want to feel welcomed, for others to give us the benefit of the doubt, and to be judged by our good intentions. We all tend to relax and become quite affable and amenable when met in this way. Conversely, no one wants to feel criticized, struggle to be heard, or be misunderstood. In such conditions just about anyone will shut down, fight back, or pretend everything's okay when it's really not. Same goes for the living energies we meet inside when doing parts work.

2. Your inner system of parts truly operates like a family. Members of literal family systems settle into identifiable roles such as "the achiever," "the peacemaker," or "the black sheep." Similarly, parts are distinct personalities, performing complementary roles and functions within the inner ecosystem. Again, when parts are met the way any person wants to be met, there is an inclination toward harmony. However, when literal family members feel neglected, when teenagers are forced into parentified roles, when children are scapegoated or resented for being "too much," when only certain emotions are safe to express, and so on—the system can easily fall into a dysfunctional mode of conflict and estrangement. It's entirely possible for a family to achieve a harmonious and healthy baseline with each other. In most literal families, however, one runs into beliefs and attitudes that basically boil down to "This is just the way we are." For example, "We're the Smiths, and we don't talk about our feelings"; "We're the Garcias; we're difficult and that's just that." It's sad that so many families don't believe they could evolve into a more functional and mutually supportive state. Similarly, harmony from the inside out is possible for us as individuals. Yet many of us don't hold this as a value or believe that it's something worth working toward. Another striking parallel is just how many of our parts hold the belief, "This is just the

way I am and that's that," when the truth is parts are products of their conditioning.

I think to the ancient Hindu mantra ACHINTYA BHEDA ABHEDA TATTVA, often translated as "the inconceivable truth of simultaneous oneness and diversity." The mantra actually has theistic origins and describes how, in one system of understanding at least, God is one with all things and yet all things are "part and parcel" of God. However, I believe this also describes the way in which we are each a whole person (oneness) but made of parts (diversity) at the same time, which is indeed inconceivable. It doesn't quite make sense, but it also has a global corollary (one among many): the ways in which all humans are one species, one family—and yet great diversity abounds. Both things are true and important at once. All of which is to say, your parts are none other than you and yet they also have a life beyond you. Parts themselves have sentience, volition, and hold the content of our past experiences that we often don't even realize is there.

Many IFS practitioners come to believe that their parts are real, separate beings leading lives of their own inside us. Another theory is that parts are an anthropomorphization of the nervous system. Personally, I default to an agnostic stance on all things unseen. Despite all my confirmed experiences, who knows what's really going on in this wild universe? Still, no matter what position one takes, the truth is that parts are living, feeling, and responsive beings by virtue of the fact that we are. Thus, all parts deserve our attention, care, and respect no matter what. This contrasts from the culturally prevalent view that there are parts of us who need to shut up, go away, or suffer an "ego death."

PARTS ARE MORE THAN THEIR BURDENS

We generally begin noticing a particular part when some sort of affliction arises, be it in thought, feeling, or body sensation. That's how parts get our attention. They really don't have another language to use—not one we'll pay attention to anyway. Like infants who cry out because they're hungry or something is wrong, parts instinctually know that generating disruptions is the best way to call our attention to something that needs it. Given that our parts generally present with the burdens they carry, it could be easy to think of a part that's generating anxiety, say, as "my anxious part." The truth is, though, just like people, parts aren't their burdens. They actually have a full range of emotions. It's just that they tend to get trapped in repetitive cycles for fear of a worse alternative. Again, none of our parts actually *want* to be caught in such exhausting roles, though they do consistently defer to whatever they perceive as the lesser of two evils.

There's a promising truth to this as well: each of our individual parts also have Self Energy, a deeper nature born of compassion. The opportunity in working with our parts is to help them reclaim this deeper nature, a mission that's synonymous with the advent of Self Energy in our lives as a whole—something we'll be discussing more in-depth in chapter 6. At their core, all our parts intend to be useful. Healing, then, isn't about getting rid of or fixing parts of us but rather helping them resolve their confusion and reclaim their lost goodness.

NONPATHOLOGY

Because we tend to only recognize and engage with parts when there's a problem, it can be easy to pathologize them. The drive to diagnose our problems as a disease or disorder is pervasive in our culture. There are days when every third post in my Instagram feed is from someone lacking any clinical qualifications yet liberally labeling people as having personality disorders. Alas, we all have brains that naturally categorize experiences and people for efficiency's sake. Our tendency to slap objectifying and dehumanizing labels on folks is an unfortunate outcome of this. It's especially heartbreaking when we do this to ourselves—vis-à-vis our parts. You might recall my caveat about diagnoses at the beginning of chapter 1.

All of our parts are fundamentally interested in our survival and well-being in some way. How many of us spend years looking in the mirror wondering why we got angry at someone, when the truth is that something in the situation made us feel vulnerable first? We commonly hate our panic attacks but fail to recognize the conditions that trigger them. We commonly judge our depressions without truly listening inside to the real reasons why we suffer this response. The parts of us that engage in such judgment and self-recrimination really aren't to blame, either. No one likes to suffer. There also exists a tremendous and unreasonable social pressure to appear "problem-free" in our society. "The notion that we should always be happy," writes the holistic physician Andrew Weil, "is a uniquely modern, uniquely American, uniquely destructive idea."[1]

While conventional psychology has used the language of *irrationality* to describe afflicted states of being, this too-simple determination fails to appreciate the elaborate complexity with which all beings operate. Our parts truly constitute an ecosystem wherein every aspect is important. We only react when we perceive a threat, and we only hold pain for as long as it's not processed. We only manage and flatly administrate our lives when we sense it *has* to be this way *or else*. We must begin to understand that our parts always have rationales for their perspectives and behaviors. They obey a logic that makes complete sense to them. The trick with parts work, then, is to tap into the logic of our parts and relate in a "language" they'll be able to hear.

PARTS TRAVEL IN PACKS

We are a dynamically interwoven system of "Mini-Me"s inside; no part of us operates in isolation. Rather, they form clusters that generally center around one main issue in our lives. While the formations of these clusters can be highly unique, they generally have at least one Exile, one Manager, and one Firefighter in the mix. More often than not, I find people will have at least a couple Firefighters and Managers gatekeeping one wounded Exile (you'll find an example of parts clusters at the end of chapter 12). That one Exile often has several attendant defensive parts reflects the evolutionary imperative of safety—even if things can get convoluted to the point of harmful behaviors.

In the previous chapter, I told a simple story about getting anxious at a friend's house. There was a part of me that wanted coffee, a part of me afraid of expressing needs and disrupting the good time we were having, and then another part of me judging the part that was afraid. This is an illustration of a cluster of parts in operation around one issue. In fact, it's an example of a cluster of Manager parts who were all concerned with preempting further discomfort. If I had gone into a deeper inquiry with these parts, I would've discovered vulnerable Exiles beneath the surface of my experience. After all, why was I afraid of speaking up about a simple need? Well, I could give you a thousand examples of times when I've let my needs be known and either they haven't been met, they've been ridiculed, or they've angered someone. It logically follows that I have at least one Exile holding unprocessed pain from those experiences. That Exile would be part of the same cluster as the Managers I described.

In the story, my friend responded to my request for coffee very positively. What if they hadn't? What if they'd been upset that I wanted to leave their apartment where they thought we were having a perfectly good time? It's likely that this would've triggered the hypothetical Exile, which in turn would activate a Firefighter. Such a Firefighter might get angry at my friend for being inflexible. Another Firefighter might utilize the "fawn response" by pretending my needs don't matter and carrying on. Such Firefighters would also be part of this hypothetical parts cluster centered on the issue of speaking for my own needs.

Hang on to this idea for the next chapter where we'll discuss how parts within a cluster can hold different aspects of an experience much more intense in nature.

THE SUBTLETIES OF SELF ENERGY

If you are getting the sense that your inner world is a vast cosmos, you are on the right track. The reassuring thing about all this is you only have to get to know one star at a time and you have the rest of your life to do so. So, what about the sun that lies at the center of your personal galaxy: Self Energy? People can have some deflating misconceptions about this inner force, especially those who have difficulty experiencing things like compassion and self-love.

When we talk about approaching parts from Self, you might think you need to have mastered a state of curiosity, calm, clarity, and compassion before you can do this. If so, I come with good news: Self Energy is not a binary, either-or situation. You do not need to be 100 percent curious or loving in order to be "in Self." When the IFS folks talk about "being in

Self," it might mean as little as 2 percent Self Energy mixed in with all the rest of what and who is most active within our personal Milky Way. One ray of light is enough to sunbathe in. One glimmer of hope is enough to grow on. One nanosecond of curiosity is a seed planted that can sprout into something great.

Consider the Buddha's sermon about the hell realms of existence. The teaching goes that there are multiple *buddhas*—"enlightened ones"—who incarnate in all the various realms of existence, from the highest heavens to the hottest hells to spread the Dharma—the methods of liberation. In the hottest of all the hell realms, said the Buddha, the enlightened ones manifest simply as one cool sip of water. That's it! Nothing more. No meditation, no philosophy. One drink of water amid the flames. One moment of relief offered with the prayer that the water might give rise to an awareness that *freedom from the heat is possible*—that one can get out of this place and this is not all there is.

Once upon a time, I found myself downing Jack and Cokes on an airplane next to a very nice, older Christian lady who was all too eager to chat with me. I had an alarming liquor tolerance in those days, and we carried on very well despite my mission to get plastered while she enjoyed . . . water. We spoke of our lives and relationships and even had some friendly debates about our differing views on the Bible. Every so often she would lean in and point to my drink, remarking quietly, "You know, there's help for that." From there, she would return to our dialogue as if she hadn't said anything at all. I was struck by her approach—and grateful for her brevity. Anything more would have been a waste of breath. Still, on this long, cross-country flight, she found gentle moments to reassert, "You can heal that," even as I ordered yet another drink. I thought of her many months later as I finally entered rehab. I believe this thoughtful stranger planted some important seeds with me that day on the plane. While her words seemed negligible at the time, they circulated in memory as I walked into this strange, new territory. This is the potential of small compassions skillfully expressed.

If you don't think you could find even 1 percent of Self Energy there amid your parts, not to worry—there are workarounds that we'll begin exploring in chapter 11.

Regarding Buddhist Teachings
on "No Self" and Emptiness

Esotericism ahead! Non-Buddhists may want to skip this section.

When I speak of Self Energy being our essential nature, Buddhists are often quick to assert the core doctrine of *anatman*, "no self"—that there is nothing about us that is permanent, unchanging, solid, and not constructed of parts. We aren't a "self" in the way we think we are. Every time we go looking for some solid, discernable essence of who and what we are, what we take to be "the self" dissolves on us.

Many years ago, I randomly stumbled upon an art opening while walking in the Chelsea district of Manhattan. It was a showing of large-scale calligraphy by a great Zen monk. I stood appreciating one piece in particular, a single Japanese character. Another monk approached me and asked if I had any questions. I didn't, but I wanted to be polite. So, I asked what the character I was looking at meant. He said, "Self." I protested, "But the Buddha taught, 'No self!'" To which the monk fired back, "Does buddha nature not endure?"

When it comes to teachings on emptiness, the Buddha taught, "Things are not as they seem, nor are they otherwise." When it comes to who and what we are, "it is not as it seems"—we are made of parts as well as a buddha nature and we are not the solid, fixed, permanent, unchanging beings we often take ourselves to be. We are a construct. But "nor is it otherwise"; if you were to pinch yourself, would you not feel pain? If you were to throw your cell phone out the window, wouldn't your next thought be, *But how will so-and-so get ahold of me later?* You do, in spite being "empty of self," exist. This body of teaching is very mysterious and is beyond simple exposition. We must admit that few of us truly comprehend it. The Buddha taught on the emptiness of all things but also about their fundamental luminosity. To state things succinctly and imperfectly, our parts are what correlate with emptiness and Self Energy correlates with luminosity. The Buddha also taught the *Brahma Viharas*, the four fundamental and limitless qualities of the heart (soon to be explored here). This is none other than the expression of Self Energy we've been discussing.

We'll explore this idea a bit more later, but the label we're using, "Self," is also a misnomer. Self Energy is not personal in nature. It is, rather, the aspect of our being that is the most closely interconnected and interdependent with all things yet is somehow not a thing itself.

There's one final "emptiness-oriented" question that routinely arises: By acknowledging our thoughts and emotions engaging with their content directly, are we not reifying our thoughts and emotions in a manner that's inconsistent with Buddhist teachings on emptiness? In a way, yes. However, one does not realize the empty nature of something by ignoring it or considering it insubstantial right away. Again, if I were to pinch you or steal your phone, you wouldn't say, "Ah, this pain has no self-nature." Quite the opposite. Thus, we must start where we are, already in the reification of such things.

In the practices aimed at piercing the veil and seeing through to the emptiness of our thoughts and emotions (*Mahamudra*), we do so by first becoming highly intimate with those thoughts and emotions— and the more difficult, the better. Only through intimacy with mental formations can we directly perceive their groundless, apparition-like nature. We don't do this foolishly, either. We do it in the context of spacious awareness and compassion practices and while connected to community, *sangha*, in a continuous manner. The practice of parts work—becoming intimate with our parts and their narratives and emotions while in the space of compassion—directly parallels this. This will become increasingly apparent as we continue here. You will also see that parts work parallels the R.A.I.N. technique offered by Tara Brach, as well as Lama Tsultrim Allione's "feed your demons" distillation of Tibetan *chöd* practice.

BLENDING AND UNBLENDING

It seems that when we're too bound up in anything, we lose our sense of self and become susceptible to all kinds of disaster. This is true of our relationships with other people: we can become enmeshed and codependent and find ourselves in some confusing dynamics. This is true of our jobs amid a crushing workaholic culture. This can be true in spiritual communities, or any community for that matter. This is also true when it comes to our own mental states and the attendant thoughts and emotions presented by our parts. It is quite natural to *blend* with our parts when they become activated. Be they Manager parts, reactive Firefighter parts, or vulnerable and wounded Exile parts, they all tend to take over such that we feel like we *are* that part of us. Whatever emotions or thoughts are coming from that part of us, be it anger or insecurity or a narrative of unworthiness, we lose sight of our multiplicity and it's as if that one part is the one, true self. We tend to automatically believe there's no other possibility save for suffering that mindstate. It's a form of tunnel vision, yet another narrowing.

"You are not your thoughts" goes the famed saying associated with mindfulness practice. Indeed, the essence of mindfulness practice is to develop the core skill of standing back from experience so as to be more of a witness to our inner dialogue and emotions. The comedian and all-around fantastic human Pete Holmes summed it up pretty flawlessly on a recent *Big Think* blog post:

> When I'm depressed, [it can be good] if I can get into that quiet space, the space that's noticing the thoughts. [For example], if you think, "I'm hungry," and then you eat and the thought goes, "thank you," who's talking to who? Really, I would say that the thought is talking to your awareness, your base awareness, your witness. That's what's watching your thoughts. If you can get into that [witnessing state], you see how impartial and unswayed by your life circumstance this witness really is. It's just there, it's neutral . . . it's just watching. It's compassionate, it's involved, it's invested . . . but it's not really as connected and tied to the events of your life story as you are, as your "false self" is. So, when those depressions happen . . . this is something Ram Dass taught me— instead of identifying with the depression and saying, "I am depressed," what I'm thinking is, "there is depression, I am noticing depression.". . . It's not denial . . . but you're a little bit less in the quicksand. Ram Dass asks, "Is the part of you that's noticing the depression [itself] depressed?" . . . There is an impartial part of me that's witnessing whatever the feeling is, and I can rest in that. Like a candle that's inside that isn't swayed or flickered by the wind. And when you're in there, you don't resist the depression, you give it *space*.[2]

Although Holmes is describing the practice of mindfulness, he could equally be describing the practice of *unblending* from parts and finding Self Energy, the compassionate witness. When we are blended with parts, we are more or less on autopilot. It's often the case that an inner child or inner teenager is running the show because they are afraid of what might happen if they don't. From a Buddhist point of view, this is a form of delusion. We begin to unblend when we become mindful of the fact that we are caught up—hijacked, even. Just noticing is like turning the lights on in a dimmed room. From here, we can begin to remember that we are more than the content of our experience.

We have a relationship to our experience as well. Our relationship to an experience determines so much about the quality of that experience and the choices we will feel inclined to make within it. If we are relating from our parts, especially the ones that hold trauma, we will see and feel and react through the lens of traumatic conditioning those parts hold. If we can find what Holmes is pointing out—the compassionate witness inside, the aspect of our being that is not caught up in any of the goings-on and yet can certainly help—we begin living through the lens of curiosity and compassion. To riff on a famous quote by the Zen master Shunryu Suzuki Roshi, in a blended state the options are few; in an unblended state, the options are many.

EXERCISE: THE SIX FS: A ROAD MAP TO TRANSFORMATIVE SELF-INQUIRY

The Six Fs form a strategy that has become a core process for unblending and working with parts. It is an indispensable, step-by-step technique that many of us use some aspect of every time we engage in parts work. It gives us something of a script to follow, complete with questions that get right into the logic parts commonly obey. As the inner world can be a nebulous and confusing place, having an instruction manual for excavating the psyche is at least as valuable as having one for your new Ikea futon.

Here, I will describe the Six Fs. You're welcome to just read through and familiarize yourself with this process. Or, if you're ready to dive in, please go more slowly and actually do each step experientially. We'll revisit the Six Fs several times in the book, including as a meditation in chapter 10.

1. **Find** a part to work with.

You can find a part to work with simply by noticing what you're feeling and thinking about right now (these are being expressed by parts). You could also intentionally seek out a part, perhaps a lonely or a frustrated part that's been coming up for you a lot lately. If you wish to uncover such a part, you can look for a *trailhead* by simply remembering an experience you had when that part was activated. Relive that memory until you feel things start to come up. Then make space for whatever it is you begin to notice. As the Tibetan Buddhist saying goes, "Welcome the stranger."

Parts show up in one or more of these four ways:

- Feelings (ranging from full-on emotions to a vague sense of something)
- Physical sensations
- Two forms of thought:
  - Images
  - Words

Again, some of us get one of these, some of us get a combination, and for some it fluctuates. What's important to understand here is that there are always parts present. Once you start identifying parts, you're already beginning to unblend; you're already back in touch with your natural multiplicity.

2. **Focus** on the part.

Once you're in touch with a part, give your attention over to them. You may need to ask inside for other parts of you to step to the side. It's okay if your attention is a bit shaky. Just do your best to focus on what I'll now call the *target part*.

3. **Flesh** the part out.

As you focus on the target part, you may begin to notice more about them. For example, you might first notice them in the form of a "voice," but once you're focusing on them, you might get in touch with an emotion that goes along with that voice; there may be a body sense involved as well. You can let the target part know that you're right here with them by reflecting back to them what you notice. Some examples: *I feel the tightness in the chest, I hear the thoughts about my boss, I'm noticing you're angry*, or *I see the memory from when I was six you want me to know about.*

To further the unblending, you might imagine you're sitting with this target part—perhaps right next to them on a park bench or maybe across a table from them. They're like an old friend that's trying to tell you something, and you are beginning to listen. A student of mine once used the metaphor of being on a first date, where you want to be sure to make eye contact and convey interest.

4. Notice your **feelings** toward the part.

This step in the process never ceases to amaze me. It lays bare the simple fact that we really can consciously communicate within ourselves and get answers. If you're new to IFS, this honestly might sound kooky to you at first, but don't let that stop you.

Ask inside yourself: *How do I feel toward this part?* We'll likely find *polarized parts* (discussed in chapter 2) that are judging, critiquing, hating, dissociating from, or analyzing the target part. Polarized parts are just as interested in our well-being as the target part, only they have a different opinion about what we need. Thank them for their opinion and ask them kindly to step to the side for now. They're not wrong, but we want to open up a space here for the target part to have their say.

We then ask inside a second time: *How do I feel toward the target part now?* It's common that you'll find another polarized part. Kindly ask again if this other part will step to the side so that you can be in Self Energy with the target part.

After two rounds of this, look toward your heartspace inside. See if you can find just a little bit of clear space in there; perhaps a feeling of calm, curiosity, or compassion; perhaps an inclination to get to know the part a bit better. If so, then you're ready to proceed. If not, then notice the polarized part of you that hasn't yet stepped aside and switch to working with that part. Repeat steps 2–4: focus on them, flesh them out, and get into a space of Self Energy with them.

5. Befriend the part.

Find a way to offer Self Energy to this part. You might offer the good feelings of Self to them or simply say, *I'm curious about you right now.* Notice if the part is receptive to this from you. If they aren't, try asking, *How old do you think I am?* Don't think of the answer; just ask. You'll likely get an age younger than you presently are. This is a great opportunity to fill this part in on your actual age, that you've survived, and that you've got better resources nowadays. They may need an apology from you, too, for being shoved to the side for so long.

> **Insight:** Trauma often forces parts of us to go into arrested development. When parts are mistrusting of Self, it's almost always because that part is frozen in the past and believes we are younger (and less resourced) than we actually are. Parts might even believe the trauma is still currently happening. Asking the part *How old do you think I am?* is an IFS trick for exposing this. When we get an answer from the part that is younger than our physical age, we can begin bringing the traumatized part out of their arrested development.

From here, you want to get into a dialogue with this part of you. How that dialogue will unfold depends on what type of part you're working with. Take a moment to discern if this part is defensive in nature—either a Manager or a Firefighter—or a wounded, vulnerable Exile. You'll know you're in the presence of a Manager when they feel a bit neutral and have their mind on tasks. You'll know if they're a Firefighter when they are reactive. You'll know they're an Exile when they are more deflated; holding pain, insecurity, or vulnerability.

Some options for questions you can ask Managers and Firefighters to get to know them:

- *Is there anything you want me to know?*
- *What are you trying to accomplish?*
- *Is there anything I can do to help you trust Self Energy more?*
- *How can we be better friends?*
- *When did you start doing this job? Was there an experience we had where you took on this role?*
- *I see you're trying to address my pain in some way; can I point out to you how you're hurting me in the process?*

If you are getting answers to these questions, you're ready to move on to the sixth *F* below. If not, you could elect to simply stay connected to this part and breathe for some time. This might be as far as you get for today. Trust takes time.

———

If you find you're working with an Exile, you'll want to open a process called *bearing witness* wherein this part finally gets a chance to feel seen and heard, just as they are, in the space of Self. Below are some questions you can ask (if they feel right) to facilitate bearing witness. The main thing with Exiles is to hold space for them, really let them know you're compassionately present with them.

- *What is it you need me to know?*
- *What has it been like for you?*
- *How old are you?*
- *What's the earliest you can remember feeling this same way?*
- *Are you ready to let the feelings out? Maybe we can walk out to a giant field where you have all the space you need to let loose.*
- *Do you have any questions for me?* (If yes, answer like the most loving parent you can imagine.)
- *What's something I can offer you to help you trust Self more?*

What's crucial here is that this part is given a chance to be themselves and to express whatever is in their heart. If you're in Self Energy, you won't get overwhelmed. If at any point you do find you're overwhelmed, there are many ways to address this. Some techniques are described in the very next section of this chapter.

If you start getting glimpses of memories wherein this part became burdened by trauma, hang on to this for now. Just hold them and help them feel less alone. Let the part know that you see them and that you'll be back to rescue them. We'll get into a process called retrieval in chapter 14 where you'll have the opportunity to do just that.

6. (For Firefighter and Managers)
What does the part FEAR?

As we've been discussing, defensive Firefighters and Managers only remain in their exhausting roles for fear of a worse alternative. Our present status quo might be laden with suffering, but it's the devil we know. Furthermore, the prospect of change often arrives as a threat. Who knows what lies on the other side of healing? Do we actually trust that freedom is possible? And if we were free, do we even know what we'd do with it? More than anything, though, defensive parts fear that if they were to drop their guard, our Exiles would come to the surface and we'd be overwhelmed. Yet, our situation is often more hopeful than our parts believe.

We can become a *hope merchant* to these parts by asking these questions:

- *Do you want to be doing this job, or do you just feel like you have to?*
- *Does it ever get tiring for you?*
- *If you didn't have to protect me like this anymore, what would you rather be doing?*

Generally speaking, defensive parts will reveal their exhausted choice-lessness and welcome the idea of doing something new that will still support the system. In some cases, defensive parts feel powerful in their current role and mistake that sense of power for fun and safety. They may need your help seeing that power is not the same as fun and is an exploitative form of safety (as feeling powerful tends to entail making someone else less powerful).

From here, you can celebrate with the defender this new hopeful possibility they're conceiving. Let them know that you want this for them, too. Let them know that if they let you go deeper and work with Exile parts they're protecting, they'll move closer to that possibility becoming an actuality.

You can discover more about the Exile the target part is defending by asking: *What do you fear might happen if you were to stop protecting me like this?* The part's answer is a direct indication of the Exile that they're protecting. You can connect these dots easily. If the part tells you, *I'm afraid we'll get beat up*, then there is an Exile who's holding the pain of being beaten up before. If they tell you, *We'll make an ass out of ourselves*, then there's an Exile holding the experience of some sort of humiliation you've been through. You can extrapolate these examples to anything the defender is telling you.

At this point you have a few options:

- This might be enough for today. If so, note what you're learning about the emerging Exile. Make sure to thank all the parts you've met today and close the session with kindness.
- If you feel up for meeting the Exile part, make absolute sure to ask inside if you have permission from the defensive parts to do so. We always want to honor the boundaries of our Manager and Firefighter parts in this work. Going too far without their permission often results in a form of backlash and even parts inhibiting all future parts work.
- The Exile may already be present. If you're up for working with them today, start over at the beginning of the Six Fs. If you want to or need to close the session, spend at least a few moments offering Self Energy to this tender part. Be a good parent to them and explain kindly that it is so good to meet them and that you'll be back soon, but it's "goodbye for now."

Exile parts have their own fears of change. They often hold a belief that the burdens they hold are their identity—who would they be without them? This is especially the case for trauma thrivers for whom the wounding began at young ages. Thus, Exiles often fear that they'll cease to exist or be abandoned by us if they no longer have all this pain to get our attention with.

When the time is right (usually after several interactions with the same Exile part), we can become hope merchants for them by asking: *If you weren't holding this pain for me anymore, what would that free you to do?* Then, just as with defensive parts, we celebrate that possibility with them and inform them, *This is the mission we're on here, to make this an actuality.*

If You Get Overwhelmed

Parts can be extreme at times. Sometimes they take on the voices and attitudes of not-wonderful (and even abusive) role models we've had in the past. Sometimes they're angry with us. Sometimes they've been locked away and ignored for so long that they're fit to burst once acknowledged. Regardless, if this is happening, here are four options for getting out of overwhelm:

1. Breathe yourself bigger so you can contain it.
2. Feel your body in space surrounded by the walls of the room you're in right now and breathe deeply for at least two minutes. This will help your body switch out of fight-flight mode and calm down.
3. Imagine you walk the part out to a big, open field, one where you can see the whole sky, horizon to horizon. This part now has all the room in the world to wild out however they need to. They can tantrum or can scream at the sky, whatever they need.
4. If all else fails, it's most likely because the part needs to feel heard at a deeper level, so try this:

   • Ask the part for their laundry list of complaints.
   • Repeat back to them exactly what you hear—for example, *I hear you are upset because of a, b, and c, as well as x, y, and z.*
   • Ask if the part feels totally heard or if there's more. If there's more, repeat the previous step.
   • Then say inside, *Now that I'm getting it, I'm wondering if you can turn down the volume here so I can have enough space to work on these things?* I sometimes imagine a big volume knob when I do this, and it slowly going down from 11 . . ., 10 . . ., 9 . . ., 8 . . ., all the way to 1.

Parts can turn things down if they want to, and no one actually *wants* to be screaming. Screaming's a lot of work. Parts often generate overwhelm when they don't feel heard.

Now that this target part feels heard, you might feel up for returning to the Six Fs or you might want to simply breathe deeply for a while. Whatever you do, make sure to practice aftercare and be good to yourself today.

EXERCISE: TRACK A PART

It's important that we track the parts we meet in meditation. It helps these parts of us feel seen, and it helps us to remember them. It engenders a sense of continuity on our path, which lends a feeling of progress and will help us from slipping backward. From this point forward in the book, you'll want to keep track of the parts you meet in meditation by simply taking three to five minutes to journal about them. (Of course, you're welcome to go beyond three to five minutes, but I find that keeping it simple helps us stay motivated.)

Some guiding questions:

- How did the part appear in thought, feeling, and sensation?
- What did you learn about them?
- Is there a friendly nickname it makes sense to give them?
- Do they seem connected to other parts of you?
- What might they need from you in order to feel safe and connected?

Note: It's important to only track parts after you've met them in an experience. Many of us might have Manager parts that want to skip ahead and start writing down all kinds of parts we suspect are there. When folks do this, it can get pretty confusing. Again, take your time getting to know one star in your personal cosmos at a time. Keep it simple and only track parts after each of your parts work meditations. Soon we'll begin mapping them.

4

HEALING IN THE DARK

The Interplay of Parts

One day you will tell your story of how you overcame what you
went through and it will be someone else's survival guide.

—*Brené Brown*

*Heads up: some stories of the violence I experienced growing up are on
the way.*

We were born into a world full of confused people. The confusions of
generations had been handed down to everyone that surrounded us
during the years we were the most vulnerable. In our childhood and ad-
olescent years, we were literally trapped with them. We had no other
options. For some of us, this was a good thing. For too many, it was not.
Most likely, few of the adults around us were taught to perceive vulnerability as a strength. Few were taught how to communicate with empathy.
Few possessed emotional intelligence. Many weren't sure if kindness
was a wise choice and so they often erred on the side of flatness—if not
aggression. Many simply didn't understand how important it is to show
up in a caring way. Again, such things are often the legacy handed down
from ancestry. One part of them, at least (there are beautiful aspects as
well). And this is how they get handed off to us.

I see a large swath of society that is beginning to extinguish these
legacies of confusion. The situation by and large seems to improve with

every new decade we enter. Emotional intelligence is now a household term. People discuss their attachment styles (patterns in intimacy) on dating apps. Reliable, coherent theory on child development is readily available. Mental health treatment is no longer a stigma. For these things I am deeply grateful. My mission in life is to be part of this collective awakening. It is lifesaving. Still, I grew up in a place and time where people meant well but were confused, themselves traumatized and re-enacting that trauma all over the place. Cruelty and violence commonly abounded as a result.

THE LAST ATTACK I COULD TAKE

I'm sixteen. It's the '90s. I've committed a real crime in the eyes of my peers. It's one others feel I deserve to be followed home for, continually harassed and humiliated for, and publicly beaten for. What is this egregious sin I've unleashed into the world, you ask? My hair is too long. And instead of it being the usual black, brown, red, or blond, it's green. And I talk in a manner some would call "femme." That's right: I'm *weird*. My presentation doesn't fit neatly into a prescribed category. I'm also neurodivergent. My brain doesn't process concepts and constructs like other brains seem to—including gender norms. I'm emotional, expressive, and have ideas about things like racism and ecology and homophobia that other kids at school haven't heard of before. To make matters worse, I've discerned that the pervasive emotional and physical violence that's come my way isn't my fault, so I've dug in my heels. I refuse to bow to the forces compelling me to conform. My insistence leads others to believe I "must like the attention."

The incessant, stupid kerfuffle of "*Gasp!* He doesn't fit in, and we don't know what to do with that" began in preschool. (Why anyone felt they needed to do anything about it is still beyond me.) Then things peaked in my sophomore year of high school.

I'm at an outdoor gathering talking to friends when a clenched fist reaches from behind to knock me square in the mouth. I fall on the pavement. A steel-toed boot collides with my neck. It was aimed at my head. My attacker intended to do real damage. The word *faggot* is resonating in the atmosphere. I lie frozen, hoping the trouble has passed. I've been attacked so many times that freezing feels less like a response and more like a routine. I see the responsible party walking away in a backward baseball cap. I eventually thaw. I gather myself, half-waiting for a friend in the crowd to come to my aid. No one approaches. I turn and begin walking home. Astonished. Alone. Done.

———

I tell you about this experience because it's an extreme-enough example for us to intuit how some basic psychological elements played out. We can now look back through the lens of everything we've explored so far to help us see how our dynamic systems function as an ecosystem in the face of trauma.

It's plain to see how there would be a lot of pain, shame, and fear carried forward from such an attack. It also makes sense that I would develop some extreme reactions to that pain, shame, and fear to protect myself psychologically. It's also intuitive enough that I would need to find a way to continue to function. Down the road, I would also need to heal from this, and I did.

The window of consolidation was open. Receiving care in the wake of this horrid experience could have greatly mitigated the neurobiological effects of the experience. Now, I want to be clear that I actually don't blame anyone in my life whatsoever for what happened next. I simply grew up in an environment where folks hadn't been exposed to the contemporary ideas and processes we're discussing in this book. No one knew any better, and neither did I. Had they known better, I know they would have done better. All the same, there just wasn't really anywhere I could share about what I'd experienced and be received with compassion. This is not to mention that being met later with messages of "You brought this on yourself by acting so weird" was a trauma all its own. This was also the third (and least violent) physical assault I had suffered in six weeks. These experiences consolidated into my body in ways that would greatly influence my life's trajectory for two full decades. Triggers formed—looking back I can recognize that the key trauma reminders were males, backward baseball hats, and being outside in the open air.

Insight: When we've encountered a similar kind of painful experience numerous times, it can often be like we're holding a pot of water that's become quite full. This naturally gives rise to a sense that we can never, ever meet with the same experience again. There's often an underlying sense that even a shot glass of water would cause us to overflow—to become overwhelmed and either lose our minds or shut down completely. One aim of parts work is often to reduce the water held in the pot by helping our parts process and release this psychic material. This results in us not having to live in fear of meeting with a similar circumstance again because we've restored our capacity to handle potential distress.

Let's now think within the categories of parts I described in the last chapter.

My Firefighters had been the very first to step in. They enacted the freeze response in the moment of the attack. They kept my body lying perfectly still on the ground to dissuade my attacker from thinking there was more work to do. They scanned the environment for any further signals of danger. And even in the trauma tunnel of surreality, they discerned the sketchy outline of the male attacker walking away in a backward baseball cap. They also kept me in a state of shock long enough for me to walk myself home.

The pain, shame, and fear I naturally felt came to be held by my Exile parts. With nowhere to go, those feelings, along with the parts holding them, were sent underground where they calcified. Keeping that material locked away was a pretty big job, though. Looking back, both my Managers and my Firefighters collaborated on what to do next. They were guided, as many defensive parts are, by two words: *never again.* Never again could I be attacked, and never again would I feel so beneath someone else.

The day after the attack, my proactive parts developed a plan for how I would narrow my world to achieve "never again." Of course, many in my position may have decided to harden. Many would have gone on the warpath. Neither of these options made any sense to me. I had no desire to "toughen up." I had no desire to become like my abusers in response to their abuse.

I was of legal age to drop out of school on my own recognizance, and I did just that first thing Monday morning. My Manager parts also developed new rules I had to live by: I could no longer leave the house except for band practice and to play shows (situations wherein I felt at least somewhat safer). I went from my house to my car to another house or venue, then back to my car and home. Other than this, if I were outside for more than a few seconds, Exiles would become triggered and I'd find myself painfully terrified.

My Firefighters formed another protective layer by armoring me with big rage, resentment, and rebelliousness. These intense emotions helped me feel powerful, which was a substitute for feeling safe. I came to spend my days hiding out, but inside there was an enormous middle finger directed at the world. Enter: punk rock counterculture. With school out of the way, I immersed myself in songwriting, booking punk shows, making zines, and reading up on radical feminism and political movements. The music I wrote was an effective outlet for the rage and pain but did little to heal much. My Exiles continued to hold it for me. My scorn for the conventional world of "normal people" came to know no bounds.

Twenty years later, someone invited me to see their friend's band. The band wasn't of the punk/indie/art ilk I gravitate toward, but I decided to be open-minded for once. Walking into the show, however, was like diving into an ocean of triggers. It turned out that fans of this particular band were also huge fans of backward baseball caps. Visceral aversion arose within me. An entire cluster of parts was suddenly clamoring. In the presence of this trauma reminder—one I had all but forgotten about—Exiles began to tremble inside. I found myself desperate to go home and wanting to cry. Yet my Manager parts didn't want to be rude to my friend who'd just gotten me in on the guest list. These parts reassured my Exiles that we were grown now and, anyhow, no one there was interested in fighting me; they were there to see the show. Still, this gave some Firefighter parts a great excuse to begin imbibing alcohol. Which worked. Sort of. I managed to numb enough to let go, enjoy the night out with my friend, and shake hands with the band before departing.

I didn't make it five steps into my living room before an avalanche of traumatic stress exploded inside me. The Exiles had been activated by the trauma reminder of men in backward baseball caps, the drinks had softened my defensive Manager system, and the decades-old pain overwhelmed me. I found myself wailing on the floor, my mind perseverating the words, *He kicked you like a dog. He wanted you dead and no one did a thing. They treated you like trash.*

One benefit of having repressed pain surface many years later is we tend to be better resourced than when the event originally took place. Here, in my grown-up life, I had solid friends I could call for help. Though it was 3 a.m., a dear love woke from sleep to come and sit on the floor with me, administering the very care I had needed when I was sixteen. That compassionate friend was expressing the thing I was too overwhelmed to find within myself in that moment: Self Energy—caring, generosity, and patience. They stayed until I could finally get to sleep.

Having discovered IFS in the months prior, I used parts work to process this trauma. For six weeks, my meditation practice was weeping. What a friend calls "the ugly cry." I'd sit down, ring the meditation bell, and my Exiles would rush to the surface, knowing this was their time. I also discovered something quite awesome (in the true sense of the word): that no matter the depth of the pain, the compassion of Self Energy could expand to meet it. This allowed me to finally let it all out without becoming overwhelmed. My neighbors, however, likely concocted all kinds of theories about what sort of Greek tragedy was unfolding in my apartment each morning.

Now this might surprise you, because, on its face, six weeks of daily catharsis sounds genuinely awful. Yet with Self Energy present, there was an odd satisfaction to this experience. It felt good to be facing this pain. It wasn't masochism, either. It was the deep release of finally facing the truth, and the liberation of knowing that every time I sat, I was closer to healing, closer to taking my power back.

Insight: Crying releases serotonin and endorphins from the body, which is why we often feel better afterward. Never be afraid of a good cry (or an ugly one).

Within the space of those weeks, I unburdened the pain, rage, and terror held by my sixteen-year-old parts. I expressed appreciation to my Managers who'd helped me survive this long-term situation. I began getting to know my destructively rageful Firefighter part, who first appeared in my mind as Rosemary's Baby but later became Ferdinand the Bull. Then there came the very tender Exile who held the core wound, the epicenter of it all. Trapped at sixteen years old, they first appeared alone and disfigured in a dark room. My meditations mostly consisted of going into the vision of that room as compassionate Self and simply sitting there, letting them go through what they needed to but no longer alone. Then there came the day when this part had finally felt the pain all the way through. They were ready to leave the room, join me in the present moment, and unburden their wounds into the Earth.

The realization dawned that I had survived. I had survived that attack, the attacks that had come before it, and the chaos of my early adult years as well. I had made it out. Obviously I knew these things cognitively, but it began landing in a new way—in an embodied way. Recognizing my innate resilience became a wellspring of confidence: *If I survived this, I'm pretty sure I have less to be afraid of than I think.* That confidence became a fierce inspiration to continue helping others and to go deeper as a therapist, teacher, and healing presence in the world. It became the inspiration to go even further along the path of post-traumatic growth.

THE REFUGE OF SELF ENERGY

Kimberly Ann Johnson, author of the trauma-focused book for cis-women, *Call of the Wild*, writes, "We often think that trauma is what happened to us. But trauma is often what was not able to happen."[1] Trauma is the community you didn't have, the voice you couldn't express, the care you didn't receive in the aftermath of something truly terrible. This view expresses the power of what happens with windows of consolidation. To have Self Energy show up when a window of consolidation is reopened is the antidote.

Self Energy can be held by another person, such as a therapist or a friend. I think of this as *Self Energy surrogacy*, and it can make all the difference to parts of us who haven't yet felt safe enough to let down their guard. The Buddha also taught that all living things hold this level of compassionate energy, including the Earth. IFS teaches similarly, as do many spiritual traditions and Indigenous cultures. It is entirely possible to feel held and healed by the Earth or even by animals. (Dogs are especially good at unconditional love, no?) Yet many of us don't know how to receive such holding and healing. And even the most supportive therapists and friends often can't sense exactly what we need for lasting healing. After all, they're not the ones living inside a traumatic experience—we are.

We will be exploring increasingly how to hold Self Energy for ourselves. While we may never shed our need for interpersonal connection—and while there are some healings that can only take place in relationship with others—there is a unique power in healing something on our own. With most of my therapy clients, I might begin by holding Self Energy for them, but once I get them into their own Self Energy more and more across the course of our sessions, I am merely a guide. The client's Self begins doing the heavy lifting. When a client is in Self and completely aligned with the part they're working with, it is common that surprising answers and insights will begin to emerge. They'll connect dots and arrive in places I could never have guided them to. It is also common for so much to start happening inside them, and so fast, that I can't even keep up. In such moments, I simply rest and hold compassionate space. The Self Energy in the client takes over and does all the work. When the alchemy of awakening begins to unfold effortlessly before my eyes, there is nothing more magical. My unshakable confidence in IFS in born of witnessing such moments.

When our own experience of Self Energy engineers this alchemical process, something that couldn't happen any other way unfolds: we begin to trust. We begin to trust that we are survivors and thrivers. We begin to trust ourselves, our own resourcefulness. We gradually begin to trust our own resilience, and from that basis we can become supremely confident in the world. We incrementally begin to sense, *Come what may, I'm gonna find a way through it.* We start sensing that we needn't let vulnerability or the possibility of making a fool of ourselves stop us so much anymore. We also start seeing life lessons emerge. We get insights about how things work inside and in the world around us. We also begin to see how everyone is made of parts. People spontaneously report things like, "My husband came at me angrily and instead of reacting, I thought, 'Oh, these are his Firefighters. I wonder what they're protecting. I wonder what he's afraid of or hurt by.' And then I noticed I was in the curiosity of Self and responded from there."

In other words, we begin to discover what Buddhists call *refuge*. And when we internalize experiences of refuge, we start to regain our child-like wonder within the context of full maturation.

EXERCISE: IDENTIFYING PARTS ACTING AS A SYSTEM

Think of an adverse (but, please, not an intense or overwhelming experience you've had), and see if you can discern the various parts that got involved. Some good examples to work with might be facing a challenge at work or a disagreement with a friend.

What vulnerabilities were present? See if you can sense into what your Exiles held (generally speaking, more vulnerable emotions and beliefs).

In what way did you try to contain things or maintain basic functioning? See if you can figure out what your proactive and preventative Managers got up to.

Did you react in any way, either in the moment or afterward? What did your Firefighters do to either smooth you out, restore a sense of justice, or create a "never again" scenario.

Take five to ten minutes to journal your answers to these questions.

Note: In this exercise we are just trying to get a handle on what parts are and how they function within the category of their roles. We're still thinking and talking *about* parts. Later, we'll identify parts in a more direct way and begin talking *to* them.

5

THE SKY IS LARGER
THAN THE SUN

Post-Traumatic Growth

*We delight in the beauty of a butterfly but rarely admit the changes
it has gone through to achieve that beauty.*

—*Maya Angelou*

I seem to have a strange quality that invites an unusual degree of openness from people. This comes in handy in my line of work, of course. It also gets me into some unusual situations, like the time a server at a diner in Nashville began telling me her childhood abuse history within ten minutes of me sitting at the counter. Or when I run into people I know at the grocery store and they randomly confess to me that they haven't been meditating lately. I think this has less to do with me per se and more to do with how hungry we all are to find qualities of simple, heartfelt presence in people.

A few winters ago, I was on a stalled ski lift with a man who told me his story of post-traumatic growth. We'd been dishing the usual small talk when I mentioned that I had once worked in foster care—and it turned out he had grown up in foster care. He had suffered an all-too-common experience of being abandoned by a parent, entering the child welfare system, and getting bounced from home to home and from school to school due to the trauma-related behaviors he developed. Yet this man was on vacation at a pricey ski resort with his wife and five(!) children. (I simply lived in the neighboring town.) When I asked what he and his wife did to afford ski vacations for such a large family, it turned out that he owned and ran three unique corporations, including a real estate agency and an oil investment firm. He remarked that his past experiences of love starvation and humiliation had given him the fuel to create an extraordinary life. When I responded with some well-rehearsed clinician line about how we really can turn trauma into a gift, he gently grabbed my arm, lifted his ski goggles, and said something to the effect of, "No, Ralph, I don't think you really get it. *I truly have something other people don't get to have.* This fire I have in my belly for this life, for my children, for accomplishing things. I don't know anyone else with it. It's literally an advantage I have over other people, one they can't go out and acquire."

I think about a dear friend, among the growing many who struggle with chronic illness. When I remarked on how unusually kind and responsive she so often is, she texted back to me, "One thing chronic illness does is tenderize. I'm less likely to take anything for granted . . . doubly so with the people I love." It occurred to me in that moment that she could have gone the other way. She could've let it all shut her down: the years of difficulty grappling with a mystery illness, not being believed by doctor after doctor, and having her whole life detoured while she was still in her thirties. Becoming bitter was certainly an option; it's an unfortunate (yet understandable) end many arrive at, but she didn't.

These are stories of post-traumatic growth, and our world is full of them.

OF CHRYSALISES AND WINGED BEAUTY

Post-traumatic growth (PTG) is any time someone makes life more beautiful, more purposeful, or more powerful in response to what they've endured.

Something truly hopeful about post-traumatic growth is we don't have to be healed to achieve it. It isn't just the by-product of IFS and meditation. It is something we can manifest along the way no matter what stage of the adventure we're on. It is an accoutrement to healing that makes the adventure all the more lovely—and altruistic. I think to Beyoncé, who took the pain of her husband Jay-Z's illicit extramarital affair and turned it into the epic multimedia work *Lemonade*. *Lemonade* is not only an album full of heart-wrenching, defiant, and powerfully uplifting music. It is also a full-length movie that showcases numerous black artists, filmmakers, and dancers, arguably launching the careers of many, including that of the beloved poet Warsan Shire.

Considering PTG, I also think to the ancient Hindu myth of Hanuman, the monkey-servant of Lord Rama, who overcame great adversity including leaping across an entire ocean to help Rama save his wife Sita from the ten-headed demon Ravana. In the end, Hanuman came to be honored as a god himself, seen as an epitome of spiritual devotion and compassionate service. I think to the wordsmith and author of *You Better Be Lightning*, Andrea Gibson, who is, at the time of writing, battling their third occurrence of cancer and subsequent chemotherapy—and doing so quite publicly on social media. Why? So other people can benefit from witnessing their warrior spirit boldly facing devastation, as we all will in due time. Gibson spoke of PTG in a powerful Instagram video after chemo caused them to lose all their eyelashes, saying, "The average person has 400 eyelashes. That is 400 wishes I wouldn't have made otherwise."[1] I stand in awe of how much of a teacher they have allowed cancer to become for them. In the same video, they go on to speak of their "primary daily practice": shifting their perspective so a challenge can open their heart rather than close it.

This is the essence of a PTG mindset.

THE UPWARD SPIRAL OF RESILIENCE AND POST-TRAUMATIC GROWTH

The researcher Barbara Fredrickson coined the term "upward spiral theory" in her work on positive emotions and lovingkindness meditation. She found that when engaging in activities that engender positive emotions, the benefit of feeling good tends to facilitate secondary and tertiary gains for people. In 2008, Fredrickson and her cohort studied the generosity-focused lovingkindness meditation on participants practicing just twenty minutes per day for seven weeks. The practice led to an overall increase in participants' experience of joy, contentment, hope, pride, amusement, interest, and awe. This increase in emotional health had the secondary gain of participants experiencing a deeper sense of purpose in life, decreased illness symptoms, increased social support networks, and increased mindful presence. These secondary benefits then predicted a further decrease in depressive symptoms and an increase in perceived life satisfaction. Hence, "upward spiral."

The study validates what we'd naturally assume: if one practices generosity, one is happier. If one is happier, one will be more present and attract better people. If one is happier, more present, and feeling more connected, one will naturally be less depressed and more satisfied in life. In a way, we don't need a study to tell us this, but it's helpful to have it laid out for us that practicing generosity, even just mentally, can create a feedback loop of desirable results in one's life. I'd like to highlight a parallel here with PTG and resilience.

Post-traumatic growth, as we see from the brief examples given, is allowing the pain to propel us toward:

- Channeling emotions into creative work and expression
- Doing something that benefits others
- Deepening spirituality and/or a sense of connectivity to all beings
- Fostering community connection in any number of ways
- Play, reclaiming childhood
- Looking within for insight, realization, and healing

That list isn't exhaustive, but already it resembles another list—the most robust predictors of resilience. We know from research that there are variables in one's life that tend to predict whether one will be able to bounce back from an adverse event. Some of these factors are:

- Making meaning from the experience through creative expression
- Sense of community and social support
- Connection to something greater than oneself (spirituality)
- Emotional intelligence and emotional literacy
- Having vision and a sense of purpose (helping others is always a great place to start)

- Grittiness and tenacity
- Material resources (health, material privilege, social privilege, safety)

There's a great deal of overlap in these two (again, short and nonexhaustive) lists. From these we can logically conclude something: *When we reach for post-traumatic growth, we naturally bolster our resilience. When we bolster our resilience, we have more to manifest post-traumatic growth with the next time things fall apart on us, which then builds even more resilience . . .*

Thus, there is an "upward spiral" to the relationship between PTG and resilience. There's also the potential for a tertiary benefit here: confidence. Every time we meet with hardship, dig deep to make it through, and come out the other side stronger for it, we can feel a little more confident in our ability to meet with difficulty again. Do this enough times and what that might start looking like is freedom. Freedom, after all, doesn't mean things going our way. Freedom is the willingness to have things *not* go our way because we've cultivated enough resourcefulness in life that we trust we'll be able to handle it. And not just handle it—become better through the handling of whatever comes our way.

In her book *The Unexpected Gift of Trauma*, the clinical psychologist Edith Shiro differentiates between experiences of resilience and PTG. As a metaphor, she describes what caterpillars go through in the process of becoming butterflies, underlining many crucial elements of post-traumatic growth, resilience, and confidence.

To become a butterfly, this little creature (formally called "larva") must lose all of its caterpillar-ness. It must decompose; be stripped of everything—its shape, its ecosystem, its way of inching through the world. Everything. In fact, if you were to look inside the chrysalis midway through its metamorphosis, you wouldn't see a partially formed butterfly or a partially decomposed larva. All you'd see is what wildlife biologist Lindsay VanSomeren calls "pink goo," a nutrient-rich soup. No trace of the caterpillar remains. In other words, it had to die in order to be reborn as something completely new. At the same time—and this is important—the butterfly would never be what it is without its caterpillar-ness, without the enzymes, nervous system, and breathing tubes provided by the larva, VanSomeren says. The caterpillar even has what are called "imaginal disks," which are "small clusters of cells that match up with the structures they'll need as adults," such as wings, eyes, antennae, and so forth. Moreover, the butterfly's emergence into the world cannot be interrupted or assisted. The winged creature must be allowed to push its way out fully formed or it will die. It's a brilliant and quite dramatic example of transformation in nature.[2]

Make no mistake, achieving post-traumatic growth isn't easy, and the methods toward it that we'll be learning in this book aren't a quick fix. It is not a linear process. Gibson says in the same Instagram video I quoted earlier, "I don't have this perspective all the time, y'all. Trust me. I can throw a tantrum all the way to the moon."[3] That is, sometimes we have to melt down, all the way down to pink goo (like the caterpillar), before we find the space to communicate, process, and make meaning of our experience. Yet whenever our long-term engagement with trauma leads us to increased compassion, connection, creativity, and courage in life (some of the Eight Cs we'll be talking about more later), we are in PTG. On this path we continually touch the goal of PTG in moments of presence, even as we continue to heal wounds, patterns, and limiting beliefs. Post-traumatic growth isn't the proprietary stuff of saints or even adept meditators. It's available right here, right now.

JOURNAL PROMPT

You're probably more resilient than you believe you are. You've probably outshined some pretty difficult situations in ways that didn't seem like a big deal but actually were. We humans tend to not give ourselves enough credit and fixate more on our negative qualities. Yet you've not only survived everything you've ever been through; you're here now, still working with it, using it to propel you in new directions. Healing work is not easy; most people shy away from it. But not you. You and your parts have worked very hard to get to this point. As the saying goes, "You didn't come this far to only come this far."

Think of a time in your life when something went wrong or felt impossible, but then you got through it and came out on the other side better for having had the experience. It could have been finals season in grad school or a tough breakup or something more significant. Please don't pick a situation you're in now that you're not already to the other side of. Choose a real-life example where you experienced your own resilience even if it didn't necessarily feel like it at the time or that you learned and grew from; maybe a time when an unexpected opportunity came out of a situation where things fell apart or had an adverse experience that drove you toward cultivating something positive in your life.

Maybe someone broke your heart and you made art about it. Maybe a situation fell apart but it pushed you to go back to school, move to a new town, or become closer to a friend who helped you through it. Maybe it was a childhood trauma you suffered that prompted you to become very fierce about holding boundaries or gave you passion about a certain sociopolitical issue. Maybe it was simply a bad day but you bought yourself flowers that lifted the energy of your home for the next week.

Identify such a memory. It can be large or small—it doesn't have to be a time you had an earth-shattering realization or rose triumphantly like the phoenix. Write about as many of the most important details as you can remember, paying special attention to the good that came of it.

6

THE ENDGAME OF HEALING

The North Star of Our Work

We suffer the loss of soul when we fail to heed irrational long-ings. They are strong voices and it would be odd if they didn't have something important to reveal to us. Following through . . . could lead us into folly. But not following through could lead us to something worse: a disenchanted life.

—Thomas Moore

In my clinical practice, one of the first questions I often ask folks is, "What would life be like if none of this was in your way?" (You might recall a sim-ilar question from the beginning of this book.) With striking regularity people tell me that they had never considered such a possibility. It's com-mon for us to become so laser focused on addressing our problems that the actual goal—freedom from the problems—leaves our purview. Similarly, I'll sometimes ask groups in workshops to imagine such a life: no longer wrestling with vicious cycles, feeling free and happy. Then I'll ask, "Who's suddenly nervous?" And, counterintuitively, a multitude of hands will go up. As mentioned in chapter 3, the prospect of change—even change for the better—often registers as threat to defensive parts of us. The fear of the unknown is often greater than our fear of familiar suffering. It can be quite fruitful, then, to spend some time imagining what freedom might be like. It gives our parts a chance to become familiar with the intended new territory of freedom (even if only imagined) and can offer a useful spark of motivation to stay the course. I'd like to paint a portrait for you of perhaps the ultimate post-traumatic growth, one of many fruitional possibilities people discover over time: becoming "Self-led."

Imagine that you could begin reclaiming the best of the childlike qualities you were born with—qualities such as effortless creativity, uninhibitedness, easy laughter, trust, endless imagination, in-the-moment-ness, eagerness to learn and explore, a big capacity for love, and unstoppable vitality. If trauma unfolded in your earliest years, you might need to imagine enjoying these qualities for the very first time—which could be especially beautiful. (I think to the time a dear student of mine, a blind woman in her seventies with a devastating trauma history, reported feeling joy for the very first time as a result of her self-work. What a moment that was.) Of course, it'd be impossible to instantly reclaim all of these qualities wholesale, but imagine moving—even just a little bit—in this direction.

Now imagine you've not only begun to reclaim these qualities but are doing so while cultivating healthy mature qualities like street smarts, discernment, emotional intelligence, social intelligence, financial intelligence, professional skills, healthy boundaries, healthy communication, healthy intimacy, spirituality, sense of identity, and community belonging.

You're evolving toward a best-of-both-worlds scenario. You're increasingly embodying a vibrant, free aliveness married to a reasonable and worldly groundedness. You're becoming childlike but not childish, righteous but not rigid. You love yourself thoroughly and completely but you're no doormat (that's not love), you're not egotistical (that's not love), and you're not irresponsible (that ain't love either). After all, on every horizon the sky kisses the mountains—that is, the stuff of dreams (sky) can meet the stuff of reality (earth) in a beautiful way.

Imagine what might be different about going to your job, engaging all the complex tasks and personalities you meet there. Take a minute and really visualize yourself through all of it. What would that be like?

Imagine what might be different in your homelife, engaging with the people and roles that await you there. What would that be like?

Imagine what might be different in how you spend your free time: seeing friends, physical activity, creative passions, hobbies . . . What would that be like?

Our true home awaits us no matter what we think is possible. And I do believe in my bones that we can evolve toward what we've just imagined here. This is a portrait of what I call "enlightenment within reach."

It's true that what we're imagining together is an ideal, and there's no such thing as the perfect attainment of ideals. That said, much like the ideals of nonviolence or ending poverty, just because they can't be perfectly realized doesn't mean we shouldn't work toward them. For the many trauma survivors out there who are grappling with things much more foundational, like putting together a livelihood or staying sober or making it through one week without a panic attack, please don't think this is something you're supposed to be able to attain next week or next year. Rather, let it be a destination to set on your map and orient your compass to. Let this endgame vison be your North Star, and see for yourself where it takes you. Life is often longer than we think, and the small changes we make every day can have a wild way of gaining momentum as the weeks and years pile up.

LETTING GO AND CULTIVATION

We've already covered several of the most important ingredients for steering toward this endgame—getting a clearer understanding of trauma; learning about our parts, how to identify and work with them; and practicing deep openness toward our bodily and emotional experience. In part two of this book, we'll integrate IFS with Buddhist meditation and wisdom teachings. Before we go there, let's draw some more inspiration from the best-of-both-worlds ideal I've just described. Those two worlds encompass two key energies:

1. **Subtraction:** awakening and healing as a shedding, a letting go, an *unburdening* of all the baggage and extra layers we've picked up along the way. When we unburden exiled parts of us (a process we'll explore in chapter 14), we release the trauma from our bodies. We're no longer holding the emotional charge of those woundings. Not only does this liberate the Exiles but it also liberates the defensive Manager and Firefighter parts as there's so much less to defend. This frees up a lot of vitality in the system;

vitality that can be used to reclaim what was lost to trauma—the lighthearted, childlike qualities we've been discussing.

2. **Addition:** awakening as a cultivation, learning, evolving to possess new qualities we didn't have before. This generally happens through the process of *reparenting* (which we will explore more fully in part three). In reparenting parts, we address erroneous beliefs and irrational thought, and help our parts achieve a fuller maturation. This entails learning how to communicate more skillfully, developing a more secure way of relating in relationships, and getting our house in order with regards to material functioning (money, career, lifestyle). This is a lifelong process wherein we must discover the resources that will help us finish growing up; unburdening trauma helps us recover the vitality and inspiration for such things.

It is on these two wheels, spinning in unison, that we can ride into the sunset. It is on these two wings that we can meet the winds of life with discernment and joy. It is with these two hands that we can mold the clay of destiny.

This cannot be overstated: subtraction and addition must go together. To have one without the other would be a disaster. Reclaiming childlike vitality without maturity would be like setting a wild horse loose in the Smithsonian. Cultivating full maturity without wonder and spontaneity would be like replacing all playgrounds with DMV offices.

I'm reminded of two contrasting stories that display both the mature, tenacious aspect of an enlightened mind as well as the childlike and playful.

The Buddha initially taught a path of ethical responsibility to students: wise thought, wise speech, wise action, wise livelihood, nonintoxication, abstaining from hedonic passions and impulsivity, and, of course, a life centered on highly consistent meditation. Veritably, the earliest canonical teachings we have that are attributed to the Buddha often boil down to "Here's how to finish growing up." He exemplified the result of this path as well. For example, when someone asked the Buddha if he experienced pain, he shockingly replied, "More than you can imagine." The implication here is that the Buddha related directly to the pain of others and the pain inherent in his life; he didn't escape any of it. Yet the compassion in him was so expansive, perhaps as wide as the cosmos, that such pain no longer knocked him off-center. He remained at peace despite his direct engagement with the suffering of the world.

Compare this to the more contemporary Chan story of Su Dongpo and his teacher Foyin (Chan is the Chinese name for what many of us are familiar with as Zen Buddhism):

Su Dongpo had been practicing deeply. One day he was feeling so very enlightened that he penned a poem proclaiming that "I am the light of the boundless universe. The eight worldly winds can no longer move me"—meaning he felt he had become like the Buddha; impervious to the "eight winds" of pain and pleasure, gain and loss, praise and blame, fame and bad reputation that tend to blow us around. He then had his attendant sail across the river to the local monastery to show his poem to Su Dongpo's teacher Foyin. Upon reading the poem, Foyin wrote the word "fart!" on the back of the page and had the attendant return the poem. Su Dongpo saw this and became enraged. He personally sailed to the monastery, this time to let his teacher have it. Upon walking into the monastery, Foyin laughed, "The eight worldly winds cannot move you, but one fart blows you across the river!"

Indeed, a compassion-centered life has room for a full spectrum of expression, from solemnity to slapstick and everywhere in between.

SELF-LEADERSHIP

The endgame of healing I'm describing is congruent with what the IFS calls becoming a "Self-led person."

Self-leadership means that you have healed *just* enough for there to be a basic sense of trust within your system of parts inside. Parts trusting Self Energy to lead your life means the energies of calm, clarity, curiosity, compassion, courage, confidence, creativity, and connectedness take the wheel. It's not that you no longer have parts or that they no longer get activated by people, places, and things; it's that you're aware when your parts activate and can redirect them with care. A Self-led person has ingrained the habit of acknowledging those parts in real time, mostly keeping them to the side (unless they are needed, such as in dangerous situations), and even speaking for those parts from a place of compassionate Self.

The foundation of mindfulness and daily meditation is indispensable in this matter. The most challenging aspect of reorienting back to Self in daily life is remembering that it's an option. If we want to enjoy the cognitive and emotional flexibility of working with our parts in the midst of our busy days, we must have a habit of harnessing our attention. We must develop the ability to notice when we're eclipsed by our parts, then steer our vessel back in the direction of Self. Your attention is literally the most valuable commodity in the world—corporations are aggressively vying to grab hold of it for a reason. Given this, the superpower of harnessed attention isn't going to come about if we don't interrupt our habit of living on autopilot. We must lovingly train ourselves to be present in a consistent fashion. That comes first. Second, our parts need to experience Self Energy enough that they begin to trust compassion as a refuge. (More is coming on the concept and practice of refuge in chapter 9.)

Altruistic livelihood can be a major contribution to Self-leadership as well. One of the reasons I love being a therapist is the degree of Self Energy I experience when working with others. Many other IFS therapists tell me the same thing. Day in, day out, my parts train in allowing the space of compassion to remain wide open. When I can maintain this, I find my clients having powerful breakthroughs more often, and I don't absorb everyone's trauma like I used to. Compassion has a protective quality to it. (That said, you don't have to become a therapist to experience this. You can be of service to others in many professions, and we can all start at home.)

It's when I get an angry email, a friend dies, or I'm staring down a plate of nachos that I still struggle to allow Self to lead. This is also common among practitioners. It can be confusing. Meditators often find themselves flummoxed by how they could be in a state of love-drenched bliss one moment, but then get on a crowded subway and careen toward radical misanthropy. Such experiences aren't confusing if we look through the lens of parts work. Different parts are activated by different experiences. Who we are in any given moment is often quite dependent on the conditions we find ourselves in. We are contextual beings, forever inter-dependent with set and setting. The North Star here, the direction we're walking in, is learning to smooth out these dichotomies and transition from one context to the next in our lives without extreme parts eclipsing us. This is the task of becoming a Self-led person. It's a good challenge, an enjoyable unfolding, and an altogether fascinating possibility.

ON THE FREIGHTER SS *DOUBT*

Some of us believe that this level of letting go isn't possible. If that's you, I invite you to watch as your next exhale just sort of . . . happens. Letting go is one of the most natural functions of our being. "Yeah, but that's different," you might say. "That's present-time letting go. I'm talking about stuff from the past." True! And sorry if this is not your favorite example, but pay attention the next time you go to the bathroom. Letting go of the past is just what humans do. We do it all damn day. To *this*, you might say, "Now you're getting on my nerves. You're talking about something physical to describe something psychological, pal." And you'd be exactly right. That's the funny thing about the psyche, it's not truly distinct from the soma. Our emotions are primarily physical; our memories, cellular. Does the body not keep the score?

Again, I admit these are idealized possibilities. At the end of the day, it's about having a life that works. It's about living on a path that flows ever in the direction of harmony and wholeness. We must admit that we'll never get a life where only good things happen; that's just not the nature of the world. Uncertainty is always with us. Conflict will not cease to abound. Just because we do the work doesn't mean others will or will want to. A life that works is a life where we are no longer living in fear of these realities. We can live this way when we've healed substantially from the past through openhearted work (subtraction model). And it is through that work that we'll also eventually cultivate the tools, resources, and maturity that will allow us to walk tall and even thrive in the midst of difficulty (addition model). When you have established that situation for yourself, there is little left to fear. Either things are within your control and therefore you control them or things are out of your control but you've done the work to know how to meet the conditions as they arise.

As long as change is somewhere *over there* and not *in here*, we will never arrive. The changes we wish to seek, the accountability, the discernment, the maturity—it all comes from the heart. It still comes from relating within and being reflective about our lives. The addition model is still the subtraction model just supplied in a different way. This is the reality born of an important truth. We already have everything we need. We already are everything that we're meant to become. Just as the oak tree is already within the acorn.

Life will never not be a bumpy road, but high-end shocks are available. May we continue to install them.

JOURNAL PROMPT

The notions of spirituality and healing tend to go hand in hand. Why is that? For example, Reiki is considered a healing art that totally relies on unseen forces. In the Old Testament of the Bible is the prophecy of Jesus, "with His stripes we are healed."[1] In Latin American countries, plant medicines, which are only to be administered by qualified *curanderos/curanderas*, are considered a spiritual solution to ailments that often present as physical symptoms. Even twelve-step programs use the term *spiritual solution* to address worldly problems of compulsive and addictive behaviors. Why?

Why are healing and spirituality so closely associated with one another? What is the connection between the two? What kinds of experiences and, perhaps most importantly, outcomes do they both share?

Take ten minutes to journal your ideas.

PART TWO: BRANCHES

Becoming a Self-Healer through Meditation and Parts Work

7

HOW CHANGE WORKS

Causes, Conditions, and
the River of Self-Love

Individual peace is the unit of world peace.
—*David Lynch*

The material cosmos is a dynamic, ever-changing place, with stars and planets and black holes constantly churning, evolving, dying, and being born. This is fortunate, as a static cosmos wouldn't be able to hold matter.[1] Matter bends space due to it having mass. This is something scientists can see especially with large bodies such as planets. Thus, if we dropped a planet into a static, rigid, unchanging cosmos, the whole thing would fold in on itself—which, ironically, would mean this static cosmos would be *forced* to change. Thus, to say that change is the only constant is true but buries the lead. That the universe (and all things in it) has an ever-changing nature is what *allows* you and me to exist in the first place.

It's curious that so many of us have struggled to change. It's curious also that anyone should ever believe that they are stuck. Stuckness does not exist. If the nature of all things entails change, the notion of stuckness couldn't be more of an illusion. You're already changing—even right now. For instance, as your perceptual systems take in these words, consider them, and simultaneously fire off thoughts about, for example, whether you agree, disagree, or couldn't care less, neuroplasticity comes into play. The physical structure of your nervous system and biology changes ever so slightly with every passing sentence. This is true of every experience we have. It's all building and renovating neural pathways—incessantly so.

And yet as we saw in part one of this book, trauma can be defined as a kind of stuckness of the nervous system: the record skips over and over again at the same spot (our triggers), our bodies compulsively produce the same stew of stress chemicals, and we feel anchored to experiences that are months, years, or even decades in the past. While we can never really lose our ever-changing, flowing capacity, how do we restore the *experience* of flow that we know is happening at various levels in and around us all the time?

A river doesn't work to flow; flowing is what the river does. Rivers do, however, change course, and for that to happen, what's actually needed is for the *riverbed*—what's channeling the river's flow—to shift its shape. The shift that's needed to change course in our lives is in how we *hold* the change that's already happening. Hold yourself with enmity or endless judgments and the river of your being will flow accordingly. Hold yourself with love and compassion and the river of your life will flow accordingly. Apply tons of harsh effort to making a shift and get ready to see aggressive rapids in the river. Hold it all lightly—with levity even—and the river may start to feel much homier and more inviting. This bodes well for us as attitudes are easier to change than emotional patterns. It's simpler to open your heart than to change entrenched behavioral habits. It's easier to love than to figure it all out. "Optimization" and self-help are exhausting and expensive. Holding space for our parts is both free and freeing.

WHAT GOVERNS CHANGE

They say there are no guarantees in life, but it's just not true. There are many things we can count on and trust. When it comes to healing, I don't believe in offering guarantees—and yet there is still the promise of something the Buddha termed *causes and conditions*. Indeed, while it is the nature of the river to incessantly flow, there are causes and conditions that come together to determine the shape of the riverbed and whether the river overflows or dries up.

The phenomenon of precipitation gives us further examples of certainty when it comes to change. Rain, after all, does not fall randomly from the sky. Nor does it ever fall from a clear blue sky. For rain to fall, we first need clouds to form from certain causes and conditions. Clouds form when enough water droplets on the ground are met by warmer air, which causes them to evaporate, become lighter than air, and thus rise into the atmosphere. When that rising water vapor is met by colder air up above, it condenses back into water droplets; if we get enough water droplets to hang out together, we can then call it a cloud. Under the right conditions, not only will a cloud form but there's no way for a cloud *not* to form. It's guaranteed.

Rain, then, happens when enough condensed water particles bump into each other and combine, eventually becoming so heavy that the sky can no longer hold them. So back down to Earth they go. My point: under certain conditions not only might it rain but it is certain to rain. Yet if the air is under thirty-two degrees Fahrenheit (or zero degrees Celsius), it is impossible for that rain to remain liquid. It turns to snow and, in fact, can only turn to snow. If, as the snow falls, the air closer to the ground is as cold or colder than the temperature water freezes at, the precipitation can only arrive as snow or ice, never as rain.

The question before us isn't *Can we change?* but rather *How would we like to change?* In light of everything we're discussing, I think this is the most important question of all: *Is the riverbed of your life formed by the traumatic conditioning you have endured—or by something more expansive and loving than that?*

It's understandable that people often have a tough time opening to the kind of caring attitude and self-compassion that transforms the riverbed in a healing way. Yet the guarantee of change offers us another clue: perhaps we're attempting to muscle our way into it. Perhaps our parts are working too hard. Quite frequently, someone I'm working with will say, "I'm trying to be compassionate toward this part of me, but I just can't get there." My suggestion: Try less. Breathe and soften the effort. Don't make a job out of it. Relax *into* Self.

Setting forth good causes and conditions in our lives works just like planting seeds in a garden. If one plants a basil seed, that seed needs only to meet with the right conditions (nutrient-rich soil; the proper amount of water, sun, and shade; not being eaten by a gopher) for the basil plant within the seed to be realized. In due time, it's guaranteed. Under the right conditions the seed *must*, in fact, sprout. Furthermore, one will never plant a basil seed and get cilantro. The seed will sprout basil every time. The same goes for your good intentions. The same goes for becoming Self-led. Hold those intentions and water them with love and they will bear fruit. Keep doing your self-therapy and your meditation and becoming Self-led is inevitable.

There's another teaching to be extracted from this metaphor: the day we plant the seed is not the day we taste the fruit. What we experience in the present moment is an echo of the past. Who we are now is a result of the seeds we planted some time ago. This is why the changes we seek don't tend to come from decisions we make in the moment. We've all tried, saying to ourselves, for example, *I'm going to stop being so judgmental* or *Starting Monday, I'm only eating healthy*, only to have those changes crumble on us. Deep, abiding change is possible, but it's more involved than that. Such declarations are merely a small seed. While formidable things often come from the tiniest seeds, those seeds need to meet with the conditions for germination, including time. And while patience is often its own challenge, time passes on its own without any work from us. Blink your eyes twice and three years will have gone by. The intentions and aspirations you start holding now could be like gifts you're giving yourself in the future. What kinds of gifts would you like to receive in three years?

Self Energy, buddha nature, the openhearted state, Source, love—pick a term that sits well with you. Whatever you call your basic nature, it's already here. The search is over. Go inside and get started. Plant your seeds and tend your river from this place. This is the spirituality of healing our lives—of outshining trauma.

THE PROMISE OF PRACTICE

Meditation is an ideal arena for such gardening endeavors. It's an intentional space wherein we can set the causes and conditions for everything we're talking about in this book. Straightaway, we are planting seeds of harnessing attention, investing in our inner world, and committing to ourselves despite any resistance (there is always resistance). By establishing a daily practice, even if just ten minutes a day, we create a stable base in our lives; a place we can return to again and again no matter what is happening. This can be a small revolution in our lives if we grew up with no sense of a stable foundation or consistency. Meditation is an act of self-love every time we sit down. If all trauma ever pushed you to do was build a daily meditation practice, that would be some powerful post-traumatic growth.

Meditation is also the ideal arena for doing parts work on our own. We'll explore this combination in detail beginning in chapter 10 and then continue through the remainder of this book—seeing how, for instance, meditation saturates the body with awareness in a way that can allow Exiles or hidden parts to emerge. Yet this isn't something to just dive into. We've got to plant some seeds first. For one, it's crucial that we learn how to slow ourselves down and regulate our emotions. It's essential that we learn how to hold our experience. To simply be there with our breath and our mind in a kind way. Learning how to set the breath in its natural rhythm is the most direct route to finding these abilities. Learning to hold the breath with our attention also shows us exactly how to hold the inner children we'll be encountering in parts work: with receptivity, warmth, and interest. It's also crucial that we're somatically focused so that we build new neural pathways of embodiment with our practice. If we engage parts work in a disembodied way, it's far less powerful. We're also susceptible to being tricked by our imagination and other forces.

For the next couple of chapters, we'll be exploring iterations of *shamatha-vipashyana*, or "calm-abiding–clear-seeing" meditation. Although it's been taught in varying ways and with different interpretations across the centuries of Buddhist history, this foundational practice is common to nearly all Buddhist schools. I offer it here in a manner that might be different from what you've encountered before, given that we are approaching it as a preparation for parts work. We'll work with this practice in five progressive steps that gently deepen as we go. We'll practice this first, and I'll offer you more detail about the nature of these instructions in the next chapter.

For all meditation sections that follow (as mentioned in the "How to

Use This Book" section), you're welcome to read them through and then set aside the book to try them; or in many cases, you can try them in brief pauses as you go along. But please do take a moment at any point to explore or savor what you're experiencing that interests you.

MEDITATION: THE FIVEFOLD FOUNDATION

The Fivefold Foundation is informed by methods for setting the body and nervous system in the parasympathetic state, which is the opposite of the fight-flight-freeze state. This fivefold process is a complete meditation unto itself, and it will also serve as the opening act to all our future meditations. If this is new to you, go slow. Familiarize yourself with these simple methods. Notice the body and the effect of this process with some detail. Whatever you do, don't struggle. This is the work of opening, not the work of achieving.

1. Posture | *1 minute*

We build a posture from the ground up with these five points.

- **Pelvis:** Whatever you're sitting on, feel the trustworthy support from beneath you. Let it remind you of the option to surrender and receive support. The weight of your torso ought to land squarely on your pelvis in front of the sitz bones (the two egg-shaped bones in your glutes). Take a breath and see if you can really sink into this support.
- **Spine and neck:** Allow a sense of energy to rise up the back body. To undo some of the cell-phone hunch in the neck, lift from the crown of the head to elongate the uppermost region of the spine. You could even gently stretch the neck for a moment or two in this manner if it feels good to.
- **Head:** To put the neck in proper alignment, simply tilt the forehead forward one centimeter and allow the chin and ears to slide back one centimeter. Ideally, you feel your ears, shoulders, and hips stacked over one another. If you don't sense that stacking or aren't sure, don't worry about it, simply notice; it will refine over

time. Take a breath and let the eyes soften. This includes the muscles around and even behind the eyes. Keep breathing and let the cheeks melt. Let the melting spread to the jawline and the tongue. You'll notice the softening of the facial muscles has a direct effect on your state of awareness.

- **Chest:** Let the collarbones be wide and allow the shoulders to be balanced. The chest needn't be puffed out (a sign you're working too hard) nor sinking inward (a sign you're in protective flight mode).

- **Hands:** Place the hands facing down on the thighs in a way that supports the collarbones staying wide and the shoulders balanced. For me, this is around mid-thigh. Find the placement that allows your arms to be a kickstand for your upper torso.

2. Abdominal breathing | *3 minutes*

Breath is the language of the nervous system. Breathing deeply into the lowest part of the abdomen, beneath the navel and toward the tailbone, communicates to the nervous system a basic sense of safety. Such breathing engenders a feeling of acceptance, that you're allowed to be just as you are here in your practice. Breathe fully with no strain or ambition. See if you can allow the breath to expand both in front of you and in the lower back. It takes about two and a half minutes for the body to get the message of safety, so keep breathing, allowing various regions of the body to soften as you go.

3. Natural breath | *2–3 minutes*

Take a few more deep breaths to begin. Then begin allowing your exhales to simply drop out of the body. Don't breathe back in right away. Let the exhale give way to space between breaths. When you feel the body wanting to breathe in, gently breathe in. Stay soft about this whole endeavor. The next exhale simply drops again. The space between breaths is an invitation to let go, to float, to experience stillness. There lies a tender mystery here. Each breath will be slightly different as the breath is given the freedom to do its own thing. As the breath is given space to regulate itself, the nervous system follows suit.

4. Knowing the body in space | *2 minutes*

As you continue to breathe, gently take note of one wall anywhere around you. You don't have to look for the wall or "feel" for it with your mind's eye. You already know the walls around you are there and you can simply open to noticing them. In doing so, you're already opening your awareness to the space that surrounds you, too. Breathing into the body with a spacious awareness of the room right now helps the nervous system to run on a map of the present moment (in which you are relatively safe) as opposed to any of the maps of the past it might hold (when perhaps you weren't as safe). Don't think about it too much, though. Simply know the body situated in space breathing one breath at a time.

5. Heart breathing | *2–5 minutes*

Keep the natural breath with spaces in between. Find the center of your sternum, the center of your chest. Begin acting as if your breath is flowing in and out from this spot. Then trace a line directly back to your spine. Imagine you have an extra nose just in front of the spine. Let your breath and your attention go all the way back, deeply into the body. Breathe into the heartspace and out from the heartspace. What's it like here? What can you feel? Are there tight spots, soft spots, spaces that feel open? Let yourself explore.

In some traditions the heartspace is the abode of *ziji* (zee-gee), "the mind of delight." I personally find it's easiest to access the calm, clarity, curiosity, and compassion of Self Energy when I breathe into this spot. No matter what's happening with my parts in the foreground, I can breathe behind it all, into the heartspace or ziji-space, and remember the reality of the compassionate witness: the Self.

Keep breathing, enjoying the spaces between breaths and softening the body as you go.

EXERCISE: KEEPING A MEDITATION JOURNAL

A good way for the spirit of your practice to show up more often in daily life is to simply journal your daily experiences with it. If you can, it's a good idea to have a dedicated notebook and pen to keep right next to where you do sitting meditation practice. That way you never have to go looking for it. End your practice and note what your experience was like. This could take the form of your standard journal entry, a poem, possibly a haiku, or even a drawing that sums up what today's session was like. Later, we will map out the parts we meet in parts work meditation. For now, establish the brief and simple habit of tracking your experience. Just a couple of minutes can go a long way.

In addition to deepening integration in the moments after your meditation practice, it can be powerful down the road to pick up that notebook and see all your writing in it. Even if you never read your notes again, you have concrete evidence of how you've been showing up and investing in yourself.

Some things it might be good to keep track of:

- Positive emotions that arose in your practice like calm and spaciousness, even if they were only there for a split second
- Sensations you noticed in the body, including the new ones you'll discover as your awareness refines
- Insights and little "light-bulb moments" that dawned
- Small victories, like treating yourself with kindness and mercy
- Questions about the practice or your experiences you'd like to ask a teacher about

Keep it light and, whatever you do, just keep going with it.

8

EMBODYING SELF-COMPASSION

Gentle Practices for Relief

The Fivefold Foundation offers a fairly simple progression, but there is quite a bit of depth informing the techniques. In this chapter, we'll take a closer look at some of the embodiment techniques. We'll also work with something quite germane to all healing endeavors: our own resistance to the work.

NATURAL BREATH

When the mind is crowded, it can be quite difficult to meditate. A busy, noisy mind is indicative of parts being on autopilot, lost in the trance of habitual mental activity, and clamoring for center stage. We could spend quite a bit of time trying to work with these talkative parts, asking them to pipe down and give us some working room, or we could simply introduce this breathing pattern that invites them all to relax and take a well-deserved break.

Natural breath, coined "setting the breath in its natural rhythm" by the Buddhist teacher and author B. Alan Wallace, is a direct invitation into stillness. It is the most useful method I have on tap for downregulating the nervous system and creating space in an otherwise crowded mind. As described in the previous chapter, you might take a deep breath first and then simply allow the exhale to flow naturally out of the body, allowing for a short space between breaths, and then keeping the inhale very gentle. The trick is to stop pushing the breath out so much and to be very light when pulling it back in. Don't be the breather of the breath so much as the breath's shepherd. Each breath will be different from the last. They will elongate and settle into a nice flow over the course of a few minutes without any work from you.

Whereas most meditation teachers will tell you to pay attention to the breath, I ask you to prioritize the spaces between breaths. Soften into them; float, even. If you can be present for the duration of this space between exhale and inhale, you're far more likely to be present for the breath itself.

Natural breathing asks us to surrender into that space, to relinquish control, and to trust that the breath will come back to us. These themes of surrender, control, and trust are powerful, as they are often conflated with our need for safety. Thus, some practitioners find themselves quite anxious when it comes time to allow the space between breaths. This doesn't necessarily mean natural breathing isn't for you or that you should stay away from it. It simply means it's triggering your parts. The breath is like a mirror that allows you to see this.

If you find your parts getting anxious, you might take this as an opportunity to show them some care. First, be aware that these are parts and they are very much like people, as we've been discussing. Second, acknowledge and affirm to these parts that trust and giving up control is indeed a scary thing. Third, be like a loving parent who shows the parts that this is a very small and manageable act of surrender. It's maybe a second or two of letting the breath and body settle down, and then the breath comes right back. It comes back every time and has been doing so your whole life. Thus, you can invite your parts to view this natural breathing as a safe opportunity to work on trust and to see for themselves if letting go and surrendering is always as dangerous as you've come to believe.

This style of breathing is written about in the Hindu tantric text *Vijnana Bhairava* (A.D. 800), translated as *The Radiance Sutras* by Lorin Roche. See if you can sense even a little bit of what's here for you:

At the end of the exhale,
Breath surrenders to quietude.
For a moment you hang in the balance—

Suspended in the fertile spaciousness
That is the source of breath.
At the end of the inhale,
Filled with the song of breath
There is a moment where you are simply
Holding the tender mystery

In these interludes,
Experience opens into exquisite vastness
With no beginning and no end
Embrace this infinity without reservation
You are its vessel.[1]

There's something special and mysterious in the spaces between breaths. There's a pocket of true stillness after the outbreath. We can also shift directly into Self Energy in a rather effortless way, though this might take just a little bit of practice.

Go ahead and try this now, and after about three minutes, ask yourself: *Are calm, clarity, curiosity, or compassion somehow more available inside than when I began?* Even if it seems minute and negligible, it matters. Note what this feels like.

INHABITING THE BODY

Your body is the most sophisticated thing in the known universe. Its numerous complex systems interlock with a nuance not seen elsewhere. The number of cells, each of their own substance and function, that must come together to make even one moment of your life happen is truly vast. It's one of the great tragedies that the magnificent living organism of the body is what becomes weighed down by the burdens and stresses we increasingly carry. Furthermore, the body itself can come to be perceived as a liability by trauma survivors for any number of valid reasons. Yet no trauma can erase the body's true, underlying nature. We can start to recover this and reclaim our bodies right now by using our attention as a vehicle of reconnection and remembrance.

First, begin to notice your hands. (If you do not have two hands, you can notice instead your feet or any other body part that you have two of—arms, thighs, front of torso and back of torso, etc.) Notice first the skin of one hand: the temperature, the tingling, the quality of the air being sensed, whatever it is you find there. Now, go deeper—into the muscles of that hand. It gets subtle but begin to feel the countless fibers and sinews within the hand. Then go further and find the feeling of the bones inside; the dense, heavy, interlocking network of skeletal structure that makes your hand what it is. Spend some time here, in the aliveness of this one body part. Then go to the other hand. What feels different—on the skin, in the muscles, with the bones? Notice how they contrast one another; the qualitative difference in texture, temperature, and general aliveness. Then switch back and forth between hands for some time. Notice what it's like to dance your way from one hand to the other. Things begin to change in quite an interesting fashion.

PENDULATION: PAIN RELIEF THROUGH EMBODIED PROCESS

Most of us deal with some form of physical pain on some level just about all the time—and more of us deal with chronic pain and illness than one might realize. Building off the exercise of feeling our two hands respectively, *pendulation* is a practice developed by the founder of Somatic Experiencing, Peter Levine, offering us a new way to relate to difficult sensations. Let your attention move now to any area of the body where you feel any distress, fatigue, or outright pain—physical or emotional. As unfun as it may be, let your mind sit right there, going ever closer to it. Is this discomfort:

- Tight or loose?
- Heavy or light?
- Sharp or dull?
- Pulsing or constant?
- More warm or more cool?
- More like water or more like electricity?

Then ask yourself:

- How much space is it taking up?
- Does it have a shape?
- Does it have a color?

Then move to any region of the body that feels relatively okay, even if it is just the tip of your pinkie finger. Notice the sensations of non-pain or even pleasure that await you there. Are these more comfortable sensations:

- Tight or loose?
- Heavy or light?
- Sharp or dull?
- Pulsing or constant?
- More warm or more cool?
- More like water or more like electricity?

Then ask yourself:

- How much space are they taking up?
- Do they have a shape?
- Do they have a color?

Go back to the pain place. Engross yourself again in the sensations by noticing the sensations in detail once again. Stay there a few moments. Go back to the less painful place. Engross yourself there. Really be in the sensations. Go back to the painful place again. Stay for a moment. Swing back into the nonpainful place. Stay for a moment. Swing back to the painful place. Wait a beat. Swing back to the nonpainful place. Like a pendulum, keep swinging back and forth like this for some time. It's like you're sharing the resources of the part of your body that is well with the part of the body that isn't so well. You're linking them, creating a bridge. Notice what happens to the pain after some time. Your brain is starting to get a new form of signaling: that it's not *all* pain, that there is more happening than discomfort. This exercise might not take the pain away, but usually within even a few short minutes, people report that things feel less overwhelming and more manageable. If this is true for you, know that you just did that with your mind.

SPACIOUS KNOWING AND THE PARASYMPATHETIC RESPONSE

I've been guilty of repeating a common Buddhist party line about the body: it is always in the present moment and therefore a great anchor in the here and now. Yet the body keeps the record of the past and builds maps according to what's happened to us as well. The body quite often acts as if what's happened to us before just might be happening now or is about to happen even when nothing could be further from the truth. In the words of Bessel van der Kolk, "[Trauma] is not about something you think or something you figure out. This is about your body, your organism, having been reset to interpret the world as a terrifying place and yourself as being unsafe. And it has nothing to do with cognition."[2]

A key to showing the body that we are in the here and now and that it doesn't have to run on maps built of past experience is *spacious knowing.*

Go back to paying attention to your two hands (or any other two body parts) both at the same time. There's no need to feel into anything this time, just know that they are there. Breathe for a moment. Notice there are walls around you: to the left, to the right, in front and in back of you. There's also a ceiling and a floor. Even with your eyes closed, you know they are there. You don't have to look for them or use your mind's eye to feel for them. Just know they are there and, most importantly, that there is space between you and the perimeters of the room you're in. Your two hands are situated in space, the space of that exists right now, and your body knows this because it is in space in relationship to the objects around you.

Stay here. Breathe. As you do this, your body is starting to build a new map, a map rooted in the relative safety of the environment you're in right now (assuming you are actually safe wherever you are reading this book). As you continue to notice your hands in the space of this room, you will start to feel little microshifts in the body. You'll feel bones settling and little releases in your tissues. You won't necessarily relax, but you may get tired. You won't necessarily feel better, but if you were in any way overwhelmed when we began, it's likely you'll feel less so than before. You are shifting into the parasympathetic response. It's not a dramatic effect. Rather, it's slight and almost imperceptible when it's new, but the actual impact is quite meaningful. This can require some practice initially, but once your body starts to get the message that *the space around me in this present moment is relatively safe*, it should only take you sixty to ninety seconds for the body to switch modes. If you do this simple process once an hour for just one minute, the shifts you feel will become more apparent.

WORKING WITH RESISTANCE

It turns out that intending to meditate and actually meditating are two completely different activities. Most of us like the *idea* of meditation, but when it comes to sitting down and actually doing it . . . *well*, we slept in too late, there's just no time, we suddenly wonder, *Is it even working?* Or our dog needs a walk, and the kitchen utensil drawer is in desperate need of reorganizing. How very curious. And isn't it this way with just about every healthy habit we try to insert into our already overstuffed lifestyles? What's worse is when we slump into cycles of shame for not following through, as if that's ever helped anyone get on track.

Resistance to the work is generated by defensive parts who associate change with threat. It's been a lot of work to survive and develop up to the point where we are now, after all. It's entailed tremendous effort from our Manager and Firefighter parts—work that they usually don't get enough credit for. When we begin conceiving of a more evolved way, it is often as if these Managers and Firefighters are offended at the lack of appreciation for all they've done, and resistance ensues. Oftentimes, our defensive parts just want a bit of appreciation and thanks for how they've held the ship together.

Resistance to healthy habits rears its head especially for the rebels among us; we who found a sense of autonomy in childhood by becoming contrarian. We develop this sensibility when we notice the folks in charge either don't have it together or they keep steering us toward things that don't work for us personally. I wasn't too far into elementary school when I realized, *Whatever they tell me to do, I'm pretty sure I'm better off doing the opposite.* I know I'm not alone in that. This mindset saved many of us from heaps of suffering at one time. I'm just not certain that it needs to persist so strongly in those of us who are now all grown. Especially when we're simply trying to do things that help us feel better.

We're also met by far too many stressors. We're not built for overflowing inboxes and incessant decision-making throughout our day, and that's just the tip of the iceberg. Modern lifestyles overtax the prefrontal cortex of the brain, which is involved in stress tolerance, decision-making, and discipline. When meditation and healing work arrive as *yet another thing* to keep up with, our parts predictably raise the banner of resistance. Even setting aside any issue of fatigue or busyness, many of our parts are quite addicted to the dopamine-rich sensationalism of our social media–driven culture and come to misperceive things like peace and rest as tedious and boring. Truth be told, genuine peace is anything but boring.

No matter our degree of misery, the status quo of the present is the devil we know. The promise of happiness and freedom might be on the table, but are we sure it's better? We've been tricked before—especially if we have been around the block with healing modalities and spiritual traditions for some time. Furthermore, parts often hold a hidden fear that they might be abandoned or cease to be useful if we level up. Hence, in the Six Fs, it can be important to ask these parts what they would choose to do should we begin to heal. We also ask these parts what they *fear* might happen if we go deeper. In this way, we become *hope merchants*, reassuring our parts that better ways do exist and that no part will be left behind. In fact, there's no such thing as psychic surgery; leaving parts behind isn't even an option.

EXERCISE: THE SIX FS FOR PARTS THAT RESIST LETTING GO

If you are feeling any relief after having done one or more of the preceding practices, it's because your parts are getting a new kind of message from you that you are trying new but trustworthy things. The message tells them that maybe relief is at hand after all and maybe we don't have to remain in the patterns we've suffered through our whole lives.

If you're *not* feeling any relief here, it's likely that parts of you didn't trust what was happening, didn't feel safe within it, and found a way to jam things up. If this is you, let's see if you can get their permission to let you try new things. We'll do this utilizing the Six Fs framework.

First, take a few breaths and notice your inner experience of thoughts, emotions, and sensations.

1. **Find** a part: Attempt one of the practices you were just noticing resistance to—or just imagine you're doing such a practice. Let it activate and trigger the part.

2. **Focus** on the part for a moment.

3. **Flesh out** the part by noticing if you feel them emotionally, physically, or if they're "talking" to you with thoughts that come as words or images. Then acknowledge the part. Let them know you're noticing them. You might feel a sense of the part acknowledging you back or resisting your presence.

4. **Feeling.** Shift into a mode where you're sitting with the part or across from the part. See if there's a space inside where even just a little bit of Self (curiosity, compassion, openness, friendliness) is available for the part. Again, this is a part (which I'll call the "focus part" now) that has worked hard for your survival. Still, if other parts are complaining or analyzing them, effectively blocking Self, you can kindly ask them to step aside. You might need to ask a few times; just be very friendly about it. Then check again to see if anything resembling the kindness of Self is available inside.

5. **Befriend** the part. Once the feeling of Self Energy is on tap, let the part know how you're feeling toward them. Perhaps there's more they'd like for you to know. Perhaps they need a chance to let out their frustration (there's such things as inner tantrums, inner screaming, and even inner crying). Perhaps they just need a big thank-you or an apology from you. Maybe they seem like they're quite young for some reason, exhibiting a childlike or teenaged quality. In this case, you might ask them to notice you, the grown-up who's here in a very thoughtful way and who's interested in finding a new way forward with them.

You might not need to go past this step. They might already be calming down, or you might get the sense that just staying here is plenty for now.

6. **Fear.** Ask inside what the part thinks might happen if they were to stop resisting or if you were to develop healthier habits. Don't try to think of the answer here. Just ask and allow whatever needs to come up. Then think like a really loving friend or an ideal parent—what do you say back from a place of love and awareness? As long as you're really kind, you can't go wrong. Maybe they just need some reassurance from you. Or to simply be heard. Or to collaborate on a solution to a problem you've been having in practice (such as falling asleep or having difficulty breathing). Or to be included in the meditation. You might find it helpful to suggest that your resistant part could hang out on the sidelines while you meditate (or whatever the activity is) so they can witness what you're up to and swoop in to stop things if it gets to be too much for you.

The main thing is to extend Self to the part. You're not here to problem-solve so much as to establish a relationship and lines of communication.

Make sure to thank the part before leaving the exercise. Then journal your experience for a few minutes.

9

REFUGE

Protection beyond
Defense Mechanisms

> Gotta have something to eat, gotta have a little love in your life
> before you can hold still for anyone's damn sermon on how to
> behave.
>
> —*Billie Holiday*

Once upon a time there lived a woman who wanted nothing more than
to feel safe and at home in this world. She had experienced all the alienation, uncertainty, and aggression she could take and sought to cloister
herself away from it all. *Peace isn't too much to ask for,* she thought. *I need
shelter from the storms of life.* So, she built herself just that: a shelter, a
home. She started with the materials most readily available: mud and water. With some time and effort she had herself a house, but when it rained,
water leaked in through the cracks between the mud bricks. She built another domicile out of wood. But then a fire broke out and razed it to the
ground. Unfazed, she constructed a new and improved structure made of
concrete, only for an earthquake to level it. Determined, she spent years
mining the indestructible materials of gold and diamond and built herself
a palace. *Finally, I am home. I am safe. I have protection.* And that's when
thieves came along and robbed her of all those precious materials.

Feeling defeated and out of ideas, she was ready to admit that all of
her seeking for the safety and certainty of a home had failed her. Where
else could she possibly look? Where were the materials that couldn't be

destroyed and couldn't be stolen? There was only one place she had not yet looked: within.

DEFIANTLY AT HOME WITH OURSELVES

Without a subjective sense of safety there can be no metabolization of trauma. Safety, our most primary need, is the most primary thing traumatic experience betrays, hence we must reestablish it for ourselves. While the world will forever remain unpredictable, and while life will always entail brushes with harmful people and institutions, we can reach for emotional, psychological, and spiritual forms of safety that foster a transformational relationship to such realities. That is, we can find an inner sense of home that helps us to alchemize friction, pain, and loss into liberating insight, healing growth, and altruistic activity. To reference the eighth-century Buddhist scholar Shantideva, the world will continue to burn—and while we can't save ourselves by covering it in leather, we can make a fantastic pair of sandals and help others to fashion their own.

When a new client comes to therapy, my first objective is to make sure they feel safe—seen and welcomed just as they are. If I fail to establish a perception of basic safety, they'll never open up to do good work; it's likely I won't even see them for a second session. The same thing is true of the self-work we do on this path. A sense of security is foundational; there can be no building, no rising, without it.

That traumatic stress imprints danger signals on the nervous system complicates this. A person with unprocessed trauma could exist in the safest of external conditions but they would still be subject to projecting their internalized sense of threat onto the people, places, and things around them. In absence of this awareness, we trauma survivors often vie for facsimiles of safety through narrowing—we shut things and people and experiences and ourselves down. "What insulates *isolates*," my first clinical mentor was fond of saying. "The ship is safest when in port," writes the novelist Paulo Coelho, "but that's not what ships were built for."[1] Thus, without an inner sense of refuge, outer conditions of safety will only do us so much good. Obviously this is another moment where I soapbox the virtues of daily meditation.

Reclaiming the refuge of your embodied, inner world can be an act of healthy rebellion; a striking back against the ways we've been betrayed and left behind. An attitude of healthy defiance can be most supportive in the quest to heal. This utilizes the contrarian mindset we discussed in the previous chapter. "Maybe acceptance is less a form of surrender than an act of subversion," writes friend and author Jon Gingerich in a powerful *Guardian* piece about his experience of going blind.[2] Viewing transformative inner work as a form of personal revolution can bring some much-needed fire into the mix.

We need an inner refuge that isn't so conditional and can't easily be taken away from us. A kind of inner belonging that allows us to flex and flow with the stormy seas of life—and not just the everyday ups and downs but the true wonders and tragedies as well. An inner resource that supports the expanding and outshining of what has hurt us and how we've held on to those experiences. We need a refuge that allows us to move increasingly in the direction of connection, courage, creativity, and confidence. We need a sense of safety that our parts don't have to work so hard for.

True refuge is protection beyond defenses. Refuge is the psychospiritual safety made available when we lay down our armor and set aside our swords. I believe such a refuge is inherent within us. I'm talking about the experience of Self Energy, of course. Before we go further with that, let's first explore the concept of refuge in both the secular and the Buddhist sense.

SHELTER FROM THE STORM

The *Oxford Dictionary* defines *refuge* as "a place that offers protection or shelter." In other words, it's home. "*Home* is the most powerful word in the English language," goes the saying (often attributed to Shakespeare). Home invokes a sense of radical acceptance, a place where we are welcome to be who and what we are in all our fluctuating and vexing forms. Home is the place where it doesn't matter if we're wearing real pants or not. Home is where we don't have to worry about whether anyone else likes the art on the walls or the food in the fridge. That's what we want the space of our healing practices to be like: home—a place where we can drop our guard without having to put any psychological walls up. Perhaps we ought to begin our sitting meditation practice by letting out that same sigh of relief we make at the front door at the end of a trying day. *We made it.*

Formal Buddhists take refuge vows as a commitment to the "three jewels" of Buddha, Dharma, and Sangha: the teacher, teachings, and community of practitioners. The historical Buddha is evidence, the example: liberation is possible for any ordinary being. *Dharma* is the teachings, the canon of Buddhist scriptures. *Sangha* traditionally refers to "those who have glimpsed deathlessness"—that is, they are pretty darn close to full awakening. More generally, it's taken to mean a community of practitioners, for it is in associating with others on this path that we gain an identity of one who is focused on liberation. In making such a connection, one gains invaluable inspiration and support to go the distance.

In many traditions, one actually takes formal refuge vows, a lifelong commitment to the path of the heart. The idea here is that following the Buddhist path—its ethical precepts, its eightfold structure for wise living, its system of meditation, and its ever-deepening insights into the ultimate nature of reality—offers a psycho-spiritual protection from *samsara*, or the ills of the world. As one begins to glimpse what this system points out and points toward, one increasingly severs their relationship with suffering. Hence, refuge: a form of protection far more expansive and effective than our defense mechanisms could ever achieve.

It's curious how the three jewels intertwine with the robust predictors of resilience discussed in chapter 5. The principle of the teacher relates to the notion of something greater than ourselves, to hope and possibility. The teachings point us toward inner life, the place where emotional literacy, cognitive flexibility, and emotional intelligence are developed. Community is also chief among these protective factors.

While I find it indispensable to have formal teachers, ongoing courses of study, and communities that align with and support my spiritual growth, sacred refuge is also available in daily life. The teacher, teachings, and community can be found everywhere when we know how to look for them. We can take refuge in our own hearts, in Self Energy as a buddha, an awakened one. When we identify directly with Self Energy, healing is natural, growth unfolds organically, compassion deepens, and we get insights, guidance, and life lessons—dharma. We also best relate to our *sanghas*, our communities, when we come from love and compassion. Finally, the parts that we hold inside are also a form of community, one that functions best when connected to the heart. Thus, the heart is the wellspring, the nexus, the place where it all comes together; it is the source of everything good, of everything worth investing in. This is the spirit behind the "heart breathing" in the Fivefold Foundation; to bring vitality and build neural pathways around this precious resource.

Thus, experiencing Self Energy is quite synonymous with the essence of taking refuge. Whether working with the IFS model, with Buddhism or another spiritual school, or with your own unique mash-up of traditions and modalities, true refuge means becoming increasingly aware of an innate, inner, and yet transpersonal resource that protects you from further entanglements with suffering. Let's look at an example:

Imagine your partner does or says something that makes you feel ignored, insecure, or abandoned. You react to this habitually—perhaps confronting them, maybe shrinking away and having a private freak-out, maybe texting friends about how to respond, maybe starting a fight and possibly putting the whole relationship in jeopardy. Any way you slice it, you're quite likely to get entangled and react in some sort of narrowed manner. The worst part: it's entirely possible that you misread what happened or are projecting your own issues onto the situation, especially if you've suffered trauma in past relationships. When this happens, we are in conflict with a phantom force, treating the person as if they were someone long gone, perhaps entering a battle that has no end (because the only place it actuality exists is in our mind).

Now imagine that your partner does that same exact thing, except this time you're in a state of openhearted compassion, self-loving Self Energy. Isn't it true that you're much more likely to *respond* rather than react? You might realize their behavior was something small and worth letting go of. You might ask questions to clarify what you perceived. You might feel the sting of being genuinely wronged but communicate with less emotional charge, using words less likely to incite conflict.

You might sense that they're actually responding to something *they* perceived as hurtful. Point being: you're much more likely to do something expansive rather than narrowing. You're much more likely to respond in a way that relates directly to the difficulty of the situation without spiraling into full-blown suffering.

This is a fairly innocuous example. When we consider the power of Self Energy to mitigate the long-term effects of traumatic stress within the window of consolidation (as discussed in chapter 1), we begin to see that *protection beyond defenses* is quite literally what we can achieve.

Is the heart open or closed? This is the essential question, if not the only one. Whether we're talking about the path of outshining trauma, the path of spiritual awakening, the path of simply living well, or even the path of hedonic pleasure—there is no matter more central, no situation more conducive to what we truly want. While there are a million ways to open the heart (and multiple processes are generally needed by each of us), seeing from this vantage point brings the complex mandala of healing work into tight focus.

Cultivate the skill of opening the heart. Learn to notice when the heart is closed and be willing to open it back up. Discover how to act from openheartedness (a spectrum from sweetness to ferocity). Develop the ability to abide in the openhearted state for longer and longer. One day: enter the garden and never leave again.

REFUGE AND SECURE ATTACHMENT
WITH SELF ENERGY

"Secure attachment" is psychological jargon for an ability to experience healthy love and long-term bonding with others. It describes the interpersonal experience of refuge. Moments of secure relating ask one to be able to regulate emotions, navigate conflict healthfully, communicate one's needs, be receptive to love without overt clinging, and embody boundaries without compulsive avoidance. (Of course, no one is perfect.) Typically, one's ability to be close to others in an ongoingly secure fashion results from consistent experiences with a caregiver wherein they felt loved with this kind of energy. In the long-term presence of such a caregiver, a developing nervous system internalizes an intuitive sensibility for these sorts of things. Such an *attachment figure* is indeed a refuge to those in their care.

"Secure attachment" doesn't only have implications for one's tendencies in relationship. It connotes a certain baseline with which one can walk through the world without too much insecurity, explosiveness, ambivalence, or self-aggrandization. It correlates to a basic and overarching sense of trust—trust in the universe as basically good, trust in life to teach us what we need to know, trust in our ability to reckon with difficulty should it come our way. All of which correlates with having a sense of inner refuge as well.

Many of us didn't get an opportunity to internalize such qualities in youth. Unpacking the whys and hows is a topic for another book entirely. For our purposes, I would rather deliver the good news: If you didn't get a chance to internalize this secure way of being when you were young, the ship has not sailed. That ship is still here, docked at the port of re-parenting, healing, and learning how to abide in Self Energy. Ultimately we want our parts to form such a bond with Self Energy; that is the most direct way forward. For many of us, though, we still need something or someone external to model the qualities of security for us to internalize. Thankfully, those needed experiences and people already surround us. Tuning in to and internalizing them is the subject matter of our next meditation as well as chapter 11.

Secure bonding has a specific set of feeling tones to it. There's a simplicity to it. There's not a lot of big up-and-down drama to it. It's peaceful, sweet, steady, smooth, soothing to our nerves, and it naturally points us in the direction of balance. There's a consistency to it, a reliability. To a nervous system accustomed to more extreme energies, it's easy to miss. To a nervous system accustomed to abandonment, rage, or psychological frisson, our parts might look right at it and not recognize it as something deeply valuable. Yet this foreign territory has everything to show us.

We can find all of these qualities in the breath when it's set in its natural rhythm. The breath is consistent, reliable; it's been there for us our entire lives. We can attend to it, hold it, immerse in it—and even if we wander far away from the breath into distractionland, it'll be right there waiting for us just the same. It's smooth, simple; and it exerts a regulating influence on the body. Which is to say, we can open ourselves to the breath and allow it to reorient our nervous systems. Repeat experiences of orientating to the secure presence of the breath can and will, over time and through the grace of neuroplasticity, naturally nudge us in the direction of a more secure way of being—especially if we're consciously aware of the breath's nature while holding this intention.

We now return to the breath-based Fivefold Foundation, this time with a different awareness and a new intention.

REFUGE AND SECURITY IN THE BREATH

Every meditation in this book going forward will move in two phases—the Fivefold Foundation followed by parts work meditation. In the Fivefold Foundation phase, we'll progressively establish a base of somatic and breath awareness. It's an opportunity to settle in, welcome yourself, and remember how good it is be here—to be alive and practicing. Go as slow as you like. Luxuriate in these steps if you have the time.

The Fivefold Foundation is useful, also, as a routine entry point for meditation: something that eliminates having to reach for guided audio meditations every single time. (Silence is golden, after all.) You may have noticed that the mind is a squirrelly and shaky thing, and our attention spans are quite challenged these days. Having a reliable sequence of steps for graduating into (even a semblance of) presence can help counteract this.

Engaging this process is much like nourishing the soil before planting a seed so that it has a better chance of taking root and bearing fruit. The second stage is that seed—the work we'll be engaging in to deepen our meditation through new concepts and approaches.

The meditations in this book are intended to be between ten and twenty (or even twenty-five) minutes in length—around five to ten minutes for the Fivefold Foundation and another ten to fifteen minutes for the subsequent meditation. It's ideal if you can set a timer on your phone or watch. If you have less time, you can, of course, choose your own adventure and skip ahead to the second stage or, alternatively, linger with the elements of the foundational stage and return to the second stage another time. What matters most is that you're here, investing in yourself in an unusually beautiful way.

REFUGE IN THE BREATH

Begin with the Fivefold Foundation:

1. Posture
2. Abdominal breathing
3. Natural breathing
4. Knowing the body in space
5. Heart breathing

You can continue working with the breath in the heartspace but many might find the sensations of the breath to be more palpable in the nostrils. It may also be easier to feel the breath above the upper lip and in the very openings of the nose. Settle on the place where you can sensorily connect with the breath. Feel one inhale. Then feel one exhale. Then rest in the space between breaths. Then feel one inhale. Then keep going just like this.

Notice the qualities of the breath. In particular, notice its smoothness, its steadiness, its availability. You can allow the breath to exert a healthy influence on you. It is giving you life. It is nudging you toward balance, toward peace. You can rely on the breath to be here for you. It's been here for you your whole life. Let yourself relax into the breath and feel its support. Familiarize yourself with what it's like to have this.

Consciously acknowledge these sensations and truths as the essence of security. Consciously acknowledge your intention to allow these sensations to reorient your nervous system.

Recognize this as Self Energy, the essence of your own heart reflected back to you by the breath.

In the words of Vinny Ferraro, let this be like a love affair. Become receptive to the breath. Hold the experience of the breath with your attention. Stay right there with it, following each of its contours. Appreciate its good qualities. Commit to it, to staying present. You could even let yourself love the breath back. You can start with simply being curious.

Your attention will stray. Let that be natural, normal. When you notice you've strayed, use it as an opportunity to come home to the breath with grace. Just come back like it's no big deal (because it isn't) and reinterest yourself in the smooth, life-giving, easy qualities of the breath.

If your mind is particularly wild, you might first check to see if you're allowing those natural spaces between breaths. Parts tend to calm down in that space. You might also talk to your parts, letting them know that this is a safe time to take a break and enjoy a little rest. You could also practice counting the breaths as a way to train the mind to be present. You could count one full inhale-exhale-space cycle as "one" and continue from there. You could also count each segment of the natural breath (inhale as "one," exhale as "two," space between as "three").

As the sweet and simple security of the breath spreads throughout your body, know that it is being felt by your parts. Acknowledge this to them. Let your parts notice that this most precious resource is here for them. They too can absorb it, be permeated by it, begin to be shaped by it. If parts are still distracting you or are waiting for this to be over, especially offer them the breath. Let them feel how good of an idea it was to meditate today.

If you feel so moved, you can conclude by inviting one part of you to come and sit front and center inside. Perhaps it's a part that's been worried or lonely or exhausted. Any part that wants to come forward and be showered with the energy of the breath is more than welcome. Give this part all the space in the universe to dwell in. Stay here as long as you like.

Dedication of Merit

It's important that we acknowledge our efforts. Take a moment to think on all the work you've been putting into this path. Reading this book, trying out different practices and exercises, the meditation just now, and all your other worthy efforts to be a decent person and kind to others. You can amplify this by imagining how many other people are making similar efforts and even practicing this very same meditation—your merits joined with the merits of the universal sangha. These merits are like gold coins, precious and rare. The thing to do with these gold coins is to give them away. Imagine them scattering in the wind like so many dandelion seeds, becoming food for the hungry, medicine for the sick, and peace for the war-torn. Hold the wish for all beings to be happy, for all hearts to heal, and for each of us to be free.

10

BEYOND INNER DIALOGUE

Engaging Parts Work in Meditation

Attention is the rarest and purest form of generosity.

—*Simone Weil*

In the tumultuous summer of 2020, I somehow found myself mentoring with Richard Schwartz. It was the surprise of a lifetime really. When he first emailed me, I was positive it was to serve me with some sort of cease-and-desist order. I had, after all, taken it upon myself to blend his IFS model with Buddhist somatic practices in my first book *The Monkey Is the Messenger*. For all I knew, he saw my free-jazz riffing on his work as a bastardization. It turns out he welcomed the innovation. He later told me I'd be quoted multiple times in his next book, *No Bad Parts*. (I may or may not have squealed like a preschooler on learning this.) So, I had another healthy "fuck it" moment; I asked if he'd mentor me.

Over the months, it struck me that his answers to my questions were often pretty textbook. His advice for most issues I brought to him: apply the rudimentary steps of parts work. I'd ask him what to do with a client with a complex problem I felt stuck on; he'd say, "Well, help them identify the part of them, step back from it, and help them get into a space of curiosity with it. Once you're there . . ." I'd ask him how to work with parts holding internalized racism or homophobia; he'd say, "Well, first help the client identify the parts involved, step back from them, find curiosity . . ." So much of the time, the guidance I received was some variation on the Six Fs—and yet the outcomes I saw in people were no less profound for it.

Having such a series of steps one can memorize and refer to is invaluable. Especially when they're reliably powerful.

There came a day when I was in heavy grief some weeks after the loss of my childhood best friend Bill. So, Richard said, "Let's find the parts holding the grief . . ." and on down the rabbit hole we went. In doing parts work directly with the number one parts work guy, a part of me wanted him to unveil some super-advanced secret technique in our process together. I thought for sure he'd share some nuanced, off-the-books approach. He did nothing of the sort. Instead, he heartfully guided me through the same process I already knew and loved so well—and we basically did several sessions' worth of emotional processing in the space of half an hour.

IFS, for all of its nuance, often unfolds through the use of scripts and sequential protocols. In later stages of the work, such as the *retrieval* and *unburdening* processes we'll discuss in chapter 14, things can get pretty unique, but the opening steps to the process are often fairly rote. Most of the time, it's all in the Six Fs. This is fortunate, as the inner world is indeed a nebulous and messy one. It's a neighborhood where the roads aren't clearly marked, the streetlights are often out, there's no speed limit, and cul-de-sacs abound.

THE ACCELERANT OF MIND-BODY AWARENESS

As we approach our second exploration of the Six Fs, this time as a formal meditation practice, some might wonder why we'll continue to include the Fivefold Foundation as an opening act as opposed to just getting down to the main event—parts work. There are some therapies where you just talk things out, there are some that focus on your cognitions, others that focus exclusively on the body, and still others that focus on the symbolic and archetypal images that form in the mind. When we engage parts work meditation in tandem with the Fivefold Foundation, we are more likely to enter a field of experience that includes all of the above. In working at every level of the psyche simultaneously, we are necessarily carving many more new neural pathways. It is an accelerant to this work.

Insight: The first empirically reviewed study that established the efficacy of the Internal Family Systems model used parts work on patients with rheumatoid arthritis.[1] If you suffer from chronic pain, you may want to try parts work with the parts of you who react to the pain. You can also experiment with sending Self Energy to the pain itself.

A few caveats: For one, there *is* nuance to the technique I'm about to offer you, not because it's esoteric or advanced but because of the abundance of if-then propositions (e.g., *if* you have compassion for a part, *then* do _____; but *if not, then* _____). Keep an eye out for these crucial forks in the road.

Second, meditation is a shaky affair, especially for post-pandemic brains hooked on attention-span-decimating smartphones and social media. Forgive yourself in advance for spacing out or being wobbly. So long as you come right back once you notice you're in outer space, it's just fine.

Third, if you are kind to whatever you meet in this experience, you can't go wrong. There is no wasted effort in the process of becoming self-aware if basic kindness is present.

Fourth—and perhaps most importantly: *go slowly* and pick light burdens to begin with so you can build these skills and inner relationships before going to anything deep. Your list-making and cognitive Manager parts or mild irritations are generally wise places to start.

Finally, this is not goal-driven work. You are not a project, and your healing is not a to-do list to complete in some linear fashion. Trauma-focused healing work is circular and exploratory in nature; it evolves most efficiently when we're willing to surrender to getting to know our parts rather than trying to fix them. Parts tend to be much more like cats than dogs, especially at first. Rather than excitedly leaping on us as we walk in the door, parts often hang back until they know we are well-intentioned and trustworthy. Similarly, if one walks right up to a cat and attempts to pick them up, it's likely to not end so well; approach parts with this kind of energy, especially Exiles, and they are likely to run and hide. Just as with cats, parts are far more likely to come around when a calm and patient presence allows them to approach on their own timeline.

Ambition is often the enemy of healing. If we are feeling ambitious, impatient, or goal-driven, we are simply not in Self Energy; a part is running the show. If you notice such a thing in your own process, it's no big deal. Take a breath, ask the ambitious part to step aside, and proceed with curiosity and compassion.

PARTS WORK MEDITATION

Begin with the Fivefold Foundation:

1. Posture
2. Abdominal breathing
3. Natural breathing
4. Knowing the body in space
5. Heart breathing

Reminder: In the cultivation of self-awareness there is no such thing as wasted effort.

Find a part to work with. Perhaps one that's already activated—perhaps trying to be a good meditator—or, conversely, distracting you from the meditation. If you desire to work with a specific part of you—perhaps you've been noticing a recurrent mental-emotional state coming up for you at work or in relationships lately—you can find a trailhead by simply remembering the situation you were in the last time this part was activated. Relive the mind movie of this memory until you feel something stirring, then . . .

Focus on the part. Give them your full attention, perhaps asking all other parts of you to step aside. Switch into a mode where you're sitting with this part, perhaps right next to them like friends on a park bench. Keep a little bit of space between the two of you, just like you would with a friend.

Flesh out the part you're focusing on (what I'll now call the "focus part") by noticing—is there a body feeling to this part? If yes, where is it and what is it like? Is there an emotional tone here, even if only a vague sense? If so, can you label it? Finally, does the part seem to be saying anything, either in words or images? Simply notice and find a way to make sure the part feels noticed. You might simply say inside, *I'm here with you, you have my full attention*, or reflect back something like, *I'm noticing you're tight in the chest, annoyed, and telling me everything you hate about my boss*. Notice if there's a sense of a response. The part might calm down. There might suddenly be more space inside. The part might intensify. Whatever the "response" is, keep letting the part know that they are seen, heard, and felt by communicating inside what you're noticing.

Befriend the part by asking yourself, *How do I feel toward this part right now?* Just ask; don't think of the answer. Then notice any reactive parts surfacing. Whether it's an analytic part, a part that doesn't like the focus part, a part that distracts, or a part that dissociates, it doesn't matter. Simply ask all other parts to step aside so you can be here with the focus part in Self Energy. Then ask yourself a second time, *How do I feel toward the focus part now?* Notice again if any reactive or polarized parts arise and kindly ask if they'll allow some room.

Next, look inside for a little space that feels clear, open, perhaps tingly—or a general sense that you want to know more or be of help to the focus part. If you can find this, please continue to the next step. If you can't find this, it's because your other parts haven't stepped to the side. Some options on how to proceed (you might use more than one of these):

- Ask inside if any parts need to be heard before they step aside. If you get a sense of "yes," then allow whatever part this is some space to express themselves. Affirm and reflect back whatever information you receive from them. Then ask them again to step aside.
- Ask inside what that part fears might happen if they let you proceed. Respond to those fears from a place of love. They're most likely afraid you'll get overwhelmed in some way. (You did learn some techniques for dealing with overwhelm back in chapter 3.)
- You might need to communicate inside that the parts' feelings are heard and appreciated before pointing out some new information from them. Some sample responses:

- "I hear that you're sick of this and feel we should've gotten over it by now, but the focus part simply isn't over it and I want to help them release their burdens so they can get over it. Could I have your permission to do that?"
- "I see that you fear what we might uncover if we continue. Perhaps you could help me work with it just a little bit at a time. I can also dog-ear the section in this book on overwhelm to refer back to in case that happens."
- The question to ask any time a part is mistrusting of Self is: "How old do you think I am?" You'll most likely sense they think you're younger than you are. Make sure they find out how old you really are and all the ways you've grown since you were younger. (Note: this doesn't necessarily mean life is better now, just that you're less vulnerable than a child is and you've learned a lot since then.)
- Should all else fail, you can switch to working with the polarized part that won't step aside. Make them the focus part and start over from the beginning.

Once you're (imperfectly) in Self Energy with the focus part, you're ready for bearing witness.

Questions for Befriending Firefighters and Managers

- What are they trying to accomplish by doing the job they're doing?
- When is the earliest this part can remember feeling this way?
- Is there anything they need from you to help them feel better?

Maybe there's a boundary you need to set in your life, a behavior change that's called for, or a reassurance they need from you.

- Do they like what they're doing now, or do they just feel like they have to be this way? Does it ever get tiresome?
- If they didn't have to be this way anymore, what would they rather be doing?
  - If you get a sense of a healthy alternative, stop and celebrate this vision with them. Not only is it possible for this part to make this switch; it's literally what we are working toward right now! Let this part know that if they permit you to work with and heal

whatever Exiles they are protecting, they too will be set free to make choices that feel better.

- If you are feeling the confidence of Self, you could even ask their permission to work with the Exile they are protecting right now. If you get a sense of "yes," allow this protector to move to the side and welcome in any hurt energies that were being guarded. Then skip ahead to the next section on bearing witness.

- Finally, what does this part **fear** might happen if they were to drop their burdens and take on a new, freer role in the inner system?

They are likely afraid you would fall apart in some way if they stop protecting you. This fear will be directly related to the Exile they're protecting. This is often an important discovery.

Many things could be coming up at this point. You might feel the tenderness of an emerging Exile. You might feel a dawning sense of clarity that gives rise to fresh insights. You might be connecting the dots of this experience to memories, perhaps in a surprising way. What matters most in these final moments is to hold the part in the space of Self-compassion. You may get other intuitive ideas for how to relate and interact with this part. Follow those intuitions. It's likely that this is coming from the *creativity* of Self and can lead you to some interesting off-the-map experiences inside.

If you've been working with the defensive system (Managers and Firefighters), you may very well be done for the day. Honor this and avoid ambition. Only proceed to the next section if it feels right, you are in Self Energy, and you have the permission of your defenders.

Questions for Bearing Witness to an Exile

Ask inside what this part needs you to know. Become receptive and simply "listen." There is no need to respond or to problem-solve. Simply witness what comes up as you sit with the question. Hold it in the space of Self, in the space of compassion; such is the essence of bearing witness. Help them to feel held. (Many people get a sense that their Exile needs a hug and visualize such; you might also get a sense that the Exile is crying or screaming internally, even though it's not happening externally.)

Remember: *Treat parts like people you want to treat well.* Allow them the space to express everything.

The best move here might be to simply offer the part refuge in the breath or allow them to bask in the sunlight of Self. *That much could easily be the rest of this meditation.* It also might be all the part is really up for just yet.

It might feel appropriate to lovingly respond or affirm this part's feelings in the manner an excellent caregiver might. It can also be most appropriate to ask further questions inside so you can continue getting to know them. Choose from this list in whatever way feels appropriate:

- *How old are you?*
- *How long have you been holding these kinds of feelings for me?*
- *Can you see me? How old I am? That we survived?*
- *Can you notice the love I'm feeling toward you right now?*
- *Is there something I can offer you that would help you?*
  - Note: We are working inside your mind right now. You can give this part the moon and the stars if that's what they want. Anything is possible.
- *If you no longer had to hold this pain for me, what would you rather be doing?*
  - It's always good to stop and relish whatever answer this part offers up to this question. It is a real possibility for their energy to be reclaimed and redirected in this way.

Ending

Bid your parts a fond farewell and thank them for working with you today. Begin taking deep breaths. Make sure to breathe in as big as any of the feelings that have been here. Assume the attitude of coming down from this experience, returning to your ordinary status quo. Any parts that might ordinarily protect you by assuming a normative role or wearing a socially appropriate mask are more than welcome to come in and do so. Keep breathing for some time.

Acknowledge your good efforts, the merits you've accumulated. Send your merits out to the world. Wish for beings less fortunate than you to somehow receive all your healing, all your insight. When we give our merit away, it only multiplies. Multiply it! Then give it away again and multiply it some more. Wish for the happiness and freedom of all beings, that your practice might be a contribution to peace in our world.

An optional move is to smile at the end—whether real or fake, inner or outer. Doing so can trigger serotonin from the brain, which might be a nice reset. (I recognize the common and frustrating experience of women being told to smile by strangers on the street, and I assure you, this isn't that.)

Note: If you struggled at all to find even 1 percent of Self Energy in this practice, hang tight. We'll explore many alternatives in the following chapter.

11

YOU ARE NEVER ALONE

Self Energy Surrogates

It is by going down into the abyss that you recover the treasures of life. Where you stumble, there lies your treasure.

—*Joseph Campbell*

Fun fact: "Buddha" wasn't the dude's name. The word *buddha* isn't actually a proper noun. It's just a regular ole noun, a title. It means "one who is awake." In the Mahayana (later school) Buddhist teachings, there are many buddhas, or awakened ones, who appear all over the place and throughout time to help beings develop spiritually and attain the full expression of their buddha nature—a.k.a. Self Energy. Thus, when you see "Buddha" capitalized, it's only to distinguish that we're talking about the historical figure from 2,600 years ago. But the word *buddha* actually points to a living state of being that is universal and impersonal in nature.

The term *buddha nature* is translated from the Sanskrit *tathagatha garba*, which literally translates as "the womb of awakening." It is the primary task of fully realized buddhas to help beings mature into the recognition of their own true nature. That is also the primary objective of Self Energy. Like a womb, it nourishes, freely sharing its resources to nurture, protect, and usher development along. Most of us have had the experience of being in nature and sensing ourselves begin to loosen up, let go of stresses, and feel restored in some way. Indigenous cultures the world over teach that the Earth itself is a healer. (This is less so for Western people conditioned by the Eurocentric "Enlightenment" of the eighteenth century, but I digress.) Like the Earth, buddha nature promotes the well-being, insight, and healing of all that it interacts with. That's the wonder of your own heart at its depths.

Like the word *buddha*, the term *Self Energy* can easily be misunderstood. As mentioned before, Self Energy is something that's simultaneously personal and universal. We all have it and can experience it personally. But that's the thing—we *all* have it; it's part of a unified field that connects us all. (In Buddhist terms, this is sometimes called *Indra's Web*.) We can find this basic nature in animals, trees, and the Earth itself. The word *Self* here doesn't mean it's your true personality or personhood. Self is more spacious than that, and it is something shared by us all, that connects us all. It's also an *energy*: it transcends individual personhood and personality. It was with you before you had a name, before you developed memories of being here. As mentioned before, the element of space itself holds the essence of Self, and we can find the secure qualities of Self in sensations of the breath as well.

A student once wrote to the Zen master and peace activist Thich Nhat Hanh, "I've lost my smile, but don't worry. The dandelion has it."[1] In a similar way, if we can't seem to access Self Energy within yet, there is no need to worry. The Earth, the breath, and space itself all hold it for us. We can consider these to be our surrogates of Self Energy, and we can access the essence of Self by relating to these living forces directly in our practice. It is not terribly unlike when a therapist holds the compassion for a client in a therapeutic relationship until a client can get to self-compassion on their own. Similarly, there are many common meditation practices where one visualizes a healing mentor, deity, or bodhisattva and taps into their compassion. Such practices, which call upon the imagination to influence the brain and our parts, can be an important gateway to Self. As discussed in chapter 9, this can be especially key for those of us who have never had even one model of what healthy love looks like. If this is you, you have options. Compassion surrounds us, even if we don't yet recognize it or know how to tap into it. That's what the practices in this chapter are about.

MEDITATION AS FAMILIARIZATION
WITH BUDDHA NATURE OR SELF ENERGY

You might be asking, *Well, if buddha nature or Self Energy is everywhere, why have I never experienced this before?* I would actually posit that you've been experiencing glimpses of this your whole life, just without exposure to insights and ideas that allow you to perceive it and name it as such. The human brain is just like a computer in that all it can apprehend is the result of its inputs. Experiences abound where something is right in front of us, staring us in the face, and we just don't have the neural receptors built to perceive it yet. We've also all had the experience of someone describing something to us and finally putting into words something we've experienced, perhaps dozens of times, but couldn't quite name because no one had ever given us the language for it.

I was five years old when my mother walked in on me with my hand jammed in the electric can opener. (If you're getting the impression that I've been a troublemaker from the start, well . . .) When she asked just what in the hell I was doing, I calmly informed her that I'd discovered a new way to trim my fingernails. She rushed me to the doctor's office, but until I saw the nurses, I was cool as a cucumber. When my mother unwrapped the towel my hand was in, it revealed a fingernail that had been sliced right down the middle to its lunula, its root, and into the sensitive tissue beneath it. The two nurses shrieked, aghast. The sharp sting of my injury came rushing in. I began wailing uncontrollably. I remember this moment clearly because up until then, I'd felt no pain whatsoever. The reaction of the nurses signaled to me that I *ought* to be in pain, and so that's when my body produced a pain response. It's uncanny that this type of perception is such a big piece of how we work, and we'll discuss our brain's primary function of *simulation* in chapter 17.

This phenomenal capacity of our neural circuitry comes into play with the most positive and even transcendent of experiences as well. Without having names for things, we aren't as likely to recognize them fully. We might miss the experience of them entirely. In beginning to name and recognize an experience that is novel for us, we not only gain greater access to said experience but we also gain a clearer capacity for familiarizing ourselves with it. The Tibetan word most commonly used for meditation is *göm*, which actually means "familiarization." For it is in becoming familiar with something that our intimacy with it grows, and it is in intimacy that we pierce the veils of our illusions and begin to see people and experiences for what they truly are. Hence, the Tibetans named meditation as an act of familiarization with mind itself, a process of becoming intimate with our inner workings with the express aim of finally experiencing the mind's true nature—buddha nature, that which is closer than our own skin.

All of this is to say, compassion may surround us at all times, but it is wholly possible for a person to not experience that if their eyes have not yet been opened to this truth. Having laid this groundwork, let's dive into three different Self Energy surrogacy practices.

THE SELF ENERGY OF EARTH

Begin with the Fivefold Foundation:

1. Posture
2. Abdominal breathing
3. Natural breathing
4. Knowing the body in space
5. Heart breathing

Imagine you're walking to your favorite spot in nature. It could be the beach, the desert, a snowy peak, the forest, or out at the center of a lake. It could be real or totally made-up. You're feeling your legs moving under you—or perhaps your arms rowing a canoe. You're looking all around to take in the sights, shapes, and magnificent colors. You hear the sounds of this environment, big and small. You smell the smells that await you here. You feel the qualities of the air—temperature, density, humidity—on your skin, on your face. Most importantly, you begin to get in touch with what it feels like to be here. Notice anything that's beginning to shift.

You arrive at a good place to sit down and allow your body to rest upon the Earth. You take your left hand and place it just underneath the Earth's surface, feeling the texture of the sand, the dirt, the water, whatever it is. You're beginning to feel the Earth's energy infiltrating and permeating your hand. When I say "Earth energy," I'm pointing to the living presence of the Earth, the force that is propagating everything you need for your life to happen: the food that eventually becomes the cells of your body, the clothes on your back, the raw materials that made your home. The Earth provides. It's all springing up from the Earth at all times. The Earth is also the grand creatrix, the greatest artist that ever was. It's almost endless—the majesty, the vistas, the ever-changing, living grandeur. This is the Self Energy of the Earth made apparent. And you're feeling its essence right here in your left hand.

As you continue to breathe, you feel this good energy in the fingers, in the palm, in the upper hand, and in the wrist. With each inhale, it's like you're pulling the love of the Earth up; further into the forearm, into the elbow, into the upper arm and left shoulder. This goodness flows into the neck, the head, the face, the brain, softening and enlivening everything it touches. You can stop, breathe, and enjoy this for as long as you like at any point.

This Self Energy of the Earth flows now into the right shoulder and down into the right arm and all the way into the fingers. It continues its journey in the chest, the upper back, making its way into the heartspace. You feel it moving down the spine, shining in the lungs, the lower back, and into the belly, touching each of the organs. This good Earth energy lands right in the pelvis. Breathe and take your time here. We hold so much tension, so much trauma, in this area—the inner organs, the hip flexors, the glutes, and even the bones. Really allow yourself to take in the healing Self Energy of the Earth here. Allow anything that is tangled up to simply unfurl and surrender to gravity. When you're ready, let the softening move into the inner thighs (the home of the psoas muscle, sometimes called "the holy grail of well-being"). As this region relaxes, you might feel a release inside the pelvic bowl and in the abdomen as well.

Finally, as you breathe, the Earth energy makes it way down the whole of the thighs, into the knees, into the feet and toes. It travels back into the source, the ground below, creating a circuit, a loop if you will, through the vehicle of the body. Breathe spaciously into the whole body now. Notice any shifts. In particular, check to see if any calm, clarity, curiosity, or compassion—Self Energy—is somehow more available inside you.

Ask inside if there are any parts of you that have been struggling or becoming exhausted lately that would like to come rest on your lap for some time. Just ask. Then notice if you get even a vague sense of anything moving to the foreground. Allow this part some space and surround them with the goodness you feel inside. Breathe with them. Rest here as long as you like.

If you're up for it, you could return to the meditation on the Six Fs in chapter 10 and process further with this part. That much is up to you.

THE SELF ENERGY OF AN ENTELECHY

Begin with the Fivefold Foundation:

1. Posture
2. Abdominal breathing
3. Natural breathing
4. Knowing the body in space
5. Heart breathing

Contemplation: *Entelechy* (pronounced en-TEL-eh-kee), a word derived from Greek and often associated with Aristotle, is sometimes translated as "realized potential." Its true meaning is deeper than that, though. It is the force within us that already holds the realization of that potential. It is the force that vies for that potential to be realized. For example, it is the entelechy of a tiny acorn to become the mighty, towering oak tree. The destiny of the oak tree was programmed within the minuscule acorn all along; it just needed to run into the right conditions for growth, then the rest was guaranteed.

Suppose you're an alien and have never seen an acorn before. You've never observed seeds and don't know how they work. If I held up an acorn for you and then pointed to a fully grown oak tree, telling you, "This becomes *that*," you'd never believe me. But it's true; the gigantic oak is already there, right there in the tiny seedling. It wouldn't matter, either, if you believed me or not. It'd still be true.

If the entelechy of the acorn is the mighty oak, what is the entelechy of your heart? Of your life? Minuscule as you might seem, as tattered and torn up as you might feel some days, it doesn't matter. Beliefs about your worthiness, what you're capable of, or your purpose here do not matter. Your divine potential isn't up to you.

Imagine before you—about arm's-length distance from the center of your chest, and about the size of your hand—your realized entelechy. This is you, except it's the you that you'd be if you had a thousand lifetimes to walk this path. This is the future you that's done all the work, healed all the hurts, and has perfected love and compassion in the process. And this future, entelechy you is looking right back at you. Their face is effulgent, serene. Their gaze is so loving you can barely stand it. Their body is emitting a rainbow hue that is incredibly inviting. They're smiling right at you, chuckling even, because they know how your story turns out. They know that everything you struggle with now, as impossible as it seems, eventually becomes the fodder for your very transformation. It's irritating how tickled they are! Just the same, those eyes, burning with the perfect love, are gazing at *you*. There's no point in hiding. This entelechy you already knows everything about you now; it's safe to drop your guard and let yourself feel completely seen, radically held in their presence.

Take some time to thoroughly bask here. Take their beaming energy fully into the body. Notice what it's like to absorb this.

You could end right here. You could also find a part of you to work with here in this supported presence. If you choose this adventure, the Six Fs are there to guide you in chapter 10.

Another option: Grab a pen and paper, then ask the entelechy, *What would you have me know?* Then let the entelechy write through you. Let it come however it comes. Keep writing for at least a page or two.

What would Love Itself have you know?

SELF ENERGY BRAIN HACK

Begin with the Fivefold Foundation:

1. Posture
2. Abdominal breathing
3. Natural breathing
4. Knowing the body in space
5. Heart breathing

Think to a time when you felt caring for someone else. It might have been a fleeting moment, it might have been for someone who was in need, it might have been for your dog. It doesn't matter which one you choose. Find one memory of a time when you genuinely felt caring affection for another being.

Imagine what it would be like if you could feel this now. What would the sensations be like in the body? What would you feel in your chest, on your face, in your belly, in your hands?

When you get a sense of this feeling, let it expand. Notice the newness of this feeling; it wasn't here a moment ago. Notice how meaningful it is to feel love for another. Notice again the specific sensations happening in the body. Notice how intense it is on a scale of 1 to 10, and even if it's just a 1 or 2. See if maybe you can move it up a notch or two—or five.

Regardless, this is Self Energy. This is it. Right here. This feeling, this place. Take a screenshot of this place. Let your parts know that this is the place you've been trying to show them. Isn't it so good? Don't they want to feel this from you more often?

You are now positioned well to work with any parts of you holding any kind of distress or fatigue.

12

MAKING THE UNSEEN SEEN

Parts Mapping

When I understand myself, I understand you, and out of that understanding comes love.

—Jiddu Krishnamurti

Our view: healing is what happens when we compassionately get to know ourselves at deeper levels. It's a deceptively simple-sounding proposition, because once we begin to turn the lights on inside, we see that there's more to us than we previously imagined. "Everything dissolves under analysis," the Tibetan proverb goes. That is, just like physicists peering into matter to discover the molecule, into the molecule to discover the atom, and then peering into the atom to discover quarks—every time we think we've found the basic building blocks of who we are, we uncover more layers of nuance—we find more parts. On one level, you could say this is further evidence of the grandeur of our being. On another level, it gets to be a lot to keep track of.

Parts mapping offers us another means of getting to know ourselves and our parts. It is another way of helping our parts to feel seen and claimed by us, or of "making the unconscious conscious" (as Carl Jung so famously stated was a precursor to enlightenment). Parts mapping is a simple style of journaling our parts work meditation. It isn't extensive, but I find it pays dividends in the end. I was first exposed to this practice through Michelle Glass's book *Daily Parts Meditation Practice,* which has become part of the core IFS canon. Glass points out that mapping our parts will help us recognize which specific parts are triggered in moments of activation (which can help us make better choices in the moment). It can also prevent parts from taking on further burdens. I've found that mapping helps parts to not slide back into the vague recesses of mind; it holds them freshly here in my conscious awareness. In short, it helps us integrate this work into our daily lives. Integration is what happens any time we make our inner experience external in some way. It can also be an incredibly grounding activity.

I'll admit, I experienced a ton of resistance to parts mapping at first. My Manager parts all groaned, *Dude, you want* more *paperwork in your life?* I am a social worker by training; paperwork is practically its own trauma type for me. It wasn't until a crisis hit and I needed to get serious about processing a specific issue in therapy that I began to map parts. I wanted to be sure the parts involved in this mini crisis made some real progress quickly, and I sensed that being slightly more organized than usual would help—and it did. It turns out my parts felt like I was taking them more seriously. An implicit message was being communicated: *Our healing is* so *important that, yeah, some paperwork is involved.*

HOW TO MAP PARTS

There are countless ways you could map your parts. What I'll present to you here, with visual examples on the coming pages, is one way that really seems to be working for both myself and my students. It involves drawing something of an egg cooked sunny-side up. You sketch out one big oval for the egg whites and then place a circle for the egg yolk at the top of the oval. The yolk represents Self Energy, the core of your being. To represent your parts, you'll draw new circles, placed on the map according to category. You can label the part with a nickname, writing that nickname in the center of the new circle, and then draw lines extending out from that circle to give you spaces to fill in with details about that part. Exile circles are drawn intersecting with the egg yolk of Self. This is because they're the parts that get the most buried in the psyche. Manager circles are drawn on the outer line of the egg white. They're on the surface of the egg because they're the parts spending the most time at the surface level of our lives. Firefighter circles get drawn outside the egg entirely. This is to represent how Firefighters aren't always active per se, but they certainly swoop into the egg of our being when Exiles get activated.

As we discussed in chapter 3, parts operate in clusters that generally organize themselves around specific issues in our lives. I personally have a cluster of at least seven parts that shows up in intimate relationships as my attachment style. I have two Exiles that hold woundings from childhood as well as adult love relationships; three Managers—one who knows how to woo someone, one who knows how to play it cool, and one who scans partners for faults and finds reasons why it'll never work; then two Firefighters who swoop in when I feel I've been wronged or insulted in some way. These parts can show up in very disorganized ways, play the victim, lash out, and find subtle ways to sabotage connections if I go to sleep on them. If, instead, I am present with them and keep them connected to Self through meditation and therapy, they tend to show up in much healthier ways and allow for Self Energy to lead in most situations. Alas, romance is the final frontier for me. It's beyond even a master class in healing for my parts. It's more like a double PhD that I'm still writing the dissertation for. Hopefully my engaging in this ridiculous level of self-disclosure helps you see how I am only able to keep up with this level of self-awareness with mapping. I wouldn't be able to keep up if not for the paperwork. And it's crucial that I do, as love and partnership is also one of the most joyful arenas of life for me.

EXPLORING EXAMPLE PARTS MAPS

For your first parts map, you'll likely only identify one Manager, Firefighter, or Exile. This is a great start. As you continue, you'll identify more parts and begin to see how your parts act as a system.

BASIC PARTS MAP

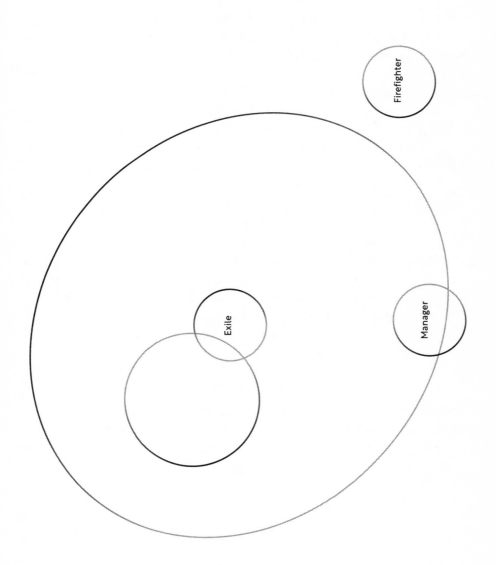

PARTS MAP: CLUSTER OF PARTS IN A PERSON WHO EXPERIENCES A LOT OF ANXIETY

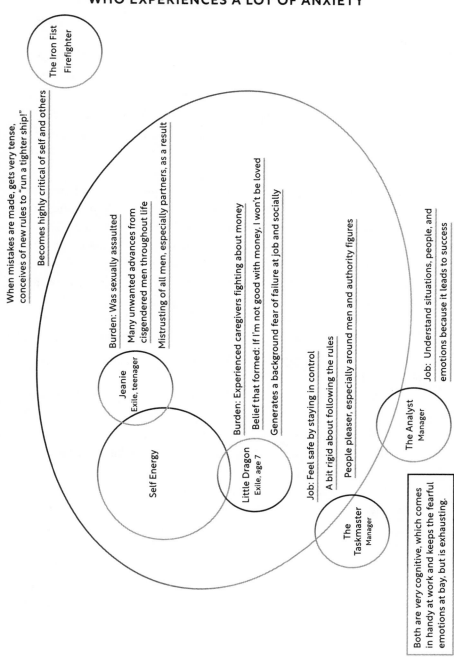

The Iron Fist Firefighter

When mistakes are made, gets very tense, conceives of new rules to "run a tighter ship!"

Becomes highly critical of self and others

Jeanie
Exile, teenager

Burden: Was sexually assaulted

Many unwanted advances from cisgendered men throughout life

Mistrusting of all men, especially partners, as a result

Self Energy

Little Dragon
Exile, age 7

Burden: Experienced caregivers fighting about money

Belief that formed: If I'm not good with money, I won't be loved

Generates a background fear of failure at job and socially

The Analyst
Manager

Job: Understand situations, people, and emotions because it leads to success

Job: Feel safe by staying in control

A bit rigid about following the rules

People pleaser, especially around men and authority figures

The Taskmaster
Manager

Both are *very* cognitive, which comes in handy at work and keeps the fearful emotions at bay, but is exhausting.

On the previous page, we have a map of a cluster of parts in a (hypothetical) person, "J," who routinely experiences anxiety. When anxiety arises for J, they typically have a surface-level perception of it, such as *Things are just really stressful at work right now*, but there is actually much more to the story.

J is a cis female. Although other identifiers and identities—such as age, race, sexual identity, and economic status—definitely play a factor in J's experience, I won't go into those here, as I want to keep this map as general and universally applicable as humanly possible. I offer the cis-female identifier as it pertains to the nature of J's trauma history.

In this particular cluster of J's parts, two Exiles hold two respective burdens. We have the Exile named Little Dragon, who experienced her parents fighting fervently over finances when she was quite young and came to conflate financial matters with being both lovable and safe. J also experienced sexual assault in early adulthood, a horrific experience that was absorbed by another Exile part, named Jeanie. Jeanie had already been absorbing the unwanted advances of cis men since she was incredibly young, and this traumatic material mixed right in with the extremity of the assault.

The emotional content of these unprocessed experiences is quite intense. These parts naturally hold a lot of fear. While Little Dragon fears failure, Jeanie fears anything that feels intrusive. There are other emotions and triggers here as well.

J would not be able to function if she lived with these fears in the front of her mind, so two of her Manager parts have developed jobs that help hold Little Dragon and Jeanie in the background. The Taskmaster is one such Manager part. The Taskmaster feels safest when following the rules, which also earns them praise from others. The Taskmaster goes into high gear when in the presence of authority figures (bosses, police, doctors, religious leaders) and people who present as male. In such situations, J thinks to herself, *I like it when I know exactly what to do and am liked by the people in charge*, but really that's the Taskmaster feeling very safe and out of harm's way. The Taskmaster works in tandem with the Analyst, who tries to "read" situations and people for cues as to how to act and curry their favor, which contributes to a sense of being successful and competent in the world. Both of these Manager parts generate a lot of nervous cognitive activity. This effectively keeps J's mind separated from her body, where her fearful Exiles live. The basic point is this: there's a tremendous sense of vulnerability underlying these Manager parts, and their incessant work at keeping the Exiles out of conscious awareness generates what J experiences as "anxiety."

We also have a Firefighter, the Iron Fist, standing guard. This reactive defender swoops in when J feels triggers of anything resembling failure or being intruded upon. The trigger could be as small as forgetting to pay a bill or feeling trapped in a conversation that J wants to be over. In the presence of such triggers, J's Exiles begin generating intense fear—but the Iron Fist shuts this down by becoming very judgmental and rigid. Sometimes this critical activity is directed at J, who finds herself fixated on every little thing "wrong" with her and her life. J might also find herself mentally criticizing others (though keeping it to herself to maintain appearances). The criticism might be pointed in both directions at once.

In the name of keeping the map somewhat simple, I didn't depict this, but we can be certain J also has at least one "polarized part" somewhere in the defensive system. This might look like a part that—despite all the rigidity, guardedness, and rule-following of this cluster—really enjoys numbing out with alcohol and food. Another plausible example of a polarized part in this system might be a part who thinks all of this is pathetic and that J shouldn't care so much what others think.

We can see from this map how each of these parts are dynamically interwoven around a bevy of issues that span J's emotional, interpersonal, vocational, and even financial world. In the presence of a trigger, everything about this subsystem intensifies. Here's an example:

One day, J makes a small but significant mistake at work. She is called into her (male) boss's office and reprimanded. Her boss isn't very skillful; he raises his voice and tells J this makes her "look bad to the whole company." She is given a disciplinary notice that could lead to probation and eventual termination should further errors be made.

Jeanie feels violated by the unexpected experience, the raised voice, and the unwanted critique and threat; and she responds by swelling up in big, expressive, tearful terror. Little Dragon senses the vulnerabilities related to livelihood and money and feels a more cowering, shrinking kind of fear.

The Analyst and the Taskmaster have essentially "failed." What's more, the two Exiles, Jeanie and Little Dragon, have flooded the system with big, fearful, and hurt emotions. J runs to the bathroom and cries uncontrollably. This triggers the Iron Fist to step in with big judgments of everything and everyone in the situation. Though still scared and tearful, the Iron Fist crowds out most of these emotions with intense, very anxious, inner-critic activity, assailing J for every little flaw. The Iron Fist generates mental activity that tells J, *I can never again try that thing I did that caused this. Maybe I don't belong in this line of work and should just give up. I'm going to have to keep my head down and my mouth shut and work extra hard for the next several weeks until everything's back to normal.* There is intense, punishing anguish that comes with all of this, but the Iron Fist feels it is the only way.

Later that evening, J has a birthday party to attend; she senses she cannot cancel (because that would be breaking "the rules" of social norms) and must comport herself in a fun and engaging manner (because that's what she believes is expected of her), but she still feels a bit raw. This gives rise to social anxiety about how to perform socially at the party. Under these conditions, drinking alcohol feels like the only way forward.

J might think the answer here is to learn to control her anxiety, to become better at regulating her big emotions, and to stop making mistakes at work. What would offer much more substantial, lasting, and empowering relief, however, would be for J to heal her Exiles. While this would be longer-term work that would begin with befriending the Managers and Firefighters involved, J could eventually unburden both Little Dragon and Jeanie, effectively discharging the stored energy of their early traumas from J's body. This would leave space for J to encounter future stressors without overflowing. Along the way, J's Manager and Firefighter parts would also develop a relationship to Self Energy and could begin allowing Self to lead with their qualities of calm, clarity, creativity, and curiosity at work and in relationships.

PARTS MAP: CLUSTER OF PARTS IN A PERSON WITH A TENDENCY TOWARD DEPRESSION

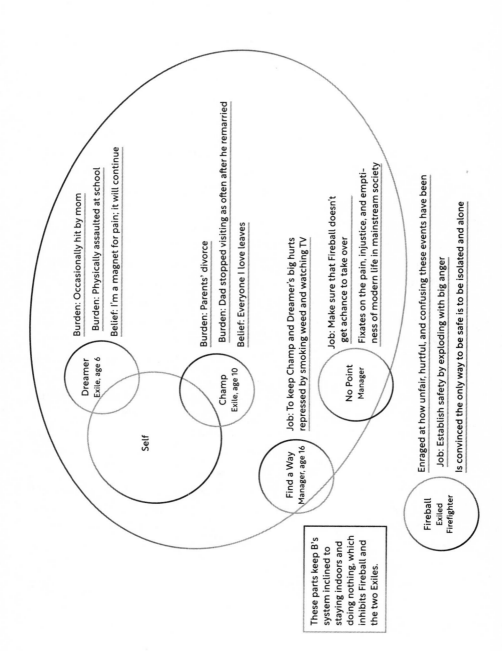

On the previous page, we have a map of a parts cluster that lives within "B," who suffers from depression. I want to be careful to say that this parts map in no way exhaustively describes all the parts that could potentially be involved in someone's depression (or chronic anxiety, as with J). This is just the tip of the iceberg (and one tip of one iceberg out of many potential depression icebergs, for that matter). Still, hopefully this map helps us see the nature of how parts clusters work and gives us at least some marginal insight into how depression itself often works.

B, who was assigned male at birth (but lately finds themselves feeling better when they relate to the idea of identifying as genderqueer), has two Exiles—Dreamer and Champ. Just one of these two would be enough to account for some real depressive episodes, because both hold big hurts. We see Champ, who absorbed the layered, complex experience of his parents' divorce and father's subsequent abandoning behaviors. It is natural and normal for any of us to experience a full spectrum of emotions at once in the midst of big life events like this, which is confusing in and of itself, especially to a developing child brain. Then we have Dreamer, who also suffered physical assault at school the same year and came to believe that there must be something about B that attracts pain. *I'm cursed*, B often thinks. Adding to this, Dreamer is actually a female part of B and generates feelings of gender dysphoria at times. In the past, this has made B that much more confused about themselves and that much more like someone who is "not like the others."

The burdens held by B's Exiles are so big that there could be a dozen or more Managers involved in suppressing them, yet we have another problem altogether: an extreme and rageful Firefighter has formed: Fireball is pissed off—at Mom and Dad, at life, at everyone and everything—for being so unfair, so selfish, so mean, and so hypocritical. In the past, Fireball has caused B to yell at people, tear apart their bedroom, and get into fights—all of which had lousy aftermaths. B's managerial system figured out at some point that their main job was to exile Fireball, since their rage was a bigger threat to the system than the pain and abuse B holds inside.

Find a Way is one Manager part who wants to have some pleasure in life and hold back the pain held inside, and necessarily must do their part to repress Fireball's rage. They accomplish all three of these ends with smoking weed and watching TV. This allows B to dissociate and have some modicum of "fun," but it leaves B too depleted of vitality for much of anything. This strategy also works synergistically with that of No Point, our second Manager part. No Point plays off the fatigue Find a Way generates by producing convincing, fact-based thoughts about how life is hopeless and how everyone always lets them down. This drags the entire system down even further and reinforces the beliefs held by B's Exiles. This serves another purpose that aligns with Find a Way's strategy of binge-watching TV and getting high: it convinces B they should stay home as much as possible since there's nothing good to be found "out there." By staying home B minimizes their potential for encountering triggers—and yet this also keeps B depressed as it minimizes their chance of doing things we know might mitigate the depression, such as going to therapy, moving their body, forming social connections, and so on. It is indeed one big vicious cycle, a loop that feeds off of itself to inhibit the arising of too much pain and too much rage.

Meanwhile, Fireball just sits in the background, sort of rotting. One might think of their hot, hot fire having nowhere to go, and their nasty, dense smoke becomes the grayness of depression. Same goes for Champ and Dreamer, B's Exiles. While B wrestles in the drama of their Managers, not only do their core wounds go unattended but B continues to believe that there would be "no point" in trying to address their woundedness and the burdens these Exiles hold become increasingly calcified as time goes on.

Hopefully, by now, the notion of a "vicious cycle" makes a bit more sense at a granular level, and the same for why depression can often appear an intractable situation. That said, breaking down the experience of depression into its moving parts that can be offered help and healing can initiate a virtuous cycle through which a person like B can gradually get unstuck and approach life anew.

EXERCISE: MAP SOME OF YOUR PARTS

After a parts work meditation session, map the part(s) you met, utilizing the maps offered here for guidance. Getting to know every part just a tiny bit is a success. For some of us, it is huge. You are getting to know your inner world; you are resolving your own confusion.

Over time you might want to combine maps and start building more elaborate ones as you establish connections between various parts and experiences. Sometimes you'll want to return to an old map to add more information. You might also make big mistakes along the way or become convinced parts are in one configuration only to later discover your impressions were off. Whatever you do, for now keep it simple and light. Don't treat mapping as a big deal.

And don't try to skip ahead. For some with eager or perfectionist parts, you might feel an urge to go ahead and map *every* part you feel sure exists within you. I'd urge you to refrain from this and only map parts after you've met them in an inner experience you've had. Let this be a process of discovery rather than something to analyze. Go slow and be willing to not know what's going on with all your parts just yet.

13

HEARTFULNESS WITH PARTS

Buddhist Lovingkindness for Parts

There is barely any distance between a feeling of neutrality toward the world and a crucial love for it, barely any distance at all.
All that is required to move from indifference to love is to have our
hearts broken. The heart breaks and the world explodes in front of
us as a revelation.

—*Nick Cave, The Red Hand Files*

There isn't a one of us who hasn't wanted for an easier way. We've wished
for the secret mantra, the guru to take initiation from, the device to buy
online, or the Latin American plant medicine retreat that would cancel
out the need for this book. Personally, I've wished it had turned out to be
true, what I believed in my earliest years on this path—that the fix was
to leave behind the "old self" and develop a new, spiritualized self; one
who conforms to a preordained set of principles. Such *spiritual bypassing*
(using spiritual practice to go around human problems), however, only
creates more confusion in the end. I've also wished we could simply analyze and understand our way to liberation; perhaps by looking through
the lens of some sound philosophy. Such an *intellectual overpass* over our
problems will never fully heal us, though. The truth is, if these things
did work in some total fashion, they would rob us of something vitally
important: the opportunity to be with our grieving parts, our longing
parts, our wounded parts, our wonderful inner children. For these are the
parts of us that connect us most deeply to the whole of humanity. It is in

bringing compassion to our most vulnerable, protective, rigid, and cha-
otic parts that we gain the opportunity, little by little, to set them free.
It is in bringing compassion to these parts that we rediscover any lost
connections to joy, to beauty, to revelry. It is in bringing compassion to
the broken heart that we discover what Nick Cave is talking about here,
to have the world "explode in front of us as a revelation." A more conve-
nient path would indeed curtail such pricelessness.

At the surface level, we are all looking for a way out of pain and a way
to make sense out of a confounding world. Yet underneath that, we tend
to be looking for permanent freedom, for the rapture of unadulterated experience, for flow states, to feel loved and held, and for a sense of expansion, meaning, and purpose. In short, we are looking for the experience
of full-fledged openheartedness. It is the openhearted state that makes
all of the above available. Yet, Spiritual Paradox #374: in order to open
the heart, we must turn toward the very pain and confusion we'd prefer
to get away from. It is in allowing our hearts to break open that we will
find what it is we are truly seeking. The antidote to pain is discovered
through relating to the pain itself. We move through heartbreak by letting the heartbroken feelings and reality in. Yet, as we've been discussing, we don't just let our hearts break open stupidly or in an ill-informed
way. Rather, the magic is to place the pain, shame, and fear in the cradle
of the open heart. In this way, what might start as a frustrating paradox
can shake out to be quite good news.

We don't love tenderly and at our full capacity until we really see
someone else's human hardships. We don't experience the trembling
warmth of compassion until we realize suffering is right here with us and
we're willing to be there for it. Contending with our own hardships can
have the same effect of eliciting the best in us. We don't snap to attention
and get intentional about our own lives until things begin to fall apart.
Perhaps we discover, as they say in twelve-step circles, "my way isn't
working." It's a terrible truth about us humans: until we're cornered in
some way, we tend to cruise along on autopilot. It's when the rug is pulled
out from under us that we start asking real questions and looking at life
with real depth. In this way, trauma can serve an incredibly adaptive purpose (if we have the resources to meet it well). I'd go so far as to say that

the process of healing trauma could show society at large everything it needs to know to finally move toward peace and justice.

I'm grateful that Nick Cave's claim that there is "barely any distance" between neutrality and crucial love[1] checks out. For one, it is literally true: our capacity for love and compassion resides in the same place trauma gets stored: in the soma, the living body. They live right next door to each other. It's also common for trauma survivors to turn up in therapy or classes who're not sure they've ever experienced the openhearted state, who've felt closed all their life, who're maybe convinced there's no compassionate Self underneath it all for them. Quite often, however, I find that these folks do experience the qualities we're referring to as "Self," but they're just not appearing in the way they'd imagined them to be. (After all, it all sounds so romantic, doesn't it? While I think the reality of our heart capacity is indeed a big deal, it's simultaneously quite ordinary.) Thus, that "crucial love," at the very least a seedling of it, was right there all along. Then there's the folks for whom the discovery of their heart's capacity is just a few minutes or a few sessions away; not much distance at all. It doesn't matter what any of us has been through, this capacity remains intact even if it's thoroughly covered over at present.

I remember a time in 2005 when I was in a room full of fellow meditators dishing about their intense and cathartic experiences after a heavy session of practice. I raised my hand and asked the teacher, "But what if you're numb?" For me at the time, there was no catharsis. Not only had I spent a decade numbing myself intentionally but I had, in fact, been an overachiever about the endeavor. Obviously I didn't stay numb forever. What I'll share next is the practice that worked to thaw my once-calcified heart: *maitri*, meaning "lovingkindness."

THE FOUR BRAHMA VIHARAS

Whereas Richard Schwartz's Six Fs are a method for opening to this natural state, the Buddha's practice of the Four Brahma Viharas (literally, "the abodes of the gods"; most commonly translated as "the Four Immeasurables") is a way of tasting these qualities before we open to them. The Four Brahma Viharas—love, compassion, joy, and equanimity—are among the Buddha's ways to practice the natural qualities of the heart.

They are another way of describing the IFS's Eight Cs of Self Energy (and vice versa). It's important to note that the heart and its infinite qualities that the Buddha discovered is the same human heart that Schwartz realized was naturally available in even his most traumatized clients.

The first abode is *maitri*, "lovingkindness," and the second abode is *karuna*, meaning "compassion," both of which we've been discussing.

The third abode is *mudita*, or "joy," also translated as "bliss" or "rapture." Meditate long enough and rapturous experiences will visit you quite naturally. Such experiences aren't the point of meditation, but they are excellent as inspiration to keep going. *Mudita* is also translated as "sympathetic joy," pointing to the heart's natural ability to sense into the happiness of others and experience it as our own. Funny how our deepest personal joys are usually experienced in connection to others in some way. We're hardwired for connection and cooperation, which is why we feel gratification when in the mindset of genuine generosity.

The fourth and final abode is *upeksa*, or "equanimity." I also like to think of this abode as trust. We can trust in life to give us experiences that we can use to develop patience, mercy, resilience, and compassion. We can trust in ourselves, in our resourcefulness, and in the fact that we've survived 100 percent of our days so far. We can trust in Self Energy as a good thing to open up to.

As trauma survivors, we tend to mistake chaos, drama, impulsivity, and "epic" experiences for home. In counterbalancing fashion, I also like to think of upeksa simply as balance—an invitation to feel the deep, reliable satisfaction of coming from peace (for once).

I include the literal translations of these qualities, these "abodes of the gods," as they are rich in subtext. For one, each of these qualities can become an abode, a home, a refuge to us. Yet, the "abode" we are invited to here isn't a land we go to or place at all: it is a state of heart and mind that we open up and deepen into. "The mind is its own place," writes John Milton, "and in itself can make a heaven of hell, a hell of heaven."[2] Making a hell out of heaven is what trauma often prompts us to do. Yet, earth becomes an abode of the gods when the heart cracks open. There is barely any distance between the two because they both lie within.

I'll offer two versions of lovingkindness practice: a more traditional approach and then an approach I've adapted for parts work. As a precursor, I want to revisit an important idea: the key to understanding our parts is to consider them just as if they were other people. They think and feel and behave the way they do, just like other people do, because they are quasi-people—because they exist within actual people. Sometimes the key to softening into Self Energy with our parts is opening our eyes to how much they're suffering and reacting to suffering, even if their initial presentation is maddeningly obstinate. What this often asks of us is *time*: staying present to suffering long enough that we melt a bit and a more earnest capacity organically emerges. I believe keeping this in mind as we experience the mirror of lovingkindness practice just might make all the difference.

TRADITIONAL LOVINGKINDNESS

Begin with the Fivefold Foundation.

You might want to see how briskly you can be with these steps now without sacrificing quality.

1. Posture
2. Abdominal breathing
3. Natural breathing
4. Knowing the body in space
5. Heart breathing

Traditional Lovingkindness for an Easy Person

Picture a moment with someone where you felt connected to that person. It doesn't have to be a moment within a perfect or uncomplicated relationship (those don't exist); just recall an instance of uncomplicated caring shared between you and someone else. Perhaps it was a time when someone was good to you, really listened, or where there was an appreciation of their humanness. Deep down, you know that they struggle, too. Find that person in your memory bank and picture them clearly in your mind's eye.

Take a breath into the heartspace. What is it like to be here with them in this moment? What's it like in the body? Can your parts give you permission to feel this good feeling?

We'll mix in some thoughts to express this feeling. We'll sync this with the breath to deepen the integration.

Breathe in with the thought: *May you be happy.*

Breathe out and imagine that thought reaching this person.

Do this a few times, noticing what it's like. Inhale with the words, exhale out the feeling of those words.

Notice what this is like. Whether it feels robotic and flat or rich and rapturous, no matter. This is your starting point, not your destination. Keep going.

Breathe into the heart the thought: *May you be healthy.* Breathe out and imagine *May you be healthy* reaching them, impacting them. Do this a few times again.

Breathe into the heart the thought: *May you feel safe.* Breathe it out toward them.

Get into the rhythm of this.

Breathe in: *May you be free.* Breathe it out toward them. You might even picture this person feeling *so* free—dancing, relieved, feeling spacious; whatever makes sense to you.

If anything resembling a positive feeling arises here, notice it. Take an internal screenshot of it. Commit it to memory, if you can. Keep it as we go into the next category of lovingkindness.

Traditional Lovingkindness for Yourself

Picture yourself now like you're looking in the mirror. Face yourself in a clear way. This might be challenging; it might be a relief. Stay with it. If it's challenging, see if you can let that break your heart open a bit. The challenge in loving ourselves can be a terrible one. The challenge itself deserves our compassion.

Regardless of anything, breathe it into the heartspace: *May I be happy. I deserve to be happy.* Breathe out and let the words resonate inside.

Breathe it into the heartspace: *May I be healthy.* Breathe out and resonate.

Breathe into the heartspace: *May I feel safe. I* deserve *to feel safe.* Breathe out and stay in whatever the feeling is.

Breathe into the heartspace: *May I be free.* Breathe out and picture yourself being free—nothing in your way, living a life that feels radically good and healed. What would that be like? *May I be free.*

Stay here with whatever the vibe is: flat, uncaring, good, amazing. What it is doesn't matter; just stay with it.

Traditional Lovingkindness for a Stranger

Picture someone who's in your life that you know nothing about. A service industry worker or a neighbor you see around sometimes, someone from your community you barely interact with—choose someone like this. Notice what it's like to be with someone you feel kinda "medium" for. It's okay, whatever that's like. Remember: they have had heartbreak and loss and myriad challenges in their lives, just like you. Then offer up the same meditation we've run through twice now, but for them:

Breathe in: *May you be happy.* Breathe out and notice any feeling, even if neutral—especially if neutral.

Breathe in: *May you be healthy.* Breathe out and offer the heart.

Breathe in: *May you feel safe.* Breathe out and offer the heart.

Breathe in: *May you be free.* Breathe out and offer the heart.

Visualize this person being free. Notice how this makes you feel.

Traditional Lovingkindness for an Enemy

Important: Do not practice for any abusive or toxic person in your life until you've had many, many trips to this rodeo. Rather, picture someone who bothers you or someone you love but in a moment when they irritated you. If you live with a romantic partner, you might picture a moment of disagreeing or being bored with them. In any case, see them as clearly as you can in that very moment.

If you're feeling not-great things for them, you are doing this right. Part of why we're doing this is to train ourselves to keep our wits about us even when we're pressed or angry. And it's for us more so than for them. So here is your chance to work on this, but we're also going to add one extra statement—"May you have the *causes* of happiness." After all, if this person acts in any way that is harmful, is that cause for happiness? Certainly not. So, we want this person to be happy, with the acknowledgment that in order for them to be happy, they've gotta wake up.

Breathe in: *May you be happy and have the causes of happiness.* Breathe out and offer the heart.

Breathe in: *May you be healthy and have the causes of healthiness.* Breathe out and offer the heart, right here in the middle of afflicted feelings.

Breathe in: *May you feel safe and have the causes of safety.* Breathe out and offer the heart.

Breathe in: *May you be free and have the causes of freedom.* Breathe out and offer the heart.

Visualize this person being free from their own afflictions, from anything that makes them act in harmful ways. Notice how this makes you feel.

Traditional Lovingkindness for All Four Together

Finally, see this motley crew gathered together—friend, yourself, stranger, and enemy all side by side. You're about to offer love unconditionally and in spite of any parts' initial reactions. What's that like for you? Again, it's not that we just want folks to be happy and okay; it's that we want them to have the causes of happiness: integrity, healing, decency, conscious evolution. These are the causes of true happiness in this life. So offer:

Breathing in: *May each of us be happy and have the causes of happiness.* Breathe out and offer the heart.

Breathing in: *May each of us be healthy and have the causes of healthiness.* Breathe out and offer the heart.

Breathing in: *May each of us feel safe and have the causes of safety.* Breathe out and offer the heart.

Breathing in: *May each of us be free and have the causes of freedom.* Breathe out and offer the heart.

Return to abdominal breathing, natural breathing, and spacious awareness for some time. Conclude the meditation whenever you feel complete and grounded again.

LOVINGKINDNESS FOR PARTS

Begin with the Fivefold Foundation.

1. Posture
2. Abdominal breathing
3. Natural breathing
4. Knowing the body in space
5. Heart breathing

Lovingkindness for an Easy Manager

Use a Trailhead to Find a Part: Think of a Manager part of you that helps you get through the day. Perhaps a taskmaster that helps you remember important things. Perhaps an analytic or creative part that helps you at your job. Perhaps a little rebel that makes sure you enjoy treats despite all your responsibility. Perhaps a part that helps you have good style or taste in art and culture. Perhaps a part that motivates you to enjoy the outdoors.

Think of a common situation wherein this part takes charge. Live in the mind movie of whatever that is until you get a sense of the part's presence.

Focus and Flesh Out: Once you sense the part, devote your attention to them. If you sense them in the body, what are they like? Heavy or light? Sharp or dull? Big or small? Tense or loose? Is there an emotion or even a vague feeling you can identify here? Does this part seem to be saying something, even if it's just one word?

Offer: Here, we'll mentally offer the traditional lovingkindness phrases, synchronizing them with the breath as before.

Breathing into the heartspace: *May you be happy.* Breathe out and imagine the feeling of the phrase surrounding this part. Do this a few times. You're welcome to experiment with the "fake it till you make it" approach throughout this meditation.

Breathing into the heartspace: *May you be healthy*. Breathe out and imagine the feeling of the phrase surrounding this part. Repeat as many times as you like.

Breathing into the heartspace: *May you feel safe*. Breathe out and imagine the feeling of the phrase surrounding this part.

Breathing into the heartspace: *May you be free*. Breathe out and imagine the feeling of the phrase surrounding this part.

Visualize this part feeling happy and free, performing at their healthiest. Notice what that's like for the part inside.

If there's any positive feeling in you now, make sure to take a mental screenshot of it as a place you can return to.

For a Firefighter

Find the Trailhead: Think of a reactive Firefighter part that's been helpful to you in the past. Their strategy may not be ideal, but it's perceivably the lesser of two evils. Maybe it's a part of you that dissociates to help you get through stressful times. Maybe it's a part of you that's a little *too good* at boundaries or a workaholic part that has helped you get to where you are.

Focus and Flesh Out: Once you sense the part, focus on them and mentally label what you're noticing. If you sense them in the body, what are they like? Heavy or light? Sharp or dull? Big or small? Tense or loose? Is there an emotion or even a vague feeling you can identify here? Does this part seem to be saying something, even if it's just one word?

Offer: Just as before—breathing into the heart: *May you be happy*. Breathe out and imagine the vibe of the phrase surrounding the part. Repeat this phrase or any of the phrases throughout this meditation if it feels helpful to do so.

Breathing into the heart: *May you be healthy*. Breathe out and surround the part with the phrase.

Breathing into the heart: *May you feel safe*. Breathe out and surround the part with the phrase.

Breathing into the heart: *May you be free*. Breathe out and surround the part with the phrase.

Stay here in these final moments with this part as long as you like.

For a Suffering Exile

Important: Don't go straight to your biggest trauma here. Especially if you're new to this practice or to healing work, let yourself get in a "practice round" before you even consider diving into the deep end of the pool. If at any point you get overwhelmed in this practice, you can go to the instructions on alleviating overwhelm at the end of chapter 3.

Find the Trailhead: Perhaps there's a part of you that's been lost in loneliness, sadness, or listlessness lately that seems to be right there, just below the surface. If yes, welcome them in. Make a big space for them. If no, perhaps it would be fruitful to think of a time in childhood or adolescence that was somewhat challenging for you—again, not the biggest challenge you've ever faced but something "medium." Stay in this memory until you feel a part activate emotionally, cognitively, or somatically.

Focus and Flesh Out: Once you've found your part, ask yourself: *What are they like in the dimensions of thought, feeling, and sensation?* Notice and allow your awareness of the part to deepen.

Bear Witness: It's optional but if it feels right, you could ask inside, *What is it you'd like me to know?* and allow this part to tell you a bit of their story. *What have you been experiencing? How long have you felt this way? Are you ready to really let the feelings out?* If yes, give them an enormous space, one at least as big as the room you're in, in which to release the stored emotional energy; to simply let it out.

Offer: Breathing into the heartspace, mentally say the phrase for the part. Breathing out, extend the feeling, intention, or image of the phrase toward the part. Stay with each phrase as long as you like, breathing with them just as we have been doing:

May you be happy.
May you be healthy.
May you feel safe.
May you be free.

For All Parts

Finally, we practice for the whole self, your entire system, all your parts at once. Please continue breathing into each phrase. You can breathe it into the heartspace or into the entire body at once. As you breathe out, allow the sense of the outbreath to spread through the whole body. Imagine the energy, feeling, or image of the phrases seeping into your muscles, cells, and nerves.

As an experiment, you might see if it's possible to let the heart open fully here. This can feel like the sun emerging from behind the clouds to reveal its unabashed effulgence. The effect can be one of parts basking in the sun, what I call "Self Energy sunbathing."

Breathe in and out with the phrases, just as we have been doing:

May all parts be happy.

May all parts be healthy.

May all parts feel safe.

May all parts be free.

Stay here as long as you like. Then return to deep abdominal breathing for two to three minutes while thanking each of the parts you practiced for along the way.

You have just completed an incredible session of healing work. Let yourself feel good about this. You might even think of a way to treat yourself for engaging so deeply today.

Journal Prompt | *5–10 minutes*

Take five to ten minutes to journal about your meditation. What did you experience here? What aspects of this practice came easy? What was challenging? Did you have any insights, connect any dots about why things are the way they are for you? Do you have any questions? Do you have any ideas about how you can continue to show up for your parts in healthy ways?

14

THE FULL ADVENTURE

The Threefold Healing of IFS

The way to happiness is to go into the darkness of yourself. That's
the place where the seed is nourished, takes its roots and grows
up, and ultimately becomes the plant and the flower. You can only
go upward by first going downward.

—*James Broughton*

Suffering → healing → awakening: let's piece this equation together.

It starts when we're fed up with painful cycles. We can think of
pain, frustration, and all negative mindstates as the expression of our
parts, trying to get our attention. So, finally we give them our attention and elect to heal and clarify our situation. In order to do this, we
ultimately must find Self Energy. No compassion, no healing. Yet, Self
Energy is synonymous with the awakened state. Therefore, our suffering, our parts themselves, are compelling us to find awakening. It's a
mission we wouldn't go on otherwise, would we? They are egging us
on. Day and night, they remain restless and unresolved until we truly
figure out how to relate from Self Energy, how to abide in Self Energy,
and how to eventually have Self Energy run the show of our lives. We
must conclude, then, that our parts are actually our highest teachers.
They've shoved us into a most blessed opportunity. Without them we
would've ignored this, shrugged it off as woo-woo bullshit or as something we're not capable of. But our parts aren't having it. They demand,
in so many coded ways, that we make the full journey. They've pulled a

bait and switch on us. It's all an elaborate ruse to get us to do the work of waking up.

We came here thinking it was about our suffering, but all along we've been training ourselves to embody the awakened state of Self Energy—something we wouldn't have endeavored for if we hadn't been suffering. Our trauma, if experienced alongside the conditions needed for healing, has been an invitation all along.

———

The meditations we've forged into thus far all fall squarely into the category of bearing witness, the first of three stages of healing in IFS. The second step is called *retrieval*, a practice of going into traumatic memories as the present-time you, replete with Self Energy, and bringing resolution to the traumatic experience. The third is called *unburdening and integration*, where you release the fully processed trauma from the body, which then frees up vitality for parts to reclaim and integrate positive qualities. We'll explore these second and third stages—to the extent possible in book format—in this chapter. (And in part three of this book, we'll explore Buddhist *tonglen* practice as another form of unburdening.)

Although it's "just" the first stage of the process, bearing witness is absolutely essential. It allows us to get to know our parts through a new lens, and it allows our parts to experience the sunlight of Self. As we get to know parts, clarity about our history and our present situation dawns naturally. We connect dots. As parts get to know Self, they feel less alone with their experience and discover a new resource of friendliness and the seedlings of secure love inside. Hopefully by now you've seen just that much engenders relief and new awareness.

Thankfully there's more, too.

I say *thankfully* because while bearing witness is what our parts will need 95 percent of the time, it's the process of retrieval and unburdening that breaks cycles. After all, though the presence of self-compassion in the process is a game-changer, bearing witness can be a bit like what many of us have experienced with conventional forms of therapy. It's vitally important that our parts feel less alone (and deeply important that we not rush past the bearing-witness step)—yet, simultaneously, running the stories and ventilating emotions won't stop the record from skipping. Not in a final way, at least. We've yet to fully discharge the stored energy of the traumatic experience that lives in our bodies. Our parts are still living in the past, running on outdated maps. The software of our conditioning was installed in youth, but our biological hardware has outgrown it. We've been running Windows '07 on a brand-new laptop. Retrieval is the first step in installing a new operating system.

Sometimes I do find that bearing witness can move along quickly when it comes to experiences already well masticated in arenas like therapy. There are cases in which there is no need to keep tracking the same stories and memories, getting to know their every detail, trying to figure out just how it's all impacted us and what it all means. It often satisfies a part's needs for us to simply hold their struggle in the space of love and compassion *just enough*, and then they're ready for the next steps.

I'll fill you in on how the second and third stages of healing are executed in IFS therapy and offer some practices that you can do here and now on your own. The practices offered might only surf the rim of these processes, but they are powerful nonetheless. Most of us truly need a gentle process anyhow—almost always gentler than we think. It's crucial that I tell you: it's not recommended that you attempt to do the full processes on your own. There is the possibility that you'll be flooded with overwhelming emotion. There is the possibility that if other parts of you don't like what you're up to, you'll get intense backlash from within. Inner mutinies do happen.

The biggest danger is that you could do these processes without a clinician or coach to check your blind spots, erroneously believe you are fully healed, never look back to something that is in actuality halfhealed, and then be confused about why the storms of your life are persisting. When we live in the mind-fiction of *I'm healed!* while the truth is *I'm kinda-sorta healed*, we are likely to build fallacious, labyrinthine story-webs around what's going on. It can get confusing enough that this sort of thing can take lifetimes to mete out. With these caveats in mind, what I will offer you are what I believe to be safe and powerful "lite" versions that can serve you greatly and relatively free of the aforementioned risks.

RETRIEVAL AND UNBURDENING:
A PERSONAL EXAMPLE

As these steps are experiential in nature, I'll offer an example of how this could work in a simple, self-guided setting and then describe the steps proper afterward.

Participating in a safe, secure, functional love relationship is actually brand-new for me. It's been front and center in my own healing work for some time, and it's something I'm finally capable of as a result. Despite this, I've still had some crisis moments when something's come up that threatened to capsize a fledgling romance. One of them has been jealousy. I'm jealous as all get-out. I can't shake it. And not just in the rote way where I suspect my partner might step out on me. I'm jealous when she goes out to dinner with friends, catches a concert when I have to work, or has a loving relationship with her dad. Hell, I'm jealous to no end when she intuits the "right" thing to order on a menu and I end up with a "just okay" dish. For a while, I'd quite literally feel like I was kicked in the gut when this jealousy arose. I'd feel like the wind was knocked out of me, sometimes for days. It was sharp, intense, and very difficult to contain. Why was I so unreasonably jealous?

> **Insight:** Whenever there's a mismatch between a situation and a personal response, trauma is involved. If you feel kicked in the gut (for example) because someone else is simply having a good time, get curious. A part of you is trying to get your attention. Emotional responses that are more extreme than the situation calls for are almost always an indicator of an underlying trauma.

So, I got curious. One day in meditation I set out to **find** the part. I thought of the last situation that conjured the gut-punch feeling. When I began to get a hint of that specific sensation, I **focused** on it and **fleshed it out** by noticing everything I could about the texture of the feeling, making space for that part of me in the process. I acknowledged the part, got into a space of compassionate Self (my **feeling** toward the part), and asked inside, *What's the earliest we can remember feeling this exact sensation?* I sat for a good while, occasionally and softly repeating the question. Finally, the *model scene* (the core memory of the underlying trauma held in the body) emerged.

It was my first love, Melissa, and the night I came home from a bike accident, injured and limping (okay, fine, I was also on LSD), to find her in bed with the guy who lived next door. The gasp, the shock, the gut-punch of the sight. I recalled how I stood there just trying to get my bearings and her insensitive response of telling me that *I* was the one who needed to leave. I was such an insecure person at the time that I did just that. I spent the night in our spare room, my whole world freshly demolished.

All this time and without my conscious knowing, anytime someone I loved had something, anything, that I wanted, this part of me was basically reliving this scene. They were letting me know by generating this sensation in my stomach—sometimes lightly, sometimes overwhelmingly. Never once had I thought to ask myself why the same sensation was on repeat along with a vast array of jealousy-triggering experiences, but here it was and the clarity was striking.

I began the retrieval process with the part by walking into the memory of the model scene as the present-time me, as Self. I asked the past me what they needed to move on from the situation, and without any further prompting, that part of me stood up to my ex-love and the literal boy next door. The part began speaking firmly to the two in bed, fiercely acknowledging how outrageously hurtful this breaking of trust was. It went on for several minutes. Then I asked the part to turn toward me and acknowledge that it was all over. Literally over. The actual *retrieval* occurred once I asked the part if they were now ready to leave this memory and join me in my present-time life. They said yes. I then invited that part of me to come live in my body in the present moment, to join with the forty-something me who had survived all that. They were relieved at this possibility. They didn't know this was even a thing. I then showed this part a mental picture of my current partner and firmly stated *Not Melissa!* to help them see that there was no need for them to project this event onto my partner like this any longer. I gave them a little while to integrate these revelations. With this, the part was effectively retrieved from the past and brought into the present.

Unburdening happened quickly from there. I simply felt into the gut-punch sensation and asked the part if they were ready to release the pain. When I sensed an affirmative answer, I next asked what they'd like to release the pain into. It's a standard practice in IFS to use the four elements of earth, water, fire, and air as a place to release our burdens. Each of these elements have detoxifying and regenerative (some would say spiritually potent) properties. The part shouted, *Fire!*, and I visualized a beautiful bonfire, the tips of its orange-red flames dancing, sparks levitating and reaching for the moon. I allowed the fire to be like a magnet to the gut-punch sensation. I breathed and felt the sensation release from my body until it was gone.

The last step was asking the part inside, *With this gone, what would you like to reclaim?* The answer came quickly: *I want to love and appreciate others. I want to support people in self-actualizing.* I then surrounded this part with the way I know myself to feel when I'm in that good place of true generosity—of mudita, or sympathetic joy. I imagined these qualities absorbing deeply into my friend inside.

I continue to check in on this part of me. They're called the Jumper because of a certain childlike excitement they contain. I occasionally remind the Jumper that they are healed and free to be as generous as they like without fear. I sometimes remind them of all the work I've done to have good boundaries and a high level of discretion around which people I let into my life these days, just to reassure them that we're not as susceptible as we once were. Remarkably, the gut-punch sensation hasn't returned. I still get a little "green-eyed devil" feeling when someone's green curry tops my garlic tofu at the Thai restaurant, but the intensity is very low and easy to tolerate without feeling pulled to react.

RETRIEVAL

When bearing witness to a part, there's usually a moment when memories begin to emerge. This is sometimes the moment when it's right to do retrieval—to enter the scene with Self Energy and find out what the part needs. We can also simply ask a part, *What's the earliest you can remem-*

ber feeling this way?, and that's usually enough to stir the memory bank. What's important is that there's a clear sense of the trauma. In some situations, there's no memory of the trauma because the experience caused them to blackout or because someone was too young to remember. In these instances, just getting a real sense of what it's been like to live with this is enough.

Insight: Memory is fallible, and the human ability to fabricate memories is both well documented and striking. People say to me with fair frequency, "I feel like I was abused as a child and just can't remember it." I steer clear of trying to "discover" or "jog" any memories. I urge you to do the same to avoid the generation of memories. You don't absolutely need the model scene to work with anyhow. The emotions you routinely experience, the behavioral and interpersonal cycles you find yourself in, this is more than enough to work with. The scenes of your life that you do remember offer plenty of fodder for retrieval.

Parts usually need two things:

1. Intervention
2. Rescue

Intervention means Self enters the memory to fiercely stop the harm that's happening. Self can also confront those inflicting harm on the part's behalf. Sometimes the part themselves wants to do the confronting, with Self standing at their back. The best thing about this is that this is your mind. No retaliation is possible because you are the one in control of the event now. You are here to give the part the love and protection they missed out on the first time, and if you're this far along in the process, you have what it takes to ensure that.

We must honor the ethical imperative of doing no harm. As discussed in chapter 1, the window of consolidation is open here. Whatever happens is going to be reconsolidated back into your body. No violent fantasies ought to be played out. We want to build neural pathways of love and resolve. If a part wants to get aggressive, they may need some skillfully spoken inner parenting from you to direct their wants toward a healthier place.

Rescuing the part and taking them to a safe place inside is where it gets quite fun. They could go anywhere—to the most fantastical place you can dream up, even. They could come home with you where you build them their own room and they decorate it just as they wish. They could join their favorite rock star or poet onstage. They could build a hut on the beach and have a wolf or a dog to protect them. Don't think up a place to take them, though. Just ask inside where they want to go. They'll tell you. The sky's the limit. Allow them to make it wonderful and very, very safe.

As retrieved parts begin to add up, some folks find it liberating to begin building a parts commune of sorts inside—a place where all the healed parts go to live within the psyche. It could be a tree house, a mountain village, a compound on Jupiter . . . With the part successfully rescued and never having to go back—again, because it's *over*—we're ready for the next step.

UNBURDENING AND INTEGRATION

Unburdening is the organic outgrowth of retrieval. With the part finding safe harbor, you can ask if they're truly ready to be free of the burden they have been holding on to. You might get a sense of yes, or you might get a sense of not yet. It's important not to rush this step. It's a momentous occasion for a part to be unburdened.

You might first visualize taking the part to a beautiful natural environment. Next we ask the part, *Can you show me where the burden is and what it's like?* At this point, things are at least a little bit visual; the part will show you where they hold the burden, but you just might sense the burden in your body at large. Either way, we must sense it with them for the window of consolidation to be open.

Then comes the letting go. The burden needs to go into something that can take it and recycle it. The four main elements of earth, water, fire, and air are indispensable for this. Sometimes, I concoct a whole ritual by visualizing a sacred circle with an elaborate shrine with the elements represented on it and then inviting ancestors and lineage guides to join me in the effort. Sometimes it's as simple as just saying to the part, *Earth, water, fire, and air, baby—which of these calls to you?* Many of my parts like the mountains and the beach, so sometimes I'll just imagine we're in one of those places and then the part can release the burden into the waves or into a tree. It's entirely up to the part; make sure to ask. Then simply breathe with them and feel the elements whisking the burden right out of the body.

The open space where the wound once lived opens the important opportunity to absorb new qualities and behaviors. We lose so many of our best qualities along the way due to trauma. Thus, we ask what sort of qualities the part wants to integrate. Whatever they reply with, we imagine them drawing it in either through visual symbols or, if nothing else, beautiful and warm light. See them taking this in deeply. This can act as a seal that prevents the energetic burden from coming back.

We find, to an uncanny extent, that parts want to integrate qualities that are direct opposites to the burdens they've been holding. A part that's been avoidant may want to connect with others. A part that's been desperate for love may want to become the giver of love and service to others. A part that's been lost in feelings of unworthiness may want to do something that puts them in front of people, such as joining a band, writing, organizing a show, or throwing a dinner party. The post-traumatic growth tends to be off the charts here. You'll know it's real especially when the things that come up take you by surprise.

FOLLOWING UP WITH PROTECTORS

Unburdening isn't just for Exiles holding traumas. It also liberates the Managers and Firefighters who've been working tirelessly to protect the Exiles. With the Exiles unburdened, these protectors are now free to integrate new roles and tasks. Before leaving an integration scene, it's important that you invite in whatever Managers and Firefighters have been filling such roles. You might say inside, *Come, check out what this is like now. Do you see this one, free and happy? You don't have to protect them anymore. I've got them. So, what would you rather do now that you're free?*

AFTERCARE FOR THE UNBURDENED PARTS

I strongly urge you to map parts that you have unburdened. As mentioned before, this will help them to keep from becoming reburdened—which can happen. It'll help you remember to check in with the part as well. It is of the utmost importance that you check in with the part once a day for four to six weeks after an unburdening. Having the part mapped and having a nickname for the part will help you to access them easily and on the fly. This check-in can happen during your daily meditations. It can also happen on the fly while you're doing the dishes or in between meetings. A client told me that his recently unburdened inner-child part comes to the surface to paint with him and for hikes in the desert. It doesn't have to be huge, but it's important that you remind the part that they are known to you, loved by you, and have a new life now. I know of one practitioner who starts her day by simply saying inside, *I love you guys!* to keep everyone inside happy, awake, and well attended to. (Do be more specific than this with recently unburdened parts, though.)

SIMPLE RETRIEVAL MEDITATION

Begin with the Fivefold Foundation:

1. Posture
2. Abdominal breathing
3. Natural breathing
4. Knowing the body in space
5. Heart breathing

Important: Only do this simple retrieval meditation with a part you've already been getting to know through your meditations or therapy. Do not do this with a part that's new to you or that has not felt Self Energy from you before.

Start by doing the first four Fs:

1. Find the part.
2. Focus on them.

3. Flesh them out.
4. Adjust your feelings toward them so that you're in Self.

Then ask the part to turn around and notice you. Take your time with this and don't rush anything. Give the part time for all this to sink in. Do they see you, the loving adult holding space for them? The one who's working so hard at becoming the best parent they could hope for? Do they see how old you are? Show them some of your friends, support networks, and loved ones in your life. Show them your spiritual practice, your resilience, your burgeoning emotional intelligence. Show them your home now and that none of the people who hurt you before live here now. Show them some of the things you do for fun. Assure them that there is no need to expect the things that used to happen to you to keep happening. And if they do, isn't it true that you're much better equipped to handle it nowadays?

Ask this part how they feel toward Self now. Then listen. Just listen. They may need amends from you for how things have been. If so, offer it. You didn't see how things were for them before, but that's changing. Or maybe they're ready to dance in the sunlight with you.

Conclude with a few rounds of lovingkindness for them: *I want you to feel happy. You deserve to feel healthy. I want you to feel safe. I want us to be free!*

PARTIAL UNBURDENING MEDITATION

Begin with the Fivefold Foundation:

1. Posture
2. Abdominal breathing
3. Natural breathing
4. Knowing the body in space
5. Heart breathing

Start by doing the first four Fs:

1. Find the part.
2. Focus on them.

3. Flesh them out.
4. Adjust your feelings toward them so that you're in Self.

Then imagine either a big bonfire, an immense lake, a mountain, or another natural structure. Let the part(s) inside know that we're simply going to release whatever is ready to be released today. It's okay if everything isn't well digested and ready to go. Then simply be in your body with whatever discomfort or emotions are present, and breathe. On the inhale, you feel the burden; on the exhale, you're breathing out whatever burdens are "cooked" enough to be let go. The mountain or natural structure you're working with absorbs the burdened material, no problem. Trust that the elements know just what to do with this stuff. Stay with the breath.

Inhale to feel, exhale to release. Nothing could be more natural. Continue until you sense you're as complete as you're going to be for today. Then check in with your body and your parts. Check specifically for any sense of space inside. Ask inside what qualities of mind and heart your part(s) would like to have fill in that space. It could be joy, play, sincerity, healthy communication, vitality, or anything else in this vein. Then visualize these qualities flowing into you in some way. Let it be childish; silly, even. If nothing else, simply picture a beautiful light coming in and infiltrating all your cells.

There are many more ways to continue massaging loose the burdens we hold. We continue the exploration and excavations now as we turn to lojong to deepen our overall sense of this work as a life path and to give us even more practices to do with parts.

PART THREE: LEAVES

Lojong, Tonglen, and the Spirituality of Reparenting

15

ADJUSTING THE LENS

Seeing Through Core
Beliefs with Clarity

The pain that made you the odd one out is the story that connects
you to a healing world.

—Tanya Markul

The adventure of outshining trauma is an adventure of *reparenting* ourselves. That such a thing as reparenting exists is fantastic news. How
many do-overs do we get in life? Not many. I can think of several Tinder
meetups that would benefit from a *redate*, but those don't exist. Fortu-
nately, reparenting is a real thing (and *might* just be more important than
a first date with a stranger). More to the point, it's a necessary thing on
our quest for a life marked by well-being and conscious choices.

Reparenting, sometimes called *inner parenting*, describes a specific
aspect of trauma recovery. While healing work necessarily begins with
giving ourselves the love we didn't get the first time around, receiving
empathic care from caregivers is only one aspect of what we needed as
kids: the softer element. The firmer element that we needed entails receiving life wisdom: things like learning how to hold good boundaries,
regulating our impulses and compulsions, learning how to tolerate hard
things (and—*gasp!*—boring things), and developing accurate and functional beliefs about how things work. Reparenting on the path to becoming Self-led might just entail:

- Learning how to tell our parts no, even in moments of craving
- Helping our parts be gritty and stay the course with challenging things
- Supporting our parts in swallowing difficult truths
- Assisting our parts in navigating conflict in a healthy manner
- Helping our parts refrain from harmful speech
- Teaching our parts the difference between victim mentality and appropriately identifying that we've been wounded or are in distress
- Addressing deeply held and limiting beliefs

We need to know how to do all of these things lovingly without our parts coming undone or shutting down. Ingraining these important skills is a critical aspect of growing up that many of us missed out on the first go-around. How are we to accomplish these ends now? In the same way you might sip really hot soup: with mindful attention and a little bit at a time.

When someone hugs you meaningfully, there's a softness, but they also squeeze you a tiny bit—they let you know that they're really there. Tenderness and firmness—both energies are called for. Similarly, all children need to be held with the softer energy of caring but also with the firmer energy of healthy discipline and direction—the operative word being *healthy*. Our parts inside need the same kind of holding. Thankfully, Self Energy can accommodate both of these complementary qualities.

In Buddhism, it's said that one needs two wings to fly. The bird of awakening is understood to soar on the two wings of heartfulness and clear seeing—compassion and wisdom, love and integrity, or "strong back, soft front" in the words of Brené Brown.[1] Hence, we cannot merely commit to the softer side of things. Compassion without wisdom is incomplete. Heartfulness without boundaries is codependence. Expanded consciousness without expanded intelligence is spiritual bypassing. Just as childlike wonder and adult maturity only function when fused together, spiritual openheartedness and worldly skillfulness necessarily must go together.

To commit only to the firmer side of the process would also be incomplete. While it's true that everything worth accomplishing requires some grit, discipline, and fortitude, too many of us stoop to harsh forms of willpower and self-shaming to find motivation. Such is a one-sided approach. Just as love without discipline is a watery mess, discipline without love is abuse. There's a prayer to the matriarchal wisdom lineage that supplicates, "Please help us to become gentle and tough!"[2]

In the realm of parts work and IFS, many practitioners erroneously assume that loving our parts means we let them have their way all the time, that we can never tell them, "No" or "Stop" or "We're not doing this today." In truth, we can and at times *must* confront and halt our parts and weather certain storms with them. I also find that when folks bump into parts who hold traumatically conditioned beliefs—which are always standing behind things like feelings of unworthiness, constant fear of abandonment, fear of moving forward in a career, or a pervasive aversion to other people—they often don't quite know how to counsel their parts into seeing a bit more clearly. How do we lovingly introduce to our parts more compassionate ways of viewing life, the world, and relationships when we haven't had the proper modeling?

One of the answers is, we've got to develop the skills of questioning ourselves and our experience. We need to contemplate truths and ideas that strike at the marrow of existence itself. We need to engage with philosophy and poetry and the works of those who've looked deeply at life and pierced the veil of their own conditioning. We need to wrestle a bit with what it means that we're here, living these lives to begin with. And not with the intention of figuring out life's ungraspable meaning but because the wrestling itself has so much to show us. This is where I believe the worldview and contemplative processes of Buddhism can complement the work in a big way. Its meditation techniques as well as its philosophy are both born of the kind of deep looking I'm describing here. We've been benefiting from its meditation techniques as an accoutrement to parts work, and now we'll turn to aspects of its worldview and philosophy with the specific aim of shepherding our parts toward deeper harmony and healing.

TRAINING THE HEART-MIND

Enter *lojong*, a thousand-year-old practice and text that was crowdsourced as an oral tradition for generations by masters of several Mahayana Buddhist lineages. First documented by the Bengali lama Atisha, the practice of lojong works with a collection of fifty-nine aphorisms meant to offer steps along the path to complete awakening—which, as we've been exploring, has everything to do with healing our hearts. The Tibetan word *lojong* is generally translated as "mind training," with *lo* specifically meaning the thinking aspect of the psyche. While many parts tend to hang out in the subconscious mind, the essence of parts work is inviting them into the conscious realm of mental formation—the thinking layer of psyche. *Jong* translates as "training," but it also means clearing the psyche of the effects of aggression, greed, and delusion we've all suffered. This correlates directly to unburdening in IFS. Furthermore, *jong* is quite close to the Tibetan word *dzong*, which refers to physical structures such as fortresses. For me, the implication is one of building a compassionate strength that addresses the harmful effects of traumatic experience—a fortress of a spiritual nature.

The lojong slogans are rooted in compassionate awakening, yet their traditional interpretations pull no punches and carry a sense of urgency. The progenitors of this text saw life as a crucial matter that powerfully calls us to practice the methods of transformation. You'll soon see why. In fact, *crucial* is putting it lightly. One might think of a parent watching their child about to walk into oncoming traffic—the swiftness and directness with which they might grab the child's arm and pull them back from the curb. It's that kind of energy. This sense of urgency about all things awakening forms one "wing" of this text. The second "wing" is a call for us to soften our grip, to be graceful with our efforts, to hold our experience a little more lightly; with humor, even.

Gentleness tempered with grit, urgency tempered with levity, love tempered with discipline: this is the way forward. Self Energy can move with both of these energies at once. Thus, we can think of lojong practice as giving the parts of us inside a lovingly firm talking to. One that is sorely needed, especially if we were raised in the context of intergenerational trauma.

THIS BOOK'S APPROACH TO LOJONG AND A QUICK NOTE ON CULTURAL APPROPRIATION

In this and the remaining chapters, we'll be using the lojong as a springboard for addressing issues connected to reparenting and post-traumatic growth. As such, we won't be following the text sequentially, nor will we cover all fifty-nine aphorisms. Other books exist for those who would like to explore a more full and traditional approach. In truth, much of the lojong will only bear its intended fruit to the dedicated Buddhist practitioner studying within a community setting.[3]

There are some who might complain that this innovative approach is out of alignment with the intention of the text and its tradition of wisdom transmission. I wouldn't necessarily disagree with such critics, yet it's important that we remember that Buddhist teachings have always been offered in a way that speaks to the context of the student. The needs and abilities of the audience are quite often prioritized over adherence to tradition. My aim for utilizing this practice within the context of this book is to give us one framework for what reparenting might look like. As such, we will dive into the aphorisms that best fit the adventure we're currently on.

These Eastern insights and practices are being offered primarily to Western minds. This amplifies the rationale for molding them accordingly, but it also demands that we do so respectfully. For some readers, exploring this text might come across as cultural appropriation. Cultural appropriation is seen by many as inherently disrespectful, given the vast human histories of violent colonization, especially in the West. I want to affirm the instincts of such readers. I also want to remind us that this text, and the bulk of Eastern wisdom that has come to the West, wasn't appropriated so much as it was exported. It was by and large brought to our doorstep by its contemporary purveyors. This effectively began with Swami Vivekananda in the late nineteenth century and continued with such figures as Paramahansa Yogananda, Srila Prabhupada, Shunryu Suzuki Roshi, and Thich Nhat Hanh. Each of these individuals started worldwide movements to spread Eastern practices. There have also been Western-born folks who brought Eastern wisdom back home with them—at the behest of their teachers—such as Helena Blavatsky, Indra Devi, Ram Dass, and Sharon Salzberg.

Tibetans exported the lojong slogans to the West as part of a vast corpus of wisdom texts in an effort to preserve it far away from the horrific Chinese occupation of their territory in the mid-twentieth century. This fulfilled an ancient prophecy spoken by Padmasambhava (credited as the godfather of Tibetan Buddhism) that "when the iron bird flies, the dharma will move to the West." One can imagine generations of ancient Tibetans scratching their heads on that one—that is, until the day "iron bird" airplanes were invented. Soon after, the Dalai Lama would flee to India on foot along with countless other Tibetans hoping to escape the forces of Mao Zedong. Eventually the Dalai Lama sent emissaries to Europe and the United States so that their unique brand of contemplative practice and mysticism could continue to flourish. Thus, it is one thing for a Westerner to adopt something from another culture because it feels cool and exotic; it is a very different thing for a Westerner to adopt something meaningful after someone from Asia comes to them and says, "Here, please practice this. In fact, please memorize the Tibetan and Sanskrit words involved; they're important."

This is how the priceless wisdom of mindfulness-based practices, yoga, and indeed the lojong landed in our hands. This is our great fortune. We owe the forebears of these wisdom lineages a tremendous debt of gratitude for their sacrifice and generosity.

> **Insight:** When it comes to Mahayana Buddhist practices and texts like the lojong, there are three levels of truth represented at once: outer level, inner level, and secret or mystic level. That is, there is an obvious meaning to the teachings, a way that teaching can be applied psychologically, and a pointing out of spiritual matters that are beyond words.

NO POWER BUT YOURS

The truism goes "Seeing is believing," but there's much to be learned by reversing that formula: "Believing is seeing." The intense conditioning of trauma leaves survivors with a host of inaccurate *beliefs* that must be addressed. A belief is an internalized notion of how things work in life that then informs further thought, feeling, and action. Beliefs are totally necessary in helping us to organize our lives, consolidate our views, and find clues in times of uncertainty. Yet they can also do a great deal to hurt us.

Some beliefs are subconsciously held and deeply complex, while others are closer to the surface and pretty straightforward. For example, when it comes to intimate partnerships, many of us hold a fairly cut-and-dry belief such as "Others have hurt me in the past, so I'd better be careful about letting someone new get close to me." Meanwhile, someone else might hold a belief such as "I'm more resourced on every level when I'm closely connected to someone good. It's worth the risk to let people in." In this example, there is no "correct" belief. Both are guiding designations conditioned by past experience, and either will lead an individual down a particular path. Who's to judge which path is "right"?

Then we have harmful, limiting, and toxic beliefs. Some examples: "I'm not good enough; I ought to hold back"; "I'm not worthy of good things; I deserve to be punished"; "Life sucks and isn't worth it." Here we have beliefs, also conditioned by experience, that are 100 percent out of alignment with the nature of reality itself. We'll be addressing these specific beliefs in our next chapter on the Four Reminders. For now, it's plain to see that these beliefs echo the voices of abusers. They are adaptations to aggression and neglect. They are the stem of a flower whose root is trauma. Leaving these beliefs unaddressed will only allow them to blossom into something that reflects their toxicity. Thankfully, if it was conditioned *into* us, it can also be conditioned *out*.

Holding inaccurate beliefs is like charting a course for a sailing trip incorrectly—you won't end up where you intended to go. Many lojong slogans are designed to address such beliefs, and we'll start with this one:

4. METHODS OF LIBERATION HAVE NO POWER OF THEIR OWN.

Fun fact: IFS has never healed anyone. Nor has any other psychological modality or form of meditation. Not on their own. All methods of liberation are simply road maps: devices to be applied to help us discover compassion. Meditation instructions and theoretical lenses—no matter how brilliant, no matter how helpful—are only scaffolding meant to support the effort of building. Methodologies and meditation practices are all made up, even if by geniuses. They are human-made constructs and inventions. Thus, models and methods are powerless without people applying them sincerely. It is the practitioner (i.e., *you*) who brings the juice that makes these vehicles go. It is you, your effort, your earnestness, your dedication that brings about the result. If a practice lands with you as powerful, it is your own power that you are experiencing. If a practice evokes love from you, it is your own love you are experiencing. If a practice triggers irritation and resistance, well . . .

This accounts for something I've always found intriguing. If I deliver meditation instructions to five people, five unique experiences will be had. It's not unlikely that one will tell me they fell into a state of bliss, another will tell me it increased their anxiety, the next person will tell me they couldn't follow along so they did something else, someone else will tell me about the life-changing revelation they had, while the person next to them lets out an audible snore because they fell asleep.

This lojong contemplation, that methods have no power of their own, directly opposes a hope we all have inside that something or someone will come along and save us. Deep down, parts of us hold on to a belief that something out there has just *got* to have the answer for us, the key that unlocks the plaguing confusions of our existence. What we find again and again, however, are mirrors: practices, teachers, and experiences that show us ourselves and point us back to the source: our own hearts. While the literal mirrors in our homes can enable our vanity, the metaphoric mirrors in our lives can enable our humility. Everything we experience is a reflection of our own mental stock. When we step into spiritual contexts—spaces of self-evolution, service to the world, and communion with the unseen—this is especially the case. When we meditate and find ourselves bored, it's not that meditation itself is boring. The meditation is reflecting back to us our own addiction to entertainment.

You could make an epic effort, say, traveling to Latin America to sit in medicine ceremonies, as so many people do these days. What you will find, however, is that the medicine is a mirror, the ceremony is a mirror, the shaman is a mirror, the retreat center and the other participants are all mirrors; everything about the experience, right down to checking your luggage at the airport, is a mirror. Everything in such an endeavor would reflect back to you your own tendencies, your own hopes and fears, evidence of your own traumas, and your own immeasurable possibility. Medicine ceremonies can be incredibly powerful, but only insomuch as they elicit your own power.

"Methods of liberation have no power of their own" is asking us to stop giving away our power and to take ownership of our experiences. It's asking us to realize that it's coming from us more than it's coming at us. It's pointing out: the door to the cage isn't locked.

GENTLY WE GO

The message of this first lojong slogan that we're working with might seem like a lot of pressure—that you alone can take responsibility for your healing and happiness; that it's up to you to utilize the wisdom and methods you're given. Our parts might respond with something that looks like, *If it's all on me, I had better work very hard at this!* or, contrarily, *If it's all me, then I'd rather collapse into a ball of nothingness and hide forever.* This is indicative of another belief: that heavy-handed, grinding, stressed-out work is how we accomplish goals. This belief often stems from the capitalist "myth of meritocracy"—the belief that the harder one works, the more successful one will be. If you look around you, it's plain to see this doesn't add up. A complex array of factors are involved in people's success or lack thereof. After all, when it comes to material success, one important factor (alongside privilege) is often *dumb luck*—for example, "I was at the right place at the right time." Any entrepreneur will tell you this.

Nevertheless, such a mentality often creeps into people's efforts with healing work. The outcome is sensing that trauma resolution will be yet another hustle, another thing to grind away at. This leads folks to either bear down and get too serious about things or feel overwhelmed because life's already too draining as it is. The lojong counteracts this belief with another slogan:

6. REGARD EVERYTHING YOU
EXPERIENCE AS A DREAM.

Alas, we meet with the "two wings" principle again. Whereas the first wing is empowerment and ownership of our self-work, the second wing is bringing a light touch to it all—to treat it like it's all a dream.

Dreams are an alternate reality wherein there is no point, there are no goals. All is soft and hazy, and there is infinite room for magic to occur. The point of a dream is the dream itself. Our waking life tends to be quite *linear*—most of what we do is a means to an end. Everything must have a goal or a point in order to be considered worthwhile. Yet, as we discussed in chapter 10, healing work has the most fidelity and efficacy when approached in a more *circular* fashion. While it's true that there are goals involved in healing work, we need to work as if there aren't any. We won't heal from hardship by piling on more hardship. The deepest healing happens when we drop our agenda. We heal when we "tend and befriend," as the Buddhist teacher Tara Brach puts it.[4] We heal as a result of a curious process of getting to know ourselves. We become whole by recognizing that we were whole to begin with. We realize love by practicing love. The process is the point.

Hence, the lojong states:

28. ABANDON ANY HOPE OF FRUITION.

When it comes to your heart, I'd urge you to stay far away from the narrowing activity of grasping at results and dwell instead in the dreamlike dance of discovery. Stay in the adventure of expansion, of outshining. This verse doesn't mean we shouldn't long for liberation. It means we will get there by staying circular and dreamy, by doing our inner work for the sake of itself. Meditate to meditate; not to get somewhere. Attend to your parts because they're your parts, not to convince them to change. Though change is desired, the lojong is asking us to notice our quality of effort. It's asking to move closer to delight.

Frankly, this is the way Self Energy tends to move on its own. Thus, we can take this teaching as yet another clue for noticing when Self Energy is present.

We'll revisit the dreamy aphorism again soon, but do bear this in mind as we head into some pretty deep waters together. Stay positively empowered, and stay dreamy.

PRACTICE: ENTERING THE DREAMLIKE STATE

Begin with the Fivefold Foundation:

1. Posture
2. Abdominal breathing
3. Natural breathing
4. Knowing the body in space
5. Heart breathing

Next, we'll scan through the body. Begin at the top of the head, feeling all the sensations of aliveness in the top of the head, the back of the head, the interior of the head, and all down the face. Don't spend too long in any one place but rather continue to feel and explore all the aliveness that's here to be felt.

Continue in the same fashion down the shoulders, arms, hands, and fingers. Keep feeling your way, somewhat briskly, down the front and back of the torso and everything inside the torso. Feel the muscle, bone, and skin of the pelvis, both front and back. Feel your way down the thighs, knees, lower legs, and feet.

Then we'll scan the body again, but this time I want you to remember something: the molecules that compose your body are 99.99 percent empty space. They say if the nucleus of a molecule were the pitcher's mound at a baseball stadium, the nearest electron or neutron would be in the nosebleeds. Everything in between them is empty space. Thus, your body is not at all solid. It is only the rapid activity of these molecules that gives your body the appearance of solidity and keeps, for example, the wind from blowing through you. Thus, your body is far more of a dream and illusion than you take it to be.

Start back at the head and imagine it's now dissolving into open space. Breathe and imagine it dissolving, dissipating. Flow down the rest of the body, somewhat briskly again, imagining it dissolving, dissolving, dissolving: the head, face, shoulders, arms, hands, front and back torso, pelvis, legs, and feet . . . all dissolving.

Now for the inner body. Start back up top where your head used to be, and scan down through the inner body, replacing everything you find with clear, blue sky. Top to bottom, nothing left but blue sky and the illusion of breath being breathed by the dream of your compassionate heart. Take some time to savor this.

The blue sky has no boundary. It spreads out into the space of the room, dissolving every object it touches. It spreads upward, downward, to the left, to the right, in front, and behind. It spreads and spreads until all that's left in the whole room is blue sky. It doesn't end there. The sky dissolves even the walls and continues its expansion in all directions. The sky goes on forever, even as the breath continues to dance in the heartspace.

Rest in this dream for as long as you like, and then bring your practice to a close.

16

THE FOUR REMINDERS

An Antidote to Apathy and Other Forms of Sublimated Suicidality

Rewinding to the beginning, the lojong opens thus:

1. FIRST, TRAIN IN THE FOUR REMINDERS.

These Four Reminders are meant to be an antidote to apathy or taking the easy route. They are meant to shake up and confront the parts of us that lean toward depression, malaise, and even suicidality. To "train" in them is to contemplate their meaning, commit them to memory, and eventually internalize these truths so that over time our parts can embody them. We want to make it as if these ideas come to live right there in our pocket so we can access them whenever they're needed. We also want the deeper levels of their meaning to begin to reveal themselves through the repetition of these contemplations. We'll explore these ideas first, then put them into a formal practice at the beginning of the next chapter.

REMINDER 1. YOUR LIFE IS PRECIOUS AND RARE

Your life, writes the astrologer Rob Brezsny, is the product of either "a colossal secret intelligence or a series of improbable, fabulous accidents."[1] Either way, it's spellbinding to consider what it's taken for you to be here at all. The carbon atoms that compose your body are at least seven billion years old. The heavy metals (*Beavis and Butt-Head laugh*) your body needs to run, including the gold needed for your neurons to fire,

187

were born in astronomical events that happened shortly after the birth of the cosmos. You are literally stardust—yes, like in the Joni Mitchell song "Woodstock." Don't get caught up in the "devil's bargain" of thinking your life is anything less. After all, thirteen trillion cells form the skin, muscle, fascias, bones, blood, organs, sinews, tendons, and multiple collaborating nervous systems of your bodily vehicle—literally the most sophisticated and evolved thing known to science. You are not a grain of sand. You are an entire beach.

The Mathematical Likelihood of Your Existence

The author and medical doctor Ali Binazir sat down and crunched the numbers. He found that the mathematical probability of your existence is as close to 0 percent as one can get. The odds of an Earth with a habitable zone becoming host to a technologically advanced species, and then for you to be born on it, are this: *1 in 10 to the 2,685,000th power—a 10 followed by 2,685,000 zeros.*[2] This number, if I were to type it out, would fill many pages with nothing but zeros. It includes the likelihood of your parents meeting, of each of your ancestors living to an age of viable reproduction, of your body being brought to term by your parents, and scores of other variables that had to come together to make *you* happen. Stop and consider all the variables of your experience that had to come together after that to bring you here, right now, to this moment. It is endless.

Because you were born, so much is possible: Healing is possible. Transformation is possible. Awakening is possible. Buddhahood is possible. Developing the altruistic courage to positively impact countless lives is possible. The confounding problems and worldly BS. you so often wrestle with do not delete these truths. It also doesn't matter what you believe about yourself or what you're worth. These truths remain valid and will keep on being so regardless. What you struggle with on the surface pales in comparison to the vastness of who you truly are underneath it all. You lose sight of this because the tunnel vision of the world eclipsed you. You lose sight of this because of the veil of ignorance unwittingly perpetuated by misinformed caregivers and a deranged society. Are you really going to let this stand in your life? Are you really going to keep wearing the blinders that make you believe you're anything less than magnificent? Say it with me: *Fuck that.* Say it again, even louder. Get yourself a megaphone and shout it from your window for the sake of everyone else lost in a trance of their false conditioning.

You can zoom out and expand your view at any time. Your ability to choose your attitude toward and relationship with your experience cannot be taken from you. That's the power of your heart and mind, which you have the ability to direct when you want to. For example, something that amazes me about the lovingkindness practice offered in chapter 13 is that once the heart cracks open and you begin to glimpse even just a little bit of its warm energy, you can send it anywhere. You can send it to your loved ones, to your friend who's sick in the hospital, to those suffering the effects of war in far-off countries, or internally to any of your parts.

Your worthiness is similarly absolute in nature—unshakable, indestructible. Imagine for a moment I'm holding up a $100 bill. We'd both agree that this bill is worth $100, that we could walk into a store and purchase $100 worth of goods with it. Now, imagine that same $100 bill has been crumpled up and tossed in the gutter. If I were to find it down there, it'd still be worth $100. Sure, I might have to uncrumple it and wipe some muck off of it in order to take it into a store and use it, but its value remains intact. That's you: you are that $100 bill. That's the nature of your value as a person. Except there's more: You are beyond value. You are not just "enough," you are not just "worthy," you are priceless and irreplaceable. You are "God in drag," says Ram Dass.[3] There has never been nor will there ever be another person like you. You might find yourself in the gutter, in need of some decrumpling, but your immeasurable value remains intact. The poet Mary Oliver calling this "your one wild and precious life" is actually a gross understatement.[4] Your mere existence transcends the words *wild and precious.*

If we saw things as they actually are, we would live with our mouths permanently ajar in a gesture of endless awe.

REMINDER 2: YOUR LIFE IS IMPERMANENT

In chapter 7, we discussed how the changes you seek are not only possible but actually inevitable under the right causes and conditions.

This is the gift of impermanence. Here, we'll explore another side of impermanence.

Traditionally, this second reminder is about keeping death firmly in mind, not because the lojong is goth but because awareness of our mortality helps us put our house in order. We tend to live in denial about this simple, shared fact of existence—and our priorities fall askew as a result. By and large, we don't turn to face death because we are afraid and so we rob ourselves of a blessing. Our fear of the end is a powerful emotional energy, one that can be repurposed as fuel for wakeful motivation. It can give our lives fresh meaning. It can cut through our addiction to convenience and foster a life-altering forbearance and determination.

When the lights go out, what will you need to be able to say to yourself? What do you need to do in order to avoid some horrible moment of realizing that you let yourself get lost in the mire; that you failed to see the value of life, people, and experience and could have done something with it . . . and now that chance is gone. To paraphrase the Quaker philosopher Parker J. Palmer, don't ask yourself what it is you *want* to do. That question has infinite answers and you'll only end up in analysis paralysis. Ask instead, "What is the thing I can't *not* do?"[5] What's the thing you won't be able to face having not done before all options are closed?

Now, I'd urge most of us to stay far away from answers like "a vacation in Bali" or whatever your version of that would be. The luxuriating experiences you've had won't matter nearly as much as doing the things that feed your heart and mind in meaningful ways. What will you have wished that you'd cultivated *within*? Because if there is anything after death, it is your heart you'll take with you. Your well-stamped passport will vanish like lightning.

Which brings us to the final point: you think you have time, and you don't. When I was five years old and thought about how I'd one day be an adult, it seemed like it was an eternity away. Now that I'm here, with a driver's license and a career and back problems, it's as if being five years old was five minutes ago. It'll be the same feeling about this present moment when I'm looking back from my final moments. Time is relentlessly evaporating so, so fast.

I recently had dinner with a friend who's struggled with multiple bouts of cancer in recent years. The doctors keep getting it out, and the cancer keeps creeping back in. My friend has been impressively resilient through it all. He soberly looked at me over a bowl of ramen and said, "I could be gone next year, or in five years, or in twenty years, so I need to do what I need to do—now." My heart caved inwardly. I blurted out something like, "That's so dark!" He looked at me flatly with the retort, "That's you, too. That's all of us. Cancer or no cancer."

We need to do what we need to do—now.

Many people might receive this truth as a cause for anxiety, rushing, or yet another case of FOMO. Such a reaction is far too simple and will only waste more time. Don't forget to temper urgency with a remembrance that this is a dream, a passing memory. Better to let this inspire you to slow down, take your time, drink in your experiences, feel the people you're with deeply, and choose only the things that truly matter. Be selective about what and who you allow in. Quality over quantity.

On Suicidality

I know that many of you sometimes wrestle with wanting to end it all. Believe it or not, I am with you in this. For the vast majority of us, it's not that we actually think death is a good idea so much as we have parts that want the pain to end and they don't see another way out. The truth of impermanence is a guarantee, however, that no matter how endless it all seems right now, it *will* end. Everything that has a beginning must also fade, vanish, and become something else. There is nothing that escapes this, and that goes for the pain, grief, and hopelessness that some of our parts hold inside, too.

As someone who still has parts that ponder suicide on the really bad days, I'll offer you one insight that has come out of the many inner conversations I've had with them:

Don't you worry. The end is coming for us regardless. There's no need to push the fast-forward button on this, no need to work at it and make some suicide attempt that you still might survive (and that would make your problems much worse). You'll get your wish; all you have to do is wait.

For me, I've chosen to live as a suicidal person, to stay alive and loving even though sometimes I feel a strong pull toward the opposite. Not all of my parts hold a death wish, but one definitely still does and this is the agreement we've come to. My parts and I live through the lens that, yes, indeed it sometimes all feels unwaveringly hopeless, that this world is indeed broken and brutal, but looking for an easy way out has never proven worth it. I have lovingly and very firmly let my parts inside know that none of them are ever, ever allowed to take me out. We go on no matter what. We see the next sunset, we listen to the next song, we dream the next dream. We keep going, and we do our best to stay Self-led despite it all.

I think about Kurt Cobain—a man credited with changing the shape of rock music only to not live past the age of twenty-seven. I can only imagine the suffering behind his suicide. I think also to one of his final interviews in which he said, "If I'm gonna die, if I'm gonna kill myself, I should take some drugs."[6] While I want to approach this matter with compassion for Cobain's suffering, for me, this version of a "might as well [fill in the blank]" mantra is too simple, too easy. It's a mantra that eventually robbed the world of this artist's gifts, his ideas, getting to bear witness to his process. It's a mantra I once followed, almost to death. It's a mantra that killed my best friend and so many others that I love as well. Imagine if Cobain had lived long enough or had found adequate help to chart a way through bipolar disorder and his health issues (not impossible); what a story that would be and how much good he could have done for suffering people with his massive brilliance and influence.

My personal version of Cobain's "might as well" mantra is "If I want to die, then I might as well show my heart to everyone and help as many people as I can." After all, if parts of me want to die, then why not *really live*? If my parts are so unafraid of death, then why bother with my everyday fears? Might as well take a chance and fall hopelessly in love despite the risk of emotional devastation. Might as well perform at the open mic or publish exquisitely vulnerable poetry online. Might as well show up heartfully for other people. Might as well go into massive debt putting myself through social work school. Might as well make life suck a little less for others. If you don't give a damn, then you might as well give the Ultimate Damn. In a world where people are promoting the idea of "giving less fucks," I challenge you to give The Ultimate Fuck.

REMINDER 3: YOU ARE FAR MORE POWERFUL THAN YOU REALIZE

Another reason to give The Ultimate Fuck: if you accept that having a body, heart, and mind is a superpower—then you must also accept that everything you think, say, and do matters. It all ripples out (in ways both obvious and subtle) to impact everything and everyone. How you spend your time, where you spend your money, the things you dwell on, the people you associate with, the words you speak, the food you eat, and the directionality of your love—it all matters more than you realize. One moment of rage can end a lifelong, nourishing friendship. If driving on the highway, a moment of rage could end the lives of a dozen innocent strangers. Similarly, one moment of kindness could also be remembered by someone for a lifetime and thus influence literally everything about them for the rest of their days—and then all of the people they impact, and everyone *those* people impact; it goes on forever. Never forget that the deadliest animal on Earth is also the smallest—the mosquito. Never forget that the most powerful force on Earth is something self-existent, free of charge, and well within our capacity—love, generosity, kindness. The vehicles for expressing these things matter—thought, speech, and behavior—and they are therefore powerful beyond measure.

The traditional description of the third reminder is "the truth of karma." Now, most of us really ought to take whatever we've heard about karma and toss it out the window. It's rare to hear someone do this highly complex topic any justice. Far too many people think karma correlates with the universe being punitive in some way—for example, "Bad things have happened to me because I'm bad." What nonsense. In essence, what karma points us to is how very much we matter, how innate empowerment is. Karma is less about what happens and more about what you become.

Perhaps the most useful translation of the word *karma* is "habit." A habit is activity that we perform with enough repetition that it becomes ingrained in our routines. As such, we exert very little decision-making power on habitual activity and do things with little, if any, regard for their outcomes. It's something we simply repeat over and over again because it's begun to feel like home to us. Therefore, if what we think, say, and do is incredibly powerful, nothing could be more powerful than our habits and their cumulative effect.

REMINDER 4: WE LIVE IN A DEFECTIVE WORLD CALLED SAMSARA

We look out at a world of indescribable majesty and see beings who are searching for happiness yet remain ensnared in greed, aggression, and confusion. We see the war, starvation, emotional deprivation, and myriad depravities humans have succumbed to, despite the innumerable wonders that also surround us. Looking at this within the context of everything we've just explored exposes with striking clarity the insanity of it all. The nature of healing practices is to not turn away from such sufferings. Our practice is to face life and allow such matters to arouse compassion in us. Don't let it break you down; let it break you open.

Given our great fortune to be sitting where we are and not actively fighting for physical survival somehow, we remember not to lapse into self-pity, guilt, or immobilization. We open our hearts and cry out to the world in the name of love, compassion, and rejoicing in the possibility that, no matter what, we can all awaken. Another world is absolutely possible. We allow these truths to inspire us to clear conviction and dedication to our path—that which leads to equanimity and trust.

PUTTING IT ALL TOGETHER

You have this astonishingly implausible, arguably miraculous existence. It is awesome, in the true sense of the word, that you have this opportunity at all. It is a chance to experience the highest love imaginable (your own) and to realize and embody that love.

Your existence flows like a river, yet it's a river you get to steer in the direction of that love or in the direction of inane materialism—it's your call. For a brief time, you are that river of ridiculous possibility.

Nay, you are *rapids*. You are powerful beyond measure. You don't even have a choice about how powerful you are. Your power is there regardless of your awareness of it or your belief in it. You are a gift to everything and everyone, including countless beings who haven't even been born yet. Your choices will affect generations. Your choices could also heal the lineages of pain your ancestors struggled with. Whatever you do, don't you *dare* die early on us! That will affect us all, too.

It's your move, and it's an important move, too—because you exist in this world where untold numbers of people experience unspeakable, deplorable degradation and misery, a world of psychotic violence. You somehow arrived here in this precious incarnation with incredible power to impact it all every moment of every day. We need you. We need you healed, well meditated, and self-loving in all the ways you long to be. We need you to find your own true happiness, humor, and wisdom. Humanity is a chorus, and we need your note. Our song will not be complete without it. This is neither fantasy nor religious fancy. These are facts. And we'll contemplate these facts in a formal meditation at the beginning of the next chapter.

17

HOLD IT LIGHTLY

You Are Dreaming

Your reality, sir, is lies and balderdash and I'm happy to say I have
no grasp of it whatsoever.

—*Baron Munchausen*

*We'll begin this chapter with a short contemplation on the Four Reminders
that ties into the next lojong aphorism.*

PRACTICE: THE FOUR REMINDERS

Begin with the Fivefold Foundation:

1. Posture
2. Abdominal breathing
3. Natural breathing
4. Knowing the body in space
5. Heart breathing

Then contemplate the four reminders.

1. *Your life is both precious and rare.* It is next to impossible that you
   even exist. Because you do, more is possible than you can imagine. Healing is possible. Realization is possible. Becoming a wellspring of love for others is possible.
2. *It's all changing . . . and ending.* You're not stuck. Stuckness is just
   a story you sometimes tell yourself. You are the flowing river. Your

196

only real job is finding spaciousness—the kind of spaciousness that allows Self Energy to be uncovered within you. It's important that you do your job, because time is short. But the fantastic news is that this job is much easier and more enjoyable than trying to force change through willpower. Hold the energy of Self Energy–buddha-nature, and you will change in that direction.

3. *You are powerful.* Everything you think, say, and do matters. Even when you're alone and no one's watching. You are emitting ripple effects out to the world in every moment. More good news is that the best things you can exude into the world are also the things that feel best for you: kindness, generosity, mercy, openness—all derivatives of Self Energy. This is your human homework. And it's fun and satisfying homework!

4. *You live in a hurting world.* We all know that is an understatement. Everyone here is confused and caught in cycles, and the effects of that are the global situation that surrounds us. Yet you are powerful. You have the opportunity to impact it all with your healing work and your loving efforts. Not only do you belong here; you are needed and wanted.

What's next? Well, again, here's what the lojong thinks it'd be wise to do next:

2. REGARD EVERYTHING YOU EXPERIENCE AS A DREAM.

Hold all this lightly. Don't let the sense of urgency trick you into thinking this is real because it is all a passing memory. Every moment you touch vanishes instantly. There is no need to get heavy about things. In fact, you will have more space for compassionate vitality and you will do your human homework much better if you regard it all as a dream.

PERCEPTION IS PROJECTION

A Zen monk walks up to a river, only on this day the river is flowing mightily and the raft that is ordinarily tied to the shore seems to have washed away. The monk, flummoxed, looks up to see his teacher standing across the river. He calls out, "Teacher! How do

I get to the other side?" The teacher calls back, "You *are* on the other side!"

Everything in your mind is a story. What you call reality is actually your brain's best guess at what's going on. You don't have access to all the facts, and this is deeply unnerving (pun intended) to the regions of your brain—or I could just as easily say to your parts—that need you to have a coherent, cogent narrative so that you can function. In the name of this, your brain generates false perceptions based on probabilities to fill in the gaps. It does this all day every day. "What we know is so little, what we presume is so much," wrote Pablo Neruda.[1]

Perception is projection. Perception by nature is a simulation of what's actually happening. Therefore, relate to your experience with lightness. Learn to see the absurdity in things we take so seriously. Don't be too sure that what you perceive is the end of the story. Question everything, especially your own mind.

Your parts might believe the stories that they live in, and those stories might be utterly valid and important; yet, at the same time, they are just that—stories. Kurt Cobain's deducing that "I'm suicidal, might as well get high" was just that: a story. He didn't actually have to believe those thoughts, even though the pain behind them was obviously so valid. How heartbreaking to think that there might not have been anyone to show him how not to believe the story his brain was writing, that his parts believed. Such loving confrontation is often necessary. The lojong's admonishment to treat it all as a dream is that kind of confrontation.

If the lojong slogans are like tips from a wise coach, meditation is the playing field. It is a continuous invitation to witness that what we take to be real and certain is much more fragile and fluid than we take it to be. When we look closely at what's going on inside, it begins to shift on us. Many find this to be a bit distressing at first, but ultimately it is quite liberating. Like the truth of impermanence, it means we're never stuck.

Let me tell you a story about a story. One morning I woke up furious with a friend. It was a couple weeks after we'd had a text exchange in which I'd felt insulted and dismissed. At the time, I had decided to let things slide, but in the weird way emotions and parts often work, I later woke up to an assemblage of Firefighters in my head campaigning for justice.

I sat up in bed and wrote an email letting my friend know that what they'd said definitely wasn't okay. Then I realized I hadn't had coffee yet and decided it would be best to save the email as a draft for the time being, just in case. After coffee, I hammered out another email that took a softer approach—but then I realized I hadn't meditated yet. The second email joined the first in my draft folder. After meditation, I decided I should reread the text message in question before firing off either email. I'd misread the text message entirely. Instead of some rage-worthy digital missive, I found only an affable and polite message that contained a couple of keywords that my parts had fixated on out of context. I hadn't been insulted. I hadn't been dismissed. Parts of me had, in fact, projected my insecurities onto the situation, and everything going on inside of me was based on a complete fiction. I'd wasted an entire morning fixated on that fiction and came dangerously close to inciting unnecessary conflict as well. I began to wonder just how many times I'd done this in the past. Probably countless. I began to have compassion for myself as I realized how many times others have misperceived me, my actions, and my words in all kinds of ways. I began to realize the universality with which we live in delusions.

Delusion, in the Buddhist sense of the word (not the clinical sense), is just another way of describing the simulation function of the brain involved in every last one of our perceptions. There's no getting away from delusion. There isn't a one of us who's completely beyond it. Delusion just comes with our human equipment; it's part of the package. It's involved in our projections. It's involved in the erroneous beliefs we hold. It's a cog in the movie projector in the theater of the mind. It's nothing to pathologize or stigmatize at all. In fact, if we look through the lens of trauma and recovery, we see that delusion is intricately intertwined with what's reflected back to us in the mirror of experience discussed in chapter 15. When we can spot our delusions and projections, we gain good clues about which parts of us need reparenting.

Seeing the extent of our delusions and projections is a great prompt to learn to live in what the Zen Buddhists call "don't-know mind." As disquieting as such an embrace of uncertainty might initially be, it is ultimately quite freeing. To live in don't-know mind is to hold it all lightly—very lightly, in fact. Given the gravity of what life entails, this may just be the only way to stay real and continue to function, not to mention respond compassionately. It's not that things aren't real or serious: this is not an invitation to shrug accountability. Rather, it is an invitation to admit that there is more to every experience than we grasp and that what we experience isn't as solid or sure as we take it to be. This ancient verse—"Regard everything you experience as a dream"— somehow reflects leading-edge neuroscience, which will lead us down a rabbit hole to matters very much related to trauma and its healing.

Mirror Neurons

In the 1990s, the Italian neuroscientist Giacomo Rizzolatti and his team were studying macaques. The monkeys spent their day with electrodes attached to their heads so that the researchers could observe the various activations in their brains on a screen. Like so many game-changing scientific discoveries—such as the discovery of penicillin, gunpowder, LSD, x-rays, and plastics—the team stumbled onto something incredible quite by accident. One day the team had lunch in the lab and forgot to turn their lab monitors off. One monkey was active while another was at rest, and yet the monitors displayed nearly identical brain activity in both monkeys. This wasn't a technical failure; it was the discovery of *mirror neurons.*[2]

Mirror neurons are a special type of brain cell that mimics what we perceive happening with others in the moment. Our neurological systems imitate whatever we perceive in our environment, even if we are not directly involved. Thus, it turns out that we are all empaths. The brain activity involved in empathic experience is a hardwired biological reality that happens without our knowledge or volition.

Insight: When we toss into the equation the theory of neuroplasticity—that our brains are ceaselessly molded by the experiences we accumulate—we begin to see new importance in our

> need for community. Truly we become like those who we spend our time with, whether we like it or not. As the motivational speaker Jim Rohn put it, "You are the average of the five people you spend the most time with." The writer David Burkus added to this: "Your friends really are your future."[3]

More than highlighting the need to associate with those who reflect the best of our interests, this points us to the fact that what we perceive as solid is much more fluid and malleable than we presume.

Just like dreams are.

Simulation

We live in a simulation of reality. It's not a simulation like in the movie *The Matrix*, where some machine-based life-form has us all hooked into an elaborate, hallucinatory mechanism. Instead, your brain is already hallucinating your reality. We live in a simulation based on the natural way the brain generates perception. After all, your brain and neural circuitry have no direct contact with the external world. What they receive are, for example, reflections of light vibrations and sound vibrations that the brain regions involved in seeing and hearing *interpret* and then send back out as a perception of your eyes and ears. This is one of the many meanings of the colloquialism "Beauty is in the eye of the beholder." Sight happens *in* the eye. A story about what's in the eye being beautiful comes from inside the mind.

In her groundbreaking book *How Emotions Are Made*, Lisa Feldman Barrett tells the story of her daughter's twelfth birthday party. Altogether fitting for a kid's sense of humor, her daughter decided to throw a "gross foods" party. They served pizza with green food dye to look like mold, peach Jell-O with bits of vegetables in it to resemble vomit, and white grape juice in medical urine sample jars. The food literally tasted like one would expect pizza, Jell-O, and grape juice to taste like: delicious. But many guests couldn't handle it. The brains of those gathered generated a perception based on past experiences that was repulsive. Many people, especially the adults, avoided eating altogether. Some tried the food but were unable to get past the simulation their brain was generating and had to stop. Their perception functioned beyond their conscious knowledge of the reality—and perception won.[4]

Let's talk delicious things without such cruel trickery. (After all, to defile pizza in this fashion borders on criminal.) Let's consider avocados for a moment. Notice what happens as I tell you that I had the perfect avocado at breakfast today. It was vibrant green with just a little bit of yellow. It was at peak ripeness, slightly sweet, lusciously fatty, and brought to perfection with a squeeze of lemon and a dash of pink salt. Are you salivating yet? Suddenly hungry or at least craving a snack? Perhaps further repulsed—for the few of us silly enough to not like avocados? Do you see the avocado in your mind's eye? How is it possible for you to see a private avocado that no one else can see?

Your brain just hallucinated an avocado. It constructed a fake avocado based on your past experiences with avocados, and your body responded. The descriptors of fattiness and salt engaged various regions of your sensory and motor processing systems to generate a response in you as if the avocado were real, regardless of the truth. Your brain generated not only an internal response but also a sense of what action you ought to take next, such as getting a snack or slamming this book shut. Now that your brain is noticing that its hypothetical avocado isn't actually here, it must attempt to correct itself, which you may be noticing isn't so straightforward. You might still be salivating more than you were a minute ago.

Feldman Barrett writes,

Simulations are your brain's guesses of what's happening in the world. In every waking moment, you're faced with ambiguous, noisy information from your eyes, ears, nose, and other sensory organs. Your brain uses your past experiences to construct a hypothesis—the simulation—and compares it to the cacophony arriving from your senses. In this manner, simulation lets your brain impose meaning on the noise, selecting what's relevant and ignoring the rest. . . . It's a huge ongoing simulation that constructs everything you perceive while determining how you will act.[5]

As Lama Marut was so fond of remarking, "The world comes from you, not at you."[6] He meant that the quality of our perceptions is generated based on our past experiences, the ones we hold inside. It isn't that there's no world around us. Stimuli is definitely coming at us. How we perceive that stimuli, our relationship to those perceptions, and our habitual responses to those perceptions—this *isn't* coming at us. It's coming from inside us. And it is all shaped and conditioned by what we've experienced in the past. Therefore, what basis do we have for proclaiming anything we perceive as actually real, actually solid, as anything to truly hold on to and take seriously? At the very least, this is an ironclad reason for us to lighten up and regard even our perceptions as elements of a dream.

THE TIGER AWAKENS

The preceding exploration of the neurology of stories and perceptions has far-reaching implications when it comes to working with trauma. Our past experiences and their memory, the record of it all that's held in our bodies, and the stories and beliefs our parts hold as a result are definitely real and unquestionably valid. Yet, we must admit that our involuntary, biological simulation and projective capacities have been involved in it all. While this invalidates nothing, it is an invitation to breathe a little deeper, unblend from our parts, and approach our experience with more gentleness. To regard it all as a dream is permission to be so, so soft with all that is so, so sharp and heavy within us.

It's heartbreaking that trauma is among the most deeply conditioning experiences we could possibly have. When trauma comes to live in the body as traumatic stress, it impacts almost every region of our brain and colors our perception of everything from within. This is how a trauma survivor becomes capable of attacking someone they love, having a panic attack when everything is okay, or collapsing into a horrific memory of being attacked just by seeing a backward baseball cap (as I did in my story in chapter 4).

The lojong reparenting reminder to hold it all as if it were a dream can be a protection against this kind of trauma response.

EXERCISE: WIDENING THE FIELD OF AWARENESS

As you read these words, I want you to focus on them. No, I want you to hyperfixate on them. Narrow in your focus. I am serious. Take these words and the task of reading them to be very serious. It's actually personal. Your ability to read these words, comprehend them, and not become distracted actually says a lot about you, about who you are as a person, about what you're worth. So fixate. Narrow. *Focus!*

Terrible, isn't it? Sorry about that.

Now, keep reading, but we'll shift to more of an open-focus way of attending. As you read, loosen up. Continue paying attention to the words and their meaning but now, without looking away, begin to notice what's going on in your periphery. If it's hazy, that's okay. Notice that you can see out of the corners of your eyes all the objects and activity happening to your left without looking away from these words. Then notice everything on the right side without looking away. You'll only be able to do it if you relax a little bit, so maybe take a breath here.

It's the same for above these words and below. Without looking away, you can widen the field of your awareness by noticing what's in the periphery of your vision. That's because the seat of your consciousness is in a region of your brain known as the *reticular activating system* (RAS) that's also heavily involved in your vision. Now notice that you can read these words with a gentle awareness of the periphery just fine. You don't have to look at the periphery, it simply appears there. It's very passive to notice it. The active part is reading.

Last thing: From this more expanded way of focusing, do the words *hold it lightly* make more sense somehow? Is it starting to make a little more sense how one might regard this as a dream even though it's real? Check in on how present you feel. Take a few breaths into the heartspace now. Are your parts allowing more space for even a sliver of calm, curiosity, clarity, or compassion? If not, try asking inside if your parts will step back for just one second. Notice how they respond.

Set the breath in its natural rhythm for one minute and let this exercise go. Then take five minutes to jot down your experiences and thoughts about all this.

EXERCISE: ADDRESSING A BELIEF WITH A PART

You could do this as a full meditation practice, beginning with the Fivefold Foundation, or you might be adept enough to have an on-the-spot conversation with a part just as you are. Choose your own adventure.

Think to a limiting belief you hold, perhaps about your worthiness, perhaps about the unworthiness of others. Dwell on that belief until you sense the part inside who holds it. Welcome them. We're not here to judge them, just to know more. Focus on the part, flesh them out, and get into a space of Self Energy with the part. You may need to ask all other parts to step aside and give you a good space inside for Self to emerge.

Now that you're curious about the part, ask them about the belief. *Where did they first get this message? Was there any experience you had that communicated this to you? When was the first time you can remember feeling or thinking this way?* (As always, don't think of the answer; just ask.)

Once the part starts sifting through memories of how this belief came to be internalized, wait until they land on the memory that seems more central somehow. It's usually the earliest in memory, but not always.

Let the part be in the memory and feel the pain of the situation they were in. You can now reparent this part by asking some questions:

- Considering the source of this belief, are they reliable or were they confused?
- Is there an intergenerational family or cultural lineage that props up this belief? If so, where does this come from? Does the part think this should persist through further generations?
- Does the belief align with self-compassion and self-love?
- Does the belief end up hurting you in the long run, despite this part not wanting you to be hurt?
- Is there a more accurate or useful view that this part could take?
- Is the part ready to give up the limiting belief and begin living by a healthier truth?

If the part is ready to abandon this belief, ask them to show you the burden of it: *Where is it in or around your body, and what is it like for you to hold it?* You could do a small unburdening with them by asking them which of the elements they would like to have take this from them: earth, water, fire, or air. Then allow the part to release the burden into that element. Surround them with Self Energy and breathe as they do so.

After the burden is gone, ask the part what true, healthy, and useful belief they would like to hold now instead. Once they tell you, visualize the energy of that good belief entering into your body. Perhaps repeat the new belief with them several times. Let them thoroughly absorb that it really is this way. This is how we see things now.

You'll want to get a nickname for this part, map them, and remind them of their new belief at least once a day for several weeks in order for this to really stick. You might even set a reminder in your phone so that you remember to do so.

18

PLAY

Relearning the Essential

Space is the place.
—*Sun Ra*

We think we understand the rules when we become adults but
what we really experience is a narrowing of the imagination.
—*David Lynch*

The invitation to hold our experience with a gentle, dreamlike awareness
allows us to explore matters that are quite deep and intense. We counter-
balance the harshness and friction of traumatic stress with the smooth
ease of spacious compassion and steady boundaries. To go without this
light touch into the disciplined work of contending with all that healing
entails would be a kamikaze mission: we'd soon burn right out, perhaps
never returning to this all-important process. We'll be moving into more
of these difficult topics soon—we must, since they do relate to us all—but
not without first amplifying this need; the need to move a little more like
the wind through our work, our hurt, and our lives.

The lojong has many aphorisms that urge us to tread softly and kindly
into the dark and deep waters of realistic understanding of samsara's cru-
elties. Here's my all-time favorite:

> 6. IN POST-MEDITATION BE
> A CHILD OF ILLUSION.

THE ESSENTIAL NUTRIENT OF PLAY

To suffer trauma in childhood is often to "grow up too soon." Hell, to live as an adult at all is to have the weight of too many responsibilities placed on one's shoulders. For whatever reason, over time it is easy to lose sight of our inherent need for play and true adventures. You might recall in chapter 1 we discussed experience as nutrition, as psychological food that can either nourish us or make us sick. I would refer to play, then, as an essential nutrient—something we simply can't be healthy and happy without. It's an energy that some of us need desperately, and thankfully, it's one we can absolutely bring into our meditation practice.

I personally define *play* as "a beautiful waste of time." It's any activity wherein there is no point other than to feel free and alive in novel ways. I remember the first time I stepped into a rock climbing gym and thought, *This is a playground for adults!* Later, I had a similar feeling as a competitive Ninja Warrior athlete aspiring to land a spot on the reality TV show *American Ninja Warrior.* As ambitious as I became about running obstacle courses, at the end of the day I was simply a grown child, swinging from monkey bars. Pretty ridiculous!

This attitude is also something that follows me into my current fixation on creating music and on the poetry of lyrics. The activist and philosopher Angela Davis, speaking of the importance of art and music, noted, "Art teaches us how to feel free. How to feel free even as we live in the conditions of un-freedom. . . . Art is actually crucial. Art is at the forefront of social change. Artists allow us to grasp what we cannot yet understand."[1] Thus, playful modes of being embody a paradox: necessarily there is no point, and yet, somehow, simultaneously, there is a very important point.

Play is the opposite of anxiety. Many of us grown-ups, especially those of us bound to urban lives and important jobs, don't do more for fun than dinner and drinks with friends. We need to frolic, to run wild and free in nature, to laugh uncontrollably, to dance, to cast off the binds of our Manager parts and get a bit lost. Rebecca Solnit reminds us in her breathtaking work *A Field Guide to Getting Lost* that we needn't go anywhere to find this playful sense of wonder in the world: "To be lost is to be fully present, and to be fully present is to be capable of being in uncertainty and mystery. And one does not get lost but loses oneself, with the implication that it is a conscious choice, a chosen surrender.... The mind too can be imagined as a landscape, but only the minds of sages might resemble the short-grass prairie in which I played with getting lost and vanishing. The rest of us have caverns, glaciers, torrential rivers, heavy fogs, chasms that open up underfoot, even marauding wildlife bearing family names. It's a landscape in which getting lost is easy."[2]

Such a playful approach can be reclaimed in various aspects of our lives; to reclaim it in inner work and conscious presence is to be a child of illusion. It's to admit that what we call reality is indeed a construct, and it is *our* construct. Again, we can shift our attitude at any time, choose any mental reframe we like. The clay is in our hands to mold in whatever way feels nourishing, supportive, and free. In doing so, we move ever closer to yet another lojong aphorism:

21. ALWAYS MAINTAIN A JOYFUL MIND.

THE FEAR OF JOY

Many of us notice that we tend to sabotage our efforts at success and relationships. And many of us notice that we tend to avoid the positive habits and practices we know will help us to feel well, balanced, and happy. Why on Earth do we have such tendencies? I find that there is no one answer as to why humans, to paraphrase Shantideva, hate suffering yet gravitate toward its causes.[3] Rather, there tends to be a unique and complex array of traumatically conditioned experiences in each person who finds themselves in such a feedback loop. The ultimate answer to this quagmire is this: get to know your parts inside; ask them why they fear good things; and ask what they think might happen should you become strong and powerful, wise and happy.

I find that one overarching, subconsciously held belief tends to be almost universally involved: "If I have nothing, I can't lose anything. If I have good things, they could be taken away. If I'm here on a mountaintop, enjoying the fresh air, I might fall, and it's a long way to the bottom.

If I'm lying on the floor, there's no chance of falling at all." To find joy in things often comes down to a choice, especially for trauma survivors. We literally must stop and smell the flowers. That is, we often must intentionally choose to see the beauty in things. The joy of this world is definitely there, staring us in the face, but it often lies just beyond the filters of our traumatic conditioning.

ASCERTAIN THE CAUSE

Lojong aphorism 12 tells us:

DRIVE ALL BLAMES INTO ONE.

Our arresting delusions weren't born in a vacuum; they grew from the ways in which love has been withheld and betrayed, as well as the ways the world has miseducated us. We really must stop blaming ourselves for our shortcomings and for the ways we get ensnared. We must rightly ascertain that these are almost never products of some moral shortcoming or evidence that we're damaged goods. The blame lies in our lack of self-love, our inability to access Self Energy. I'll say it again as it bears repeating (a million times, really): it is not our fault how we arrived at our station, and we are also now accountable for what we do with it. We actually have a responsibility to become self-healing children of illusion. It is the only way we'll ever stop hurting ourselves and others. And if it's not the only way, it's definitely the most pleasurable.

> **Insight:** True self-love and self-compassion are the opposite of ego. The word *ego* is shorthand for "parts of me that defend against the world while being overly self-concerned and self-aggrandizing." It's also shorthand for overly identifying with our parts as opposed to identifying as the compassionate witness of Self inside. These are realities born of trauma, delusion, and miseducation. Self-love and self-compassion will always lead us to humility, wisdom, and compassionate action for others. This is the antidote to so-called ego.

When we begin to pick apart our delusions and reclaim our vital sense of loving play, we also fulfill lojong aphorism 11:

> WHEN THE WORLD IS FULL OF DELUSION,
> TURN IT INTO THE PATH OF AWAKENING.

As well as lojong aphorism 16:

> WHATEVER YOU MEET, JOIN IT
> WITH YOUR MEDITATION.

These slogans, of course, have more meaning and layers of wisdom than just this, though. They actually relate directly to the core meditation practice of the lojong, the practice of *tonglen* or "emotional alchemy." We will explore this in the coming chapter. Before we go there, here are two simple, light ways to experience part of the meaning of these aphorisms by reclaiming a more playful attitude, right here, in the middle of our messy world.

EXERCISE: GO ON A CURIOSITY WALK

Take a ten-minute walk (or longer) where your only objective is to get as curious about as many things as you possibly can. Ideally this would be a walk you take for the sake of taking a walk—not to get somewhere.

Get curious about the richness of the colors around you. Study the veins and contours of a leaf. Really take in the smell of something enjoyable. Listen to the symphony of sound around you, even if in the city. Is it possible to get curious about the next people to pass you on the street and the lives they might lead? Can you get curious about the sources of the smells around you? Can you add to this list of questions? The objective is twofold:

- Can you soften and open to a sense of wonder about ordinary things, things we take for granted?
- Can you stop and take something in for a full ten seconds? Really pay attention and engage all your senses in whatever it is. Set a timer if you must.

Bonus round:

- Ask inside if your parts will let you soften into Self Energy here. What might it be like to feel Self inside, even just a little, as you take in the world? What might it be like to send a person, an animal, or even plants and trees a little bit of Self (a.k.a. lovingkindness) as you walk? Even if you can't get there, imagining what it'd be like if you could is often a good doorway.

Then journal about your discoveries for five to ten minutes.

EXERCISE: DO SOMETHING YOU LOVED AS A CHILD

Think of something you loved doing as a child that fell away as the years progressed or got taken away from you. It could be as simple as coloring in a coloring book; it could be as complex as a trip to see the ocean. Is there a way for you to reclaim this activity? Perhaps a modified version of it? If so, go and do it and let yourself enjoy it fully. Invite your parts to be present for the activity. Let any child parts of you take the lead and relish the opportunity. Let any grumbly naysayer parts simply be. Dance past any resistance you might feel. Keep it simple and unambitious. At some point during the activity, check inside to see if there's an increase of Self Energy as well (calm, clarity, curiosity, or compassion).

19

TURNING THE TERRIBLE
INTO TENDERNESS

The Emotional Alchemy of Tonglen

Courage is not about being fearless; it's about letting fear
transform you so you come into right relationship with uncertainty, make peace with impermanence, and wake up to who
you really are.

—*Lissa Rankin*

The Buddhist practice of tonglen is the Swiss Army knife of meditation.
It incorporates all the elements we've covered so far and helps us to reparent in a multitude of ways. It increases our mindfulness. It has the
elements of lovingkindness but takes them a step further. It offers us a
skillful way of relating to the inevitable difficulty of the present moment.
It gives us a way to unburden our parts of their past trauma a little bit at a
time so as to not be overwhelming. It gives us another way to experience
the nature of Self Energy. It helps us to know more deeply and intimately
the space and power of the heart. It gives rise to great, unflinching compassion. It also disrupts in a very healthy way our clinging to comfort
and our aversion to discomfort. It is the practice championed by the lojong, and rightly so. It gives us the means to relate to lojong slogans such
as these:

11. WHEN THE WORLD IS FULL OF DELUSION,
TURN IT INTO THE PATH OF AWAKENING.

16. WHATEVER YOU MEET WITH,
JOIN IT WITH YOUR MEDITATION.

42. WHETHER YOU GET WHAT YOU WANT OR
GET WHAT YOU DON'T WANT, HOLD IT LIGHTLY.

Tonglen is translated literally as "sending and receiving." Personally, I translate it as "emotional alchemy" or simply "compassion meditation," because it models the basic nature of compassionate activity with concise precision. It is a practice of intentionally moving closer to suffering—not because the lojong is training us to be masochists but because it wants us to become alchemists. Thus, the emotional alchemy begins with drawing in suffering in order to transmute it into compassion and then offering that compassion outwardly from the heart. In this way, tonglen is a method of addressing our instinctual habit of clinging to comfort and installing a more accurate belief that, often, relating directly to discomfort not only has much more value than we believe but is also often the doorway to liberation. Please remember, however, that discomfort to the point of getting overwhelmed is unwise and won't take us toward the healing we might seek. We want to find that happy medium where we're working at our growth edge.

Like lovingkindness practice, this energy can be offered to various people in our lives, the world at large, ourselves at large, or to specific parts of us. That's an aspect of the magic here. The lojong gives us two direct verses on doing this practice:

7. THE PRACTICE OF TONGLEN
SHOULD RIDE ON THE BREATH.

10. THE PRACTICE OF TONGLEN
SHOULD BEGIN WITH YOURSELF.

Here, we will explore this practice three different ways: first, for ourselves and our difficulties at large; next, for specific parts of us; then, for the world.

SELF-COMPASSIONATE TONGLEN

Begin with the Fivefold Foundation:

1. Posture
2. Abdominal breathing
3. Natural breathing
4. Knowing the body in space
5. Heart breathing

Without looking for a trailhead, without doing any digging at all, simply scan through your body and find anything in you, physically or emotionally, that's in discomfort, fatigue, distress, or pain. Notice what it's like, whether it's heavy, sharp, agitated, dull, cloudy, or something else. Are there words coming from this part of you or are they nonverbal? Are there emotions you can mentally label? If so, mentally label them: "stress," "tiredness," and so on.

Imagine a little bonfire right in the center of your sternum in front of the heartspace. It's glowing beautifully, red and orange and yellow; it's crackling. (If the bonfire image doesn't work for you, perhaps a cool lake, a patch of earth, or the open air speaks to you instead.) This element is right there in front of the heart, with all of its transformative and regenerative properties.

Breathe the suffering you sense inside into this bonfire of the heart, like your inhale is a vacuum. The suffering goes right into the fire and gets burned up. When the breath turns to exhale, it is now compassion. You can visualize this as warm, golden, shimmering light; as a simple, easeful energy; or as open space itself. Exhale it out toward the spot where you sensed suffering. It is an offering. Sense it surrounding the suffering, coming to its aid.

Train in this for some time: breathing the difficulty in and through the fire, breathing out compassion from the heart. Once you get the hang of it, intentionally turn up the volume on the suffering. Bring it to a level that's a bit challenging but not overwhelming. Traditionally, the suffering is seen as thick, gray smoke. What matters most is that it's not comfortable to be breathing in—again, not because we're training in masochism but because we're entraining a new belief that the discomfort can have tremendous value, especially when we know what to do with it and especially when we know how to turn it into golden compassion and open space.

Once you get the hang of this practice, you could do this practice anytime, anywhere, for any part of you.

Tonglen for a Part

Begin with the Fivefold Foundation:

1. Posture
2. Abdominal breathing
3. Natural breathing
4. Knowing the body in space
5. Heart breathing

This time, look for a trailhead. Think of a part you've been getting to know or a situation in which your parts recently became activated. Think on that situation until you feel something stirring in thought, emotion, or sensation.

Now that you've found the part, focus on them and ask all other parts to step aside. Then flesh them out by noticing everything you can about them.

Notice especially whether they're a Manager, Firefighter, or Exile. Managers are administrative and tend to be neutral in feeling, if a little tightly wound. Firefighters are extreme and reactive, such as with dissociation or anger. Exiles often present as more downtrodden, deflated, and often less mature. If the target part is indeed a Manager or Firefighter, you might want to ask inside if they're willing to allow the Exile they protect to come to the foreground. If they're willing to do so, it's possible you can help to partially unburden them. When Exiles carry fewer burdens, our defensive parts have less work to do. So simply ask inside, and if you somehow begin to notice something deeper emerging, observe what this part of you is like in the dimensions of thought, feeling, and sensation.

If this doesn't happen, it's just fine. Simply stick with the defensive Manager or Firefighter you began with.

Whatever part you're working with, find a way to let them know they are seen, heard, valid, and have your full attention. Let them know you will be offering them something that will help. You don't do this with an agenda for them to change but simply so they can feel lighter.

Then place the bonfire (or one of the other elements you relate to) in front of the heartspace. Breathe any difficulty, discomfort, or burden this part is holding into the heartspace. As you breathe it all in, it passes through the transformative fire. As you breathe out, the afflictive energy has become golden, warm, open, spacious, compassionate. Use whatever imagery works for you. Perhaps it is more cool than warm. Perhaps it is more loving or sympathetic than compassionate per se. Perhaps it is fierce, perhaps it is soft. What matters is that it's relief from the heart.

Stay with this for several minutes: in with the suffering, out with the healing. See the healing energy surrounding the part. They may even begin to cheer up, revel, or dance in your awareness. Keep going.

You could stay right here in this process for a full twenty-minute practice. You could also get more specific. You could ask the part to share more with you about the burdens they hold. They might tell you a story, they might present to you the core memory they live in, they might tell you how alone or beat up they feel. Whatever they present to you, breathe it in through the fire and breathe out the compassionate help. You can continue asking them, *Is there more?* and every time they give you more, into the fire it goes. Let the compassion accumulate around them as you go.

To conclude, allow the compassionate space to really add up. There's more and more with each breath. Exhale until the compassion is ocean-sized and this part of you is just a tiny dot swimming in this gorgeous space. Say your goodbyes and thank all your parts for working with you today.

Close with five deep, cleansing breaths. Make sure to breathe in as big or bigger than any of the feelings that have been present. Make sure to breathe out big sighs of relief.

Wrapping up, you may want to dedicate the merits of this awakened activity to all those who suffer in the world. May they awaken, may all beings heal, and may we all be free.

Tonglen for the World

Begin with the Fivefold Foundation:

1. Posture
2. Abdominal breathing
3. Natural breathing
4. Knowing the body in space
5. Heart breathing

TONGLEN FOR AN EASY PERSON

Think of a moment you've had with someone where it was easy to feel benevolent toward them. Maybe they're not perfect and maybe it was just the one moment you shared that was good, but go there. See that person as clearly as you can. Bring them into the room with you, sitting across from you.

Now consider that they have pain, they have struggled, they suffer myriad confusions and projections—just like you.

Place the bonfire in front of your heart. Consider their sorrow, their difficulty, their trauma, whatever it is. See it as a thick, awful smoke wafting in and around their body. Breathe it in, right through the cleansing fire. Exhale out compassion for them. Again, compassion has one thousand faces: it can be bright or subtle, fierce or gentle, colorful or clear—just go with what makes sense for you in the moment. Let the compassion accumulate until this being is surrounded by your heart energies. Then let them go.

FOR YOURSELF

See you as your self-concept, your self-image, sitting right in front of you. Consider for a moment how hard you work at life, your own struggle, your own confusions. Let your heart break for yourself a bit here. See all of your sufferings as a heavy, terrible smoke in and around your body. Place the bonfire in front of your heart and breathe your own sufferings right through it. Exhale to release compassion. Let it gather around your self-image. Let it build up a little more with each exhale until you are ensconced in it, perhaps permeated by the compassion. Then let this image go.

FOR A STRANGER

Think of someone who's in your life but that you don't pay much mind to. A neighbor, coworker, or a service industry worker, for example. Do the same thing as before: see them clearly. Consider their heartaches, failures, and traumas. See it as smoke afflicting them. Place a good, purifying fire in front of your heart. Breathe their suffering through the fire and into the heartspace where it's recycled into compassion. Keep breathing out compassion for them until they are soaking in it. Then move on.

FOR AN ENEMY

Think of someone you don't like. Try to steer clear of someone who's hurt you intentionally! Someone who bugs you will do.

Now, you may be thinking, *Why would I want to offer this person compassion?* Well, do you want your compassion to be conditional? Isn't it that *you* feel better when you're enacting compassion? Why would you put conditions around something that brings you goodness when it could be unconditional? Also, isn't it possible that if this person had less suffering in their lives, some of the things that bother you about them would shift? This is certainly true if (you've chosen *not* to heed my advice and) you're working with someone who's been deliberately awful to you. As the saying goes: "Only hurt people hurt people."

So, see this enemy as clearly as you can. You might elect to see them as a child. Contemplate how, just like you, they've suffered tremendous loss, have been betrayed, have been abandoned. See their suffering as smoke. Put the bonfire in front of your heart. Breathe their suffering through it. Breathe out big compassion. Fake it till you make it here. But do keep going. Keep going until they're swimming in the beautiful, healing energy. Then let them go.

EXPANDING THE HEART

Keep the bonfire firmly in front of the heart as you proceed.

Expand your awareness to the immediate area around you, perhaps your street or your neighborhood. Consider all the lives being lived here. Consider how each person around you has their own sorrows, troubles, insecurities, and regrettable losses. Breathe in all the suffering and let the compassion you exhale outshine it all. Keep going for several breath cycles.

Expand even further. Consider your city. How many lives? How much trauma? Already it's unfathomable. Breathe it right in. The energy you're taking in *becomes* the compassion, so release a city-sized compassion as you breathe out. Keep going for several breath cycles.

Imagine all the beings in your state, and how each being is more like you than they're not like you. This is especially true when it comes to their suffering. Breathe it in. Release enough compassion for the whole state.

Keep going. Contemplate all the beings in your country. So, so much trauma! By now you get it. You have nothing to fear. Breathe it all in like the warrior you are. Let your compassionate exhale outshine it all. Stay here and breathe like this for some time.

Finally, consider the entire planet. Countless beings, countless lives, countless woes. Some are starving, some are fighting wars, some are enslaved. Don't look away. Become even more audacious now. Breathe in the whole world's suffering. Breathe out astronomically sized compassion. Then keep going.

As your compassion envelops the whole world, contemplate how very *not* alone you are. Whatever you're going through, others have experienced similar things, and some are experiencing them right now at the same time as you. You may want to conclude by breathing in the specific sorrows that resemble yours. Take it away from all of them. After all, you know how to transform it now. Because of this, you're among the most fortunate of all.

Post-meditation note: As mentioned earlier in this book, we integrate the work we do in meditation much more deeply when we take our inner experience and make it outer in some way. If you've experienced any relief, insight, or joy in our process here today, let that feeling carry you into some compassionate activity. This could be as simple as how you comport yourself today, it might look like pledging time or money to an organization that helps folks more vulnerable than you, it could look like a phone call to your elected representatives about an issue that impacts others. Compassion has a thousand faces, and it also has a thousand expressions.

20

LOVE WITH NOWHERE
LEFT TO GO

On Grief

But you can't get to any of these truths by sitting in a field smiling beatifically, avoiding your anger and damage and grief. Your anger and damage and grief are the way to the truth. We don't have much truth to express unless we have gone into those rooms and closets and woods and abysses that we were told not to go into. When we have gone in and looked around for a long while, just breathing and finally taking it in—then we will be able to speak in our own voice and to stay in the present moment. And that moment is home.

—Anne Lamott

49. MEDITATING ON THE DIFFICULT POINTS HAS THE MOST VALUE.

Before we begin this exploration of grief, allow me to remind you to hold this all as if it were a dream, to hold it in the spaciousness of gentleness, and to not forget your true, compassionate nature.

On the path to healing trauma, there is much to grieve. There is grieving the life that we've had to date, one where our options were involuntarily limited by the actions of others and circumstances we were subjected to. There is grieving the life that could have been, the younger years we could have enjoyed uneclipsed, the relationships we could have salvaged if not for our myriad reactions and projections. There is the grieving of our own actions that have hurt others and the pain of needing to make amends. Grief is a natural response to any kind of loss; whether it's a person or time or money or an opportunity doesn't matter. We feel the loss, and the feelings deserve space.

It's important that we start with this broad view of grief as an emotional reality connected to much more than the death of loved ones, for the work in processing any kind of loss can be strikingly similar, no matter the origin. We will explore grief in its most literal capacity here, though. It is its own trauma type, one that is too seldom explored and faced squarely and soberly.

I think to a recent class I offered, where I led a group through some retrieval work (as described in chapter 14). The bulk of the class was able to meet parts of themselves in model scene memories where abuse and neglect were going on, and my students were able to reach for some important resolution there. In such scenes, the work is sort of obvious: we go in as Self Energy, we stop the abuse occurring in the memory, and we rescue the part trapped there, getting them to safety. Yet one student said that they went to the funeral of someone they loved and asked how they could possibly reach for resolve when a life was taken too soon. Reaching for resolve here was a more complex matter. In this context, what the part stuck at the funeral needed was something different: for someone to sit down with them and say, *Yeah, this is hard. This hurts a lot. There's not really an answer here and I don't know what to do, but I'll be right here with you through it.* Often, responses of this nature are the most healing thing despite their lack of a "solution." Connection is more powerful than problem solving.

Too many of us have experienced the death of loved ones as children or adults and no one talked about it. Few of us had someone who sat down and helped us explore our feelings and thoughts. No one was willing to simply be in the confounding and painful mystery of it all in an honest and unflinching way. No one spoke courageously about it. Many of us experienced emotionally stifled funerals growing up. Many of us lost someone we really loved only to witness all the adults "staying strong" or "thinking positively," leaving us alienated and confused about what to do with our pain and loss. Meanwhile, everyone who swept their emotions under the rug were actually whisking away something vitally important.

To paraphrase the Talmud, when a person dies, an entire world dies with them. Each of us are worlds unto ourselves. When someone we care for dies, we don't just lose them as a person; we lose the whole world that lived inside them and manifested all around them. I believe I felt this truth most intimately when Bill, the childhood best friend this book is dedicated to, died in April of 2021. Suddenly and without warning, this enigma of a human that I had never known a life without was gone. Bill had inexplicably vanished. Each time I experience the death of someone close—my brother Luke (who died shortly after Bill), my sister Sally, my father David, my creative compatriot Pandora—I am met with the maddening question: *Where did you go?* There was an entire world there, a world in motion, a world of infinite possibilities, and now that world has simply evaporated? In the snap of a finger? How is any of this possible? How am I to make sense of this?

I was sitting in a Death and Dying class in my last semester of social work school. The teacher asked us to write down the names of everyone we'd known who'd died. My list filled the front of the page and halfway down the back, while some of the others in class had to leave theirs blank. Toward the end of the semester, after exploring clinical methodologies for assuaging and softening the reality of death with mental reframing techniques and what have you, I finally blurted out something along the lines of "I feel like we're doing everything except meeting the matter head-on. I can feel us squirming around in our seats all semester as if to say, 'Please tell me there's a way to make this something other than what it is. Please tell me there's some way for me to avoid this fate, too.'" The silence that ensued was more than uncomfortable. It was existentially queasy. Still, I would prefer (times one thousand) to learn how to face these matters squarely than to reach for some way to dumb and dull it all down. In the context of compassionate Self Energy, we can do this. And we ought to. I'll tell you why.

THE NATURE OF GRIEF

Grieving is respect. Grieving is honoring. Grieving, as terrible and earth-shattering as it can feel, is imperative. For shutting down our grief is not only disrespectful but it also represses a T. Rex–sized psychic reality that will only go on to be held by our parts. To continue to avoid that grief is to push living parts of us further and further into the dark recesses of the heart. It is a particularly tragic form of self-cruelty.

Grief is love wearing a different mask. Grief is our burning attachment for another that can now take no other shape because the other is gone. Grief is love that has lost its object. Grief is love with nowhere left to go. We grieve because we have loved. The shock, sadness, remorse, pain, anger, shame, and numbness are all evidence of how deeply our heart was invested in another's soul.

"But I took them for granted!" many might retort. Don't I know it. We all fall victim to underappreciating the stars in our sky. Yet, considering that the person was an entire world—nay, a cosmos—unto themselves, how could we not take them for granted? Was there any way to behold their true majesty before this? "But I could have done more!" is something I've whispered to myself in the mirror on too many occasions. At some point, a voice said from within, *Darling, you could always be doing more. Instead of wallowing, why not call or write someone now to make sure they know how much you love them?* Wishes to turn back the clock are self-flagellation. It's natural to have these thoughts, but they do little except leave more bruising. Such self-flagellation is often a sophisticated mechanism for further avoidance. Grief, once faced, has a strange beauty to it, a bittersweet taste that I've come to prefer over the bland flavor of denial.

Grief can feel enormous when we sense it in the background wanting to emerge. It's yet another reason we often feel a resistance to this path. We subconsciously sense that if we are to truly wake up, there will be many shadows to face. Yet we're already facing those shadows, since they are what we carry with us. They've been coloring our experience this whole time from the subterranean layers of the subconscious. Thus, we either face them implicitly or explicitly—and, honestly, facing them explicitly and directly is the quick and easy way. Personally, I've had a couple of experiences of being overwhelmed by grief; more times than not, though, I find that once I give grieving parts the space to be, the emotional activation isn't nearly as bad as my Manager parts had feared. The resistance to such things can trick us into thinking they're bigger than they actually are. Sometimes the resistance is actually the worst part.

TANGLED FORMS OF GRIEF

Given that the context of trauma always plays a role in how our nervous system absorbs the experience, there are, of course, different types of grief. *Anticipatory grief*, for example, is the confounding experience of knowing someone is going to die soon but their body is still around. In anticipatory grieving one's parts might long for it to be over already or for the dying to be out of their suffering, while other parts are sad or scared of what's to come. We can find our way out of any confusion this might bring us by remembering that we are made of many parts; *of course* they don't all feel the same way about what's happening. Each of those parts just needs to have their turn and their place in the process.

There's also *complex grief*, when someone's death gets mixed in with other traumas. There are situations where folks lose their homes or entire estates after someone dies. There are situations where there's just no money for a proper burial, cremation, or funeral. Grief can be complex when our abusers die. Grief can be complex when the deceased loved one hurt other people or when we genuinely and convincingly feel responsible for the death in some way—which is very common among parents who've lost their offspring to accidents or suicide. There are countless ways death can get tangled up in other factors, making it hard to feel the loss in any straightforward way. I am grateful for the wisdom of IFS, which tells us that this complex tangle is a bevy of parts who yet again simply need to have their turn and their place in the process.

Grief itself is like a stain that colors the fabric of our life for some time. These tangled forms of grief are a bit more like our fabric has been soaked in dye. Yet, in either instance, the antidote is the same: set it in the sun and the color will fade. Lay the grief in the light of Self and we will honor what we need to honor, learn what we need to learn, and feel what we need to feel in order to find resolution. The difference lies in how long that might take.

EXISTENTIAL QUESTIONS AND CRISES

Perhaps those questions and complaints that so commonly circle in our heads—what we wished we'd said, what we wished we'd have appreciated more, and the rest—offer us a crack where the light can start to get in, as Leonard Cohen sings in "Anthem." It is in facing the reality of loss that we begin to ponder crucial matters of the heart. After we get past the reactionary self-blame and regret phase of inquiry, we can, with guidance, redirect this energy to a wiser place. We can let all our pettiness fall away and acquiesce to life's supreme importance, life's supreme tenderness, and turn toward the loved ones that are still here. Indeed, we *do* take people for granted; let this be an invitation to stop holding back. Indeed, we *could* be doing more for others; let this be an invitation to show up more often, even if all we have space for is a three-word text message that says "I love you." (I think to my friend Stephe, who has a personal policy that whenever someone pops into his head randomly, no matter what he's doing, he stops and texts them something he likes about them. I'll get texts from him out of the blue that just say "You're a good dude." Nothing more. Such a simple way to be beautiful.) Indeed, facing the reality of loss breaks down our defensive and jaded armoring and exposes the truth: people matter so much more than we ordinarily conceive.

As does time. Dave Mustaine, the founding member of the bands Metallica and Megadeth—who's no bodhisattva but occasionally makes a good point—once flatly remarked, "Without death, life makes no sense."[1] This says to me—if time weren't limited, we might rest on our laurels forever. It's another thing loss does for us (and not just *to* us): it puts us in touch with the first and second of the Four Reminders, that this is all quite fleeting and yet so very important. "Is not impermanence the fragrance of our days?" wrote the Austro-German poet Rainer Maria Rilke.[2]

I'm reminded of my friend's dad, a true purveyor of the American Dream archetype. Born into poverty, by the time he hit his early sixties he found himself selling the business he had built for millions and going into early retirement. Of course, he built that business at the expense of time with his family, who often felt neglected in his absence as he steadily worked to create a better life. When he retired, his first order of business was to buy the car of his teenage dreams: a vintage Mustang. He got the car home, took it for an inaugural spin, and suffered a massive heart attack on the way back. My friend, facing the meaning of his dad's tragic passing, was shaken into wakefulness. His priorities rearranged on the spot. "Nothing matters," he became fond of saying, "except people. Maybe experiences."

These are the benefits of turning to face death's profound meaning. For better or worse, loss and grief help us to see and savor things that we'd ordinarily waltz right past. To turn away from grief and loss is not just to disrespect the dead; it is to rob ourselves of the chance to have our priorities rearranged in wiser ways. My hope is that with the warmth of Self Energy in mind, we can stop sending our grief underground to calcify and find a middle path where we can compassionately face it little by little.

HOW TO PROCESS

Again, our purpose in contending with pain is not to simply sit in it and be brutalized by it. It's to harvest the opportunity to expand. That said, the essence of grief work is to find a way to bear witness to the feelings and thoughts until our parts are ready to be unburdened. The practice of tonglen does an excellent job of conveying this implicitly: when we reckon with pain and courageously breathe it in, it transforms fuel for compassion. In a life where few have modeled to us even the principles of basic sanity, it stands to reason that we have been left bereft of models for processing grief in wise, expansive ways. Tonglen's underlying message is just that: we can face the full truth of our lives, the entire spectrum from joy to sorrow, and we can turn it into medicine.

The basic formula remains the same: Meet whatever your parts are holding with Self Energy. Do it at a pace that does not overwhelm you. And be patient enough to stay the course. Firmly remind yourself that though it seems endless, nothing is endless. There is another side to this—a brighter side.

CUES FROM WISDOM CULTURES

I find wisdom from both Jewish and Tibetan cultures to offer some solid groundwork for meeting and processing grief through to its conclusion.

The Jewish practice of *sitting shiva*, in essence and intention, is about meeting the reality of death squarely. Shiva (pronounced shee-vah) offers the bereaved a full week of suspension from reality. No work is to be done. No food is to be cooked. No one goes anywhere. None of the usual activities are to be participated in. Even the mirrors inside the family home are turned around, signifying that one is to even abandon concerns of outward appearance and presentation. Indeed, the experience of bereavement and grief is one of floating in an alternate universe, to live in suspension for some time, and the tradition of shiva offers those in mourning such an opportunity: a full week to do nothing other than face the loss and receive grieving guests.

TIBETAN BARDO PRACTICE

For forty-nine days after a member of a community has left the Earth, it is customary in Buddhist cultures of the Indo-Tibetan region to process the loss through ritual and prayer. They do so within the acknowledgment of reincarnation, that just because a person's physical body has taken its leave does not mean the person is gone. For Tibetans, the essence of that person has entered the *bardo*—the "in-between" realm where they await a new body, a new life to claim as their own. It is taught that during this time, the consciousness of the deceased is confused by the trauma of their death and may not remember just how they got there or who they were before. What's more, they are being met with the sum total of their karma, which may appear in the form of fearsome ghosts and terrifying situations. Thus, it is the responsibility of those who loved them to send prayers to this person to help them through it all.

The basic point is that since this person is now nowhere, they are everywhere. They are lost in the trauma of death and might be experiencing something truly hellish. In their confusion they intuitively are drawn to any place or person that is thinking about them or talking about them. They're likely open to receiving clarifying messages from loving parties. Thus, their loved ones become empowered to help by speaking to them directly and reminding them of their buddha nature.

When Bill died, I felt his essence all around me, as many do after the loss of a loved one. At times it felt frightening. At other times, joyous. Nonetheless, I was, for a time, lost with this. I contacted many mentors to ask their advice. I was guided to follow my intuition, which was to

follow the example, albeit in my own way, of the Tibetan Buddhist lineage: to offer thoughts in the same way one offers thoughts in lovingkindness meditation, for however many days it felt right, to Bill's spirit
in the ethers. I began urging him to go home, to not get stuck here in the
material realm, to not be confused by any experiences he might be having. I explained to him that he had died and that he could not come back.
I reminded him of Self Energy, his buddha nature. I reminded him he was
Love Itself and to go straight into the light, into the vast expanse. Whenever I'd feel his presence or thoughts of him would fill my mind, I would
exude the brightest energy I could imagine in his direction and continue
sending these messages.

Was Bill's spirit really with me? Did this help Bill? These are things
that can neither be confirmed nor denied. What I do know is it helped *me*.
It helped me to face this gutting loss directly without dressing it up as
something else. It helped me to say goodbye in a loving way—and dozens
of times at that, which it turned out I also needed. I've seen this help others as well. In my online classes, especially the ongoing ones where we've
all really gotten to know each other, anytime someone shares about the
recent death of a loved one, we stop. I have the community member tell
us a little bit more about the person, what they looked like and what they
were like as a person, and I lead the group in a short meditation where
we wish for this person to not get caught in confusion and to simply go
home into the clear light, the dawning of their true nature. Again, does it
help the person who's died? I don't know. But I know it helps the grieving
party to face the loss directly, and it gives the community around them a
way to support them in that.

THE ENDGAME OF GRIEF

Again, grief has an end, and there is a brighter side. While we may never
be the same, there comes a time in the process where we've grieved
enough and it is time to relate to the loss in a different, perhaps surprising
way: through gratitude and celebration. After all, we gained something
tremendous in getting to know this person at all. Their existence was
a gift, and knowing them was a privilege. Yes, it is right to focus on the
loss for some time, but imagine if we had never known them at all: that

would be the real travesty. They have made the journey of life and death as we all will in time, but what matters most is that they were here to begin with. Hence, grieving can indeed give way to the celebration of this truth, a grateful remembrance that they were here, they mattered, and we are forever changed because of their presence in our lives. We were lucky to have them for as long as we did.

SAYING GOODBYE

The grieving process often gets stuck when we haven't really said goodbye. Maybe we attended a funeral, told a story or two about them, and felt some things—but did we truly bid them farewell?

There are many ways to finish saying goodbye, but perhaps the most direct way is to write the departed a letter that gives them a proper send-off. It can be short or long, electronic or handwritten. What matters most is that it gives you an opportunity to feel things through in the space of compassion.

Such a letter might include:

- Stories and important memories you have of them
- What it's been like with them gone
- What losing them has made you realize
- Why it just isn't right to hang on to them any longer
- Your wishes for them in the great beyond
- Your gratitude for what their existence gave you
- How you intend to carry on in a new way

Many of us will need to write such a letter a little bit at a time; some of us will find it important to write it all at once. Either way, what you do with the letter once you feel it's complete also has significance. You could:

- Hang on to it, perhaps in a special place or on a shrine
- Hang on to it for some time, but then destroy and release the letter when the time is right
- Destroy and release the letter upon finishing it

Destroying and releasing the letter, if it appeals to you, is quite symbolic of finally letting go of the loved one. Some might want to burn the letter. Some might want to rip it up and scatter it in the wind or in a river. Some might want to treat it like one would the ashes of a cremated party: scatter the letter or bury it in some place meaningful to you, to them, or to the relationship you had.

Whichever way you go, make sure you do this all from a place of love and compassion. It's important that you practice good aftercare as well. Call on your friends. Be willing to receive support. Take a long bath. Book a spa day. Go for an extended walk. Anything that feels gentle and restorative to you will do.

OFFERING COMPASSION AND PRAYERS TO THE ONE WE'VE LOST

Begin with the Fivefold Foundation:

1. Posture
2. Abdominal breathing
3. Natural breathing
4. Knowing the body in space
5. Heart breathing

Visualize the person you're practicing for. See them in their earthly form as clearly as you can. Their eyes, their hair, their body, everything you can remember about them. You might also imagine the sound of their voice. You might not be able to visualize at all but simply have a general sense of their presence. You might stop and remember some of the things you loved and admired about them or linger in some key memories.

Surround them with a glorious rainbow-colored light, the light of transcendent love and compassion. Hold them in this light, let them bathe in it for some time. Then offer them phrases in the style of loving-kindness:

May you move on from this world swiftly and with clarity.
May the gods and goddesses and guides all come to help you.

May you go into the light, into the clear dawn of buddhahood.

May you enjoy freedom and the true causes of freedom.

Spend some time with each of these phrases. Then visualize the rainbow-colored light permeating their earthly body. Their earthly body fades and fades until all that is left is rainbow-colored light. Take some time here to celebrate what they meant to you and the possibility that they are finally free.

TONGLEN/PARTS WORK FOR PARTS OF US THAT ARE GRIEVING

Begin with the Fivefold Foundation:

1. Posture
2. Abdominal breathing
3. Natural breathing
4. Knowing the body in space
5. Heart breathing

Think of the loved one who has gone. Let your parts who hold grief, sadness, anger, and numbness all come to the surface. Breathe yourself a bit bigger, maybe even as big as the room you're in so you can contain it all.

If many parts have come to the surface, communicate inside that you'll need to work with one at a time. Create a beautiful waiting room inside of you where the parts are invited to rest until their turn. Choose one part to focus on and let the rest take a break in the waiting room.

Remember: These parts may be polarized and hold feelings about the loss that may seem to conflict. Just let them be. All reactions are valid, and we are not here to figure anything out with them. Rather, we are here to help them feel things through.

Once you're fully present with one part, flesh it out a little. Then place the bonfire of transformation in the heartspace. Begin the process of tonglen: breathing the suffering into the heartspace, letting the fire burn it up on the way in, and releasing the golden space of healing compassion on the way out. Do this until you feel a natural sense of completion.

Thank the part for letting you hold space for them today, and let them move to the side.

Then make space for the next part holding another piece of the grief. Repeat the process. Welcome them, flesh them out, place the bonfire in the heartspace, then begin the process of tonglen. Stay in that process until you feel naturally complete.

Keep going with each part, one at a time. You may run out of time. You may need to stop so you don't go too far or overwhelm yourself. That is just fine. There is time, and you can return to this process.

Whenever you're done, make sure to acknowledge all the parts inside. Make sure to let any of the ones you didn't get to today know that you will be back.

Then begin taking deep, cleansing breaths—in through the nose and out through the mouth if you can. Breathe bigger than anything that's been felt today, which might be quite big. Little by little the parts and the feelings and the memories all dissolve, dissolve, dissolve until you come all the way down.

You might end this session with a fake smile, just to get the serotonin going. The truth is, though, you deserve that smile. You're doing such courageous work. Keep going and all will come clear in the sunlight of Self. It's just a matter of time.

Conclusion

WE ARE THE NEW CARTOGRAPHERS

We don't do it to be better, we do it to be whole.

—Mark Nepo

I write from the evergreen landscapes of Kripalu, a retreat center in the Berkshire Mountains of Massachusetts where I am currently coleading a weeklong workshop. It is the golden hour, the sky palette full of yellow and pink over low-lying mountain peaks in the distance. The mosquitoes and tiny flies are out in full force, basking, uninhibited, and without any knowledge of a world that apprehends them as pests. From my seat I can see the edges of a lake, where our group spent the morning meditating and having unusually profound conversations.

I feel as I always do toward the end of retreats with any level of trauma focus: like I've given a lot and asked a lot. I'm not always the easiest teacher. I'm deeply imperfect, and I like to meet matters head-on. Try as I might to bring forth as much gentleness as humanly possible, I am always reminded that there is another version of the world outside the one I live in: one where people hide from their emotions, live in fear of facing things, and where the kinds of conversations I have every day are totally alien. This is the world where most people reside; where you, dear reader, might live yourself. The conventional world tends to find it frighteningly strange that the world I dwell in exists—one where we excavate the deep layers of what we carry so we can see it for what it is and offer compassion; one where we openly discuss the truth of what's happened and how we came to be the ways that we are. It is quite the adventure every time I share it; every time I have the privilege of holding space for a group like this one. They learn a lot, I learn a lot, and none of it is easy in the worldly sense. None of it is "normal," and yet all of it is utterly human.

It occurs to me that this is where we are in this book as well. We've had quite the adventure together. I've offered a lot, and I've asked a lot. If you've made your way through even half of the practices here, it has been quite the ride, and possibly one that is completely alien to you, that you have no context for whatsoever. It has maybe taken you to places that no one around you ever talks about visiting. If this is so—and even if it's not—please know that I am deeply honored to have offered you any exposure to these processes of awakening, even in the slightest. Tears form in the corners of my eyes as I type.

It's a broken world out there. Few of the ways we've been given are truly working for us. The models we've been handed, the things we were taught to assume about life, relationship, work, and the world—they don't check out. Fear of our own humanity is strewn throughout convention. The language we've been given to describe our lives is incomplete; we keep needing new words. The kinds of conversations we really need to be having aren't commonly had. The cultures that surround us, the assumptions people make, are rather infected with the fear of feeling and truth. In one sense, who can blame them for guarding against discomfort? May they have happiness and the causes of happiness. In another sense, it is heartbreaking that anyone should live without spelunking the wild caverns of the human heartspace.

So much could be said about how the fear-based ways the conventional world has contributed to disarray in various social systems, political systems, school systems, health-care systems, and so forth. You don't need me to help you form opinions on all of that. I think, for now at least, it suffices for me to say that every social and political ill boils down to one thing: the corrosion of compassion and altruism in human hearts—and the extent to which that's come to inform cultural norms and values.

I want to lift up your courage here. I want to highlight your beautiful audacity. I want to affirm your tenacity. This work is not easy. Many begin, but few follow through to the end. Not you, though. You're here, reading this now. This tells me something without even knowing you;

you're likely to keep going. I hope you do. Just as much, I hope you feel a deep sense of appreciation for yourself and for your parts, one by one. You deserve a sense of divine pride in the work you're doing. It is against the grain of a world mad with grasping and aversion.

This has not happened in a vacuum, though. To have the means to obtain this book, to have the education to take in its words, to have the time and space to practice, to have both the inspiration *and* the tenacity to be at this point—this is something rare. The satisfaction of such concluding moments—it's something most people do not get to enjoy. As much as I have asked, which is only as much as the journey of outshining trauma asks anyone, there are some who live in parallel worlds where they'll never have space enough to glimpse such a possibility, much less go after it. But not you. As tragic as our sense of our lives may or may not be, as fraught as we might feel situations have become, as much as we might feel tormented by the apparitions of mind and heart, we must admit that in the global sense that includes the whole of humanity, we are the lucky ones. We are the ones who have the luxury to face things head-on. I know it may not feel like that, but if we expand to the global view, there is no contest.

We are the new cartographers. We are the brave explorers of new worlds for which there is no set map. We belong to a new set of humans for whom it is right to go out on our own. We may or may not relate to guru culture. We may or may not trust conventional spiritual systems. We may or may not buy into this or that psychological modality. Still, it is true that what many of us need, at least at some leg of the adventure, is to create our own amalgam of ways and practices that suit us specifically, that meet us where we are in the process. Meditation masters often have psychotherapists, after all. Psychotherapists commonly have therapists, coaches, mentors, energy workers, and "alternative" medicine practitioners in their lives. Some of the most famous meditation teachers out there, Richard Schwartz included, began as hardcore atheists and came to spirituality as a result of the deep looking their research entailed.

It is clear that what's appropriate for most modern people is a mixture of modalities, a "sampler platter" approach that we discover on our own as we continue to engage. We might center on one set of teachings, but we will generally need to source supplements from elsewhere. This is what I've brought to you. The dynamic composite of Buddhist meditation, philosophy, and worldview; mixed with Internal Family Systems; mixed with the trauma lens is indeed just that. It is the product of this *sampler-platterism*, of tinkering smartly in the laboratory of my own personal practice, gingerly offering it to others, and then discovering with increasing confidence that it works.

It is up to us to discover our own map.

May we remember two things: First of all, "the map is not the territory," as the Buddhist teacher Reggie Ray writes.[1] Modalities will never match the granularity of experience. The processes offered to the public will always be, to a greater or lesser extent, generalized. The advice of a therapist is never provided with a full comprehension of what's happening; they only know what we tell them. Yet our lives are the point. The lived, experiential outcome of our self-work is the point. It's all a construct—and yet constructs also matter deeply, especially when they bring us to a greater state of clarity and compassion; when they put us in touch with Self in some way.

This second point circles back to the first one: that we are the lucky ones. We've come this far because of our own courage and yet nothing about us was born in a vacuum. Others simply won't have the chance that we have. This is nothing to feel guilty about. This is not some admonishment. Rather, it is a calling to own up to the interdependence of it all and to vow to do something of great importance.

The sociopolitical systems, the world that thinks we're alien for processing our emotions, the people we pass on the street: it is of the utmost importance that we treat each of these people and situations in our lives in a manner similar to the way we treat our parts—with mercy and compassion. It is also crucial that we not keep this medicine to ourselves. We don't need to go preaching IFS or meditation to folks in our lives. We carry this forward through the way we treat others, even the ones who piss us off. The way we carry this forward is in the way we show up at work, at PTA meetings, in conversations held with strangers on social media (my personal weakness). It is also in the way we withstand critique when others think we're weird for being compassionate in the world.

We have, as a society, become blended with the forces of greed, aggression, and delusion. The Buddha's prediction that we would come to live in an age of "dharma decline"—wherein the love of basic decency, critical reason, and obvious logic would fall away completely—has come to pass. We are in hot water, and yet we can live the answer. If compassion and altruism were placed as the ultimate and unapologetic guiding principle for any system, that system would transform. When you hold compassion for your parts, you hold the answer to literally everything. When you hold compassion for other beings, all the more so. *Society* is just another word, after all, for a whole lot of human hearts coming together—much like *water* is another word for enough hydrogen and oxygen molecules coming together. Be the molecule that connects, that stands for love, that holds elegant boundaries, that speaks truth to power, that models the power of generosity and kindness.

Placing compassion and altruism at the center of our efforts can protect us from designating what is true based on what makes us comfortable or "feels right." That said, we can indeed give ourselves permission here to defy norms, think for ourselves, and take accountability for our mistakes in the process. That last part might be the most important clause in the deal.

If we take this as true—that no matter what our age, ours is the generation responsible for reestablishing compassion and compassionate means—then the place to begin is our own lives, our own traumas, and our own delusions. If we hope to have any effect on society, we must begin with the microsociety within. We must open up the lines of communication within the body and develop practices of deep listening and deep resolve. We must take cues from our parts while learning how to lead from Self inside. We are invited to stop pathologizing ourselves and to honor a fundamental wholeness: that everything within us moves subjectively in the direction of safety, gratification, learning, and belonging. We need to find the ways in which that mission has become distorted and tangled and help our parts to see clearly and set their belief systems aright.

If we continued with the lojong beyond the tiny bit we've explored here, we'd find instructive aphorisms such as:

29. ABANDON POISONOUS FOOD.

30. DON'T BE SO PREDICTABLE, FOLLOWING
TRENDS AND PATTERNS.

31. DON'T MALIGN OTHERS.

32. DON'T WAIT IN AMBUSH FOR OTHERS TO FAIL.

33. DON'T STRATEGIZE TO BRING THINGS
TO A PAINFUL POINT FOR OTHERS.

34. DON'T PASS THE BUCK.

35. DON'T TRY TO BE THE FASTEST.

36. DON'T ACT WITH ULTERIOR MOTIVES.

37. DON'T MISUSE WISDOM TO
JUSTIFY YOUR SELFISHNESS.

38. DON'T SEEK OTHERS' PAIN IN
ORDER TO FEEL SUPERIOR.

39. ALL ACTIVITIES SHOULD BE DONE WITH ONE
INTENTION: COMPASSIONATE AWAKENING.

40. REPAIR ALL YOUR WRONGS WITH ONE
INTENTION: COMPASSIONATE AWAKENING.

56. AVOID WALLOWING IN SELF-PITY.

57. AVOID JEALOUSY.

58. BOYCOTT IMPULSIVITY.

59. DON'T EXPECT APPLAUSE.

When my students have coursed through these aphorisms, the initial impression is that this is a whole lot of judgmental finger-wagging over things that are common sense. Yet look out at the lives we all are leading and what you may find is that such basic principles are what we've lost in this age of dharma decline.

I agree that at first glance, this all strikes as a lot of moral judgments that feel like the Ten Commandments; hard to take if we hold a trauma reaction of hating being told what to do. That said, I believe what the lojong is actually urging us to do is find and heal the parts of us that hold these tendencies.

From there our mission is to help others heal and transform just as we have. That will forever be the last leg of the healing adventure. We won't be complete without it. Healing is never complete when done in stark isolation. Many of the traumas we hold can only reveal themselves in the context of the many forms of relationship. The basic point is we cannot keep our healing and transformation to ourselves; it is meant to be shared. Thus, every workshop you've ever taken has actually been a teacher training. Every therapy session that's ever helped you has given you a small piece of your eventual gift to the world. Every self-help book you've ever read is meant to inform your helping of others in their quest for restoration.

To declare that this is a fundamental aspect of our process is not to lay on more obligation. Hopefully we see by now that healing is not some burdensome enterprise but actually a calling into realms of curious discovery and thrilling insight. The same truth applies here. Our parts might cling to their comfort zones, but we are only being asked to trade up, to win in the bargain of stepping out into the sunlight.

Go slow, my friends. As ambitious as what I'm putting out to you might be, we only live one moment at a time and one day at a time. The Buddha taught that meditation is done one breath at a time. We need only contend with the smallest particle of the adventure: the here and now of it all. Thus, this is not a demand that you become a meditation teacher or a therapist or run to Nepal to deepen your quest. Rather, much more grounded questions are raised: How can compassion begin to show up and inform your interaction with your neighbor, your barista, and your sociopolitical involvements? Can we set aside our views and our conditionings and hold each other with care?

My goal is always practice. Philosophy is just a collection of nice words if it fails to generate a meaningful lived experience. Ideas do little. Experience does a lot. So perhaps it is most fitting if this book concludes with a contemplation that ties it all together.

PRACTICE: SELF-APPRECIATION
AND THE DEDICATION OF MERIT

Begin with the Fivefold Foundation:

1. Posture
2. Abdominal breathing
3. Natural breathing
4. Knowing the body in space
5. Heart breathing

Here, with the breath coursing through the heart, take stock of all you've experienced, all you've realized, all you've learned.

In this meditation, I will offer a rare exception: it's okay if you stop and write it down.

Next, acknowledge how much effort it's taken for you to make it this far. It's not a normal effort. It's not the effort of ambition for career or ordinary pleasures. It's different than that. It's harder than that. But you did it and you continue to make these efforts. In the Buddhist sense, these are efforts that do not generate karma—they generate *merit*. Merit is like gold coins placed in your spiritual bank account—they can never be taken away.

The thing to do with those gold coins is to make wishes on them. Make wishes that they may multiply—and not just multiply but multiply to *infinity*. Wish for them to become so bountiful that they become medicine for the sick, water for the thirsty, food for the hungry, a vehicle for those who need to seek refuge, wisdom for those lost in delusion. Wish for this, and imagine your gold coins spreading to all lands, to all beings, and envision a world where your practice provides real, concrete relief.

Conclude by speaking this out loud:

I imagine my body shining like the sun
Radiant and loving like the moon.
From my heart
Out to the world
My compassion goes.

(*Pause, take a breath.*)
I reflect on my efforts and good deeds on this path.
(*Pause, take a breath.*)
I wish that these merits be multiplied to the furthest
    reaches of space.
May they be shared with all beings.
I want so badly for all beings to awaken.
(*Pause, take a breath.*)
I will keep going—
I will keep working—
I will keep playing—
I will keep loving—
Until all beings are free
Until all beings can rest in Self
together.

To close, you might place your left hand over your heartspace. Take a moment to feel the precious life, vitality, and vulnerability coursing through you. Then take your right hand and place it over the left hand in a gesture of the protection and refuge you are so worthy of. Finally, you can lean forward in the gesture of a bow, offering your wise heart to the world, to all beings, that they might come as far as you have.

Friend, I salute you.

NOTES

INTRODUCTION: THE THINGS WE CARRY

1. Hilary K. Lambert and Katie A. McLaughlin, "Impaired Hippocampus-Dependent Associative Learning as a Mechanism Underlying PTSD: A Meta-Analysis," *Neuroscience & Biobehavioral Reviews* 107 (2019): 729–49, https://doi.org/10.1016/j.neubiorev.2019.09.024.
2. Martin Seligman, "The New Era of Positive Psychology," TED.com, February 2004, https://www.ted.com/talks/martin_seligman_the_new_era_of_positive_psychology?language=e.
3. It must be noted that seventeen years before the work of Bessel van der Kolk hit the mainstream, Judith Herman penned the groundbreaking *Trauma and Recovery*, which circulated heavily in the hands of clinicians but not so much the general public until recently.

CHAPTER 1. THE SOMA KEEPS THE SCORE

1. Irvin Yalom, *Love's Executioner and Other Psychotherapy Tales* (New York: Basic Books, 2012), 186.
2. Gabor Maté, "Gabor Maté on How Trauma Fuels Disease," *Rich Roll*, podcast, episode 702, September 5, 2022, https://www.richroll.com/podcast/gabor-mate-702/.
3. *Oxford Dictionary of Psychology*, 3rd ed., s.v. "trauma (n.)," accessed January 16, 2024, https://www.oxfordreference.com/display/10.1093/acref/9780199534067.001.0001/acref-9780199534067-e-8554;jsessionid=B0193945BCEB5B0F26D1F812E8FD45D4.

CHAPTER 2. MORE THAN THE SUM OF YOUR PARTS

1. Richard Schwartz, *You Are the One You've Been Waiting For: Applying Internal Family Systems to Intimate Relationships* (Louisville, CO: Sounds True, 2023), 41.
2. Vinny Ferraro, "The Freedom of Forgiveness," in-person talk at Spirit Rock, October 8, 2010, https://vinnyferraro.org/recordings.

CHAPTER 3. ROAD MAP TO WITHIN

1. Andrew Weil, *Spontaneous Happiness* (Louisville, CO: Sounds True, 2011).
2. Pete Holmes, "Big Think Top 10 2019: '#9: Depression Is Different for Everyone. Here's What It's Like for Me,'" *Big Think*, accessed March 1, 2024, https://bigthink.com/neuropsych/pete-holmes-depression/.

CHAPTER 4. HEALING IN THE DARK

1. Kimberly Ann Johnson, *Call of the Wild* (New York: HarperCollins, 2021).

CHAPTER 5. THE SKY IS LARGER THAN THE SUN

1. @AndreaGibsonPoetry, "How Can This Open My Heart?," YouTube, December 28, 2022, https://www.youtube.com/shorts/4yWyIdOWAww?feature=share.
2. Edith Shiro, *The Unexpected Gift of Trauma: The Path to Posttraumatic Growth* (New York: Harvest, 2023), 46.
3. @AndreaGibsonPoetry, "How Can This Open My Heart?"

CHAPTER 6. THE ENDGAME OF HEALING

1. Isaiah 53:5 (King James Version).

CHAPTER 7. HOW CHANGE WORKS

1. "The Expanding Universe," Ideas of Cosmology (website), Center for History of Physics, a Division of the American Institute of Physics, accessed March 1, 2024, https://history.aip.org/exhibits/cosmology/ideas/expanding.htm.

CHAPTER 8. EMBODYING SELF-COMPASSION

1. Lorin Roche, *The Radiance Sutras: 112 Gateways to the Yoga of Wonder & Delight* (Louisville, CO: Sounds True, 2014), 39.
2. Bessel van der Kolk, "How Trauma Lodges in the Body," interview with Krista Tippett, October 20, 2017, *On Being*, podcast, https://soundcloud.com/onbeing/bessel-van-der-kolk-how-trauma-lodges-in-the-body.

CHAPTER 9. REFUGE

1. Paulo Coelho, *The Pilgrimage* (San Francisco: HarperOne, 2021), 15.
2. Jon Gingerich, "How I Wrote My First Novel while Going Blind—and Kept It a Secret," *The Guardian*, December 27, 2022, https://www.theguardian.com/society/2022/dec/27/first-novel-writing-blindness.

CHAPTER 10. BEYOND INNER DIALOGUE

1. Nancy A. Shadick et al., "A Randomized Controlled Trial of an Internal Family Systems–Based Psychotherapeutic Intervention on Outcomes in Rheumatoid Arthritis: A Proof-of-Concept Study," *Journal of Rheumatology* 40, no. 11 (November 2013): 1831–41, https://doi.org/10.3899/jrheum.121465.

CHAPTER 11. YOU ARE NEVER ALONE

1. Thich Nhat Hanh, *Peace Is Every Step: The Path of Mindfulness in Everyday Life* (New York: Random House, 1992), 3–4.

CHAPTER 13. HEARTFULNESS WITH PARTS

1. Consider for a moment that Nick Cave is someone who spent his younger decades strung out on heroin and making brutal, intentionally coldhearted, transgressive music. It's a fringe part of his career that's lesser known. The years and contention with heartbreak tenderized him, though. And things really turned around for Cave when his fifteen-year-old son died in a tragic accident some years ago. Cave wrote the words quoted here in the wake of his son Arthur's death. When he says a direct encounter with heartbreak is a key ingredient

in awakening the heart, he's speaking as someone who's seen and knows. The passage quoted at the beginning of the chapter continues: "I suspect that trauma is the purifying fire through which we truly encounter the good in the world." See "In Your Opinion, What Is God?," Red Hand Files, no. 196, June 2022, https://www.theredhandfiles.com/in-your-opinion-what-is-god/.

2. John Milton, *Paradise Lost* (Oxford: Oxford University Press, 2005), 26.

CHAPTER 15. ADJUSTING THE LENS

1. Brené Brown, *Dare to Lead: Brave Work. Tough Conversations. Whole Hearts.* (New York: Random House, 2018), 90.
2. Chögyam Trungpa Rinpoche, "Supplication to the Mother Lineage," Surmang Foundation, accessed March 1, 2024, http://www.surmang.org/wp-content/up loads/2016/05/The%20Supplication%20to%20the%20mother%20lineage.pdf.
3. Many exhaustive expositions on this text already exist, such as Traleg Kyabgon, *The Practice of Lojong: Cultivating Compassion through Training the Mind* (Boston: Shambhala, 2007), Pema Chödrön, *Start Where You Are: A Guide to Compassionate Living* (Boston: Shambhala, 2004), and Norman Fischer, *Training in Compassion: Zen Teachings on the Practice of Lojong* (Boston: Shambhala, 2013), all teachers more qualified than I am to transmit the essence of some of the more esoteric aspects of this text.
4. Tara Brach, "Bridging the Divide: Learning to Tend and Befriend," YouTube, May 12, 2021, https://www.youtube.com/watch?v=chLPQX nzG3E.

CHAPTER 16. THE FOUR REMINDERS

1. Rob Brezsny, "Glory in the Highest," Free Will Astrology, January 3, 2013, https://freewillastrology.com/horoscopes/archives/2013-01-03.
2. Dina Spector, "The Odds of Your Existing Are Incredibly Small," *Business Insider*, June 11, 2012, https://www.businessinsider.com /infographic-the-odds-of-being-alive-2012-6#:~:text=This%20 is%20multiplied%20by%20the,being%20alive%20are%20 basically%20zero.

3. Ram Dass, "Ram Dass Quotes," Love, Serve, Remember Foundation, accessed March 1, 2024, https://www.ramdass.org/ram-dass-quotes/.

4. Mary Oliver, "The Summer Day," in *New and Selected Poems*, vol. 1 (Boston: Beacon Press, 1992).

5. Parker J. Palmer, *Let Your Life Speak: Listening for the Voice of Vocation* (Hoboken, NJ: John Wiley and Sons, 2000), 25.

6. "Kurt Cobain Talks Music Videos, His Stomach & Francis Bean," MTV News, April 29, 2015, YouTube, https://www.youtube.com/watch?v=hJtm9HomKdE.

CHAPTER 17. HOLD IT LIGHTLY

1. Pablo Neruda, "Through a Closed Mouth Flies Enter," *Five Decades, a Selection (Poems, 1925–1970)* (New York: Grove Press, 1974).

2. Cecilia Heyes and Caroline Catmur, "What Happened to Mirror Neurons?," *Perspectives on Psychological Science* 17, no. 1 (2022): 153–68, https://doi.org/10.1177/1745691621990638.

3. David Burkus, "You're NOT the Average of the Five People You Surround Yourself With," Medium.com, May 23, 2018, https://medium.com/the-mission/youre-not-the-average-of-the-five-people-you-surround-yourself-with-f21b817f6e69.

4. Lisa Feldman Barrett, *How Emotions Are Made: The Secret Life of the Brain* (New York: Macmillan, 2017), 27.

5. Feldman Barrett, *How Emotions Are Made*, 27.

6. Lama Marut, "From Victimhood to Mastery," live talk, June 5, 2012, YouTube, https://www.youtube.com/watch?v=ekAlEOoU1x4&t=3s.

CHAPTER 18. PLAY

1. "A Question of Memory—Interview with Angela Davis at OMCA, 2019," Oakland Museum of California, October 6, 2022, YouTube, https://www.youtube.com/watch?v=Jq5ck1VV_gI.

2. Rebecca Solnit, *A Field Guide to Getting Lost* (New York: Penguin, 2006), 6.

3. Pema Chödrön, *No Time to Lose: A Timely Guide to the Way of the Bodhisattva* (Boston: Shambhala, 2005), 184.

CHAPTER 20. LOVE WITH NOWHERE LEFT TO GO

1. "Decline of the Western Civilization Part II—The Metal Years," directed by Penelope Spheeris (Burbank, CA: New Line Cinema, 1988), YouTube, https://www.youtube.com/watch?v=ivSQcG4rb5M.

2. Rainer Maria Rilke, quoted in Stephanie Kaza, ed., *A Wild Love for the World: Joanna Macy and the Work of Our Time* (Boulder, CO: Shambhala, 2020), 81.

CONCLUSION: WE ARE THE NEW CARTOGRAPHERS

1. Reggie Ray, "Training and the Path," Dharma Ocean, https://www.dharmaocean.org/the-training-and-the-path/.

ABOUT THE AUTHOR

Ralph is a psychotherapist and longtime meditation instructor. He is the author of *The Monkey Is the Messenger* and *Don't Tell Me to Relax*, and his work has been featured in the *New York Post*, *CNN*, *Tricycle*, *GQ*, and *Women's Health*. Himself a survivor of PTSD, mental illness, and addiction, Ralph sees his work as an extension of his own healing path, offering the very tools he actively uses to claim a life of self-actualization, self-love, and creative effervescence.